Creativity, Innovation, and Entrepreneurship

The **LITTLE BIG BOOK** Series

Creativity, Innovation, and Entrepreneurship

The Only Way to Renew Your Organization

H. James Harrington

CRC Press
Taylor & Francis Group
Boca Raton London New York

CRC Press is an imprint of the
Taylor & Francis Group, an **informa** business
A PRODUCTIVITY PRESS BOOK

CRC Press
Taylor & Francis Group
6000 Broken Sound Parkway NW, Suite 300
Boca Raton, FL 33487-2742

International Standard Book Number-13: 978-1-138-35369-5 (Hardback)
International Standard Book Number-13: 978-1-4665-8245-3 (Paperback)
International Standard Book Number-13: 978-0-4294-2509-7 (eBook)

Library of Congress Cataloging-in-Publication Data

Names: Harrington, H. J. (H. James), author.
Title: Creativity, innovation, and entrepreneurship : the only way to renew your organization / H. James Harrington.
Description: 1 Edition. | New York : Taylor & Francis, [2019] | Includes bibliographical references and index.
Identifiers: LCCN 2018043414 (print) | LCCN 2018044570 (ebook) | ISBN 9780429425097 (e-Book) | ISBN 9781466582453 (pbk. : alk. paper) | ISBN 9781138353695 (hardback : alk. paper)
Subjects: LCSH: Entrepreneurship. | Creative ability in business. | Technological innovations.
Classification: LCC HB615 (ebook) | LCC HB615 .H3377 2019 (print) | DDC 658.4/06--dc23
LC record available at https://lccn.loc.gov/2018043414

Visit the Taylor & Francis Web site at
http://www.taylorandfrancis.com

and the Productivity Press site at
http://www.ProductivityPress.com

I dedicate this book to all the people who have complained

about me because they challenged me to be better.

H. James Harrington

Contents

Preface

INTRODUCTION

There are several words that exist outside your normal vocabulary range, such as *love, successful, quality, innovative*, and so on, to the point that you cannot agree on a standard definition. You agree that these terms exist and you know them when you see and hear them. But you see each of them as you define them which may or may not agree with the viewpoints of your family, friends, customers, consumers, employees, and/or investors. Like the old saying "What's good for the goose is good for the gander," but contrary to this old saying, the goose and the gander may not see them from the same standpoint.

I'm proud to say I am a process man. I think everything is a process and if it isn't, I do my best to form it into a process. For example, there is the process you use to get up and the process use to take a shower. And there are much more complicated processes like how to select a spouse, design a toothbrush or a laptop computer. Writing this book is a mega-process to get you to buy it. Processes come in all sizes and shapes and can be simplistic or complex. There are long and short processes and there are ongoing and project-related processes. The improvement efforts are focused around making them less complicated and straightforward. The success of an organization is dependent upon how well the processes are managed.

To proceed without a process is to recede.

H. James Harrington

Process management is not new to management and the quality professional. It is the basis of most quality improvement methodologies. The object of any process improvement activity is to understand, document, control, and reduce variation throughout the processes within the organization. Processes, by definition, are a "series of interconnected activities that takes an input, adds value to it, and produces an output." Truly, that

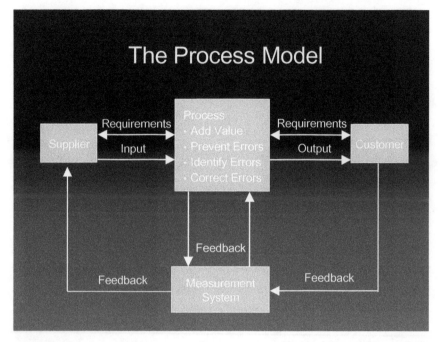

FIGURE P.1
The process model.

is the way all organizations do their day-to-day routine. Your processes define how the organization operates. There are literally hundreds, if not thousands, of processes going on daily in all organizations. Figure P.1 shows a simple process model.

Using this simple model, you can see that the following must be defined if you are going to manage a process.

- An agreed-to output requirement statement between the process owners and the customer.
- An agreed-to input requirement statement between the process owners and the suppliers.
- An effective group of activities that transforms the supplier's input into an output that meets the customer's performance and quality requirements.
- Feedback measurement systems between the customer and the process and the process and the suppliers.
- The way people are trained to understand the process.
- A measurement system within the process.

Detailed Process Model

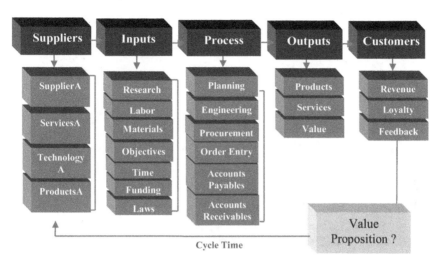

FIGURE P.2
Detailed process model.

These are six key factors that you should address when you design the process. The problem that most organizations face is that they never designed many of their support processes in the first place. They were created out of a need without really understanding what a process is. Figure P.2 outlines a much more detailed look at a typical process and its inputs and outputs.

UNDERSTANDING THE PROCESS HIERARCHY

Almost everything you do, or you are involved in is a process. There are highly complex processes that involve thousands of people (for example, electing the President of the United States) and very simple processes that require only second of your time (for example, casting your ballot). Because of these differences, you need to establish a process hierarchy (see Figure P.3).

From the macro-view, processes are the key activities required to manage and/or run an organization. New product definition is a good example of a macro-process. You can subdivide a macro-process into sub-processes

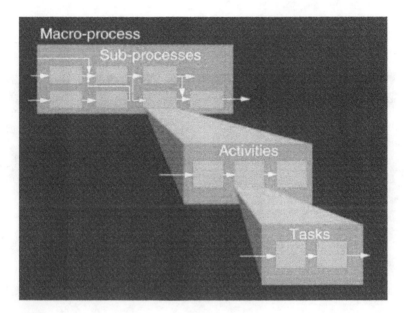

FIGURE P.3
Process hierarchy.

that are logically related, sequential activities that contribute to the mission of the macro-process. Selecting a presidential candidate is a good example of a sub-process of the macro-process of electing a president of the United States.

Often, you divide complex macro-processes into several sub-processes to minimize the time required to improve the macro-process and/or to provide focus on a problem, a high-cost area, a long-delay area, or to focus on continuous improvement.

Every macro-process or sub-process is made up of several activities (for example, assessing the status of a meeting room to determine whether it is ready for a focus group meeting). Activities are things that go on within all processes. As the name implies, they are the actions required to produce a result. Activities make up the major part of flowcharts.

Each activity is made up of several tasks. For example, some of the tasks that are part of checking out the focus group conference room would be ascertaining that:

- There are enough chairs for the invited guests.
- Water and ice are in each of the pitchers.
- A pen and pencil are placed on the table in front of each chair.

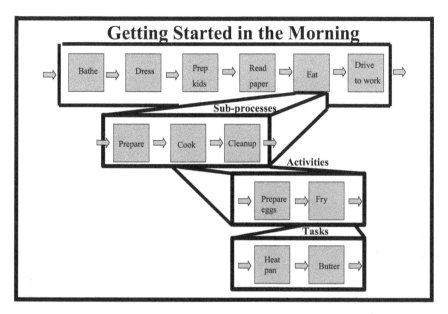

FIGURE P.4
Process hierarchy breakdown.

Normally, individuals or small teams perform tasks. They make up the very smallest micro-view of the process. Professor Robert Reid applied this process-hierarchy breakdown to getting up in the morning (see Figure P.4).

Key Process Definitions

- *Activities* are small parts of a process usually performed by a single department or individual.
- *Cycle* is any input that goes into a series of processes and/or systems and part of the output circles back to trigger a new input into the cycle.
- *External Customer* is an individual or organization that is not within the supplier's organization that receives a product, a service, or information from the supplier.
- *Internal Customer* is a person, process, or department within the organization that receives output from another person and/or process within the same organization.
- *Process* is a series of logically interconnected, related activities that takes an input, adds value to it, and produces an output to an internal or external customer.

- *Process Adaptability* is the flexibility of the process to handle future, changing customer expectations, and today's individual, special customer requests. It is managing the process to meet today's special needs and future requirements. Adaptability is an area largely ignored, but it is critical for gaining a competitive edge in the marketplace. Customers always remember how you handled, or didn't handle, their special needs.
- *Process Effectiveness* is the extent to which the outputs of the process or sub-process meet the needs and expectations of its customers. It is a lot like quality but includes more things. Effectiveness is having the right output at the right place, at the right time, at the right price.
- *Process Efficiency* is the extent to which resources are minimized and waste is eliminated in the pursuit of effectiveness. Productivity is a measure of efficiency.
- *Process Groupings* are groups of processes and systems that are grouped together due to the way they interact with each other or, in some cases, are alternative processes. (For example, you can do something by hand or electronically. In either case the task involved is very different.) In the case of the Innovation Systems Cycle, I defined 12 process groupings.
- *Systems* are groups of related processes that may or may not be connected.
- *Tasks* are steps that are required to perform a specific activity.

Note: You will note that the big difference between a process and a system is that the activities that go on within the system are not necessarily connected, whereas in a process there is a smooth, connected flow from beginning to end.

Throughout this book I will be using the term *system* in place of *macroprocess* because it better reflects today's vocabulary.

INTRODUCTION TO INNOVATION SYSTEMS CYCLE

I am a firm believer that you can view anything going on within an organization as a process and/or system (a system is a group of processors). Based upon these assumptions, you can understand why I consider the new product development cycle and/or the improvement activities which

FIGURE P.5
Detailed view of the new product cycle.

are made up individual processes as a more comprehensive system. For an innovative project I will call this the **Innovation Systems Cycle (ISC)**. There are many ways I could have represented the ISC depending upon the complexity of the model I wanted to use. It could be as simple as three steps (development, production, and sales) or it could be so detailed that it covers a total whiteboard (see Figure P.5).

In closely analyzing the innovative process, I found that there were numerous ways that I could divide it. After looking at the different options, I selected a three-phase made up of 12 process groupings—the ISC structure. The three phases are:

- Phase I. Creation. During this phase, you identify and evaluate improvement opportunities. Also, in this phase, you identify ways to take advantage of the opportunity and validate concepts.
- Phase II. Preparation and Production. During this phase, you complete a detailed value-added study and compare it to the other improvement opportunities to ensure that it provides more value-added to the organization than other available options. The potential projects that have the best value-added for the organization, its stakeholders, and/or important milestones to meet the organization's strategic objectives become active projects. The organization models the innovation to ensure that it will perform as proposed; completes the supporting engineering, sales, and manufacturing paperwork; and sets up manufacturing processes and trains people to use them

for those products that require production of a manufacturing-type process. Products start shipping to potential customers.

- Phase III. Delivery. This phase starts before the organization considers the product customer ready. Packaging design, sales compensation, advertising plans, promotional plans, and training for the sales group occurs well in advance of the first output being ready to go to the customer. The objective of the pre-first customer ship promotional activities is to stimulate consumers' interest in the product thus ensuring a successful product announcement. Phase III also covers the customer service activities required to support the product. The organization puts in place the measurement system developed during Phase II to provide hard data related to the product's value-added. The cycle ends with a transformation evaluation. Often initial indications are that the product is a big success, but over time people tend to fall back to doing things the way they were originally doing them. The transformation of the culture and the processes is a key measure of success for any innovative activity.

Table P.1 outlines a list of the three phases and the four process groupings that relate to each phase.

TABLE P.1

Innovation Systems Cycle

Innovation Systems Cycle
Phase I. Creation
• Process Grouping 1. Opportunity Identification
• Process Grouping 2. Opportunity Development
• Process Grouping 3. Value Proposition
• Process Grouping 4. Concept Validation
Phase II. Preparation and Production
• Process Grouping 5. Business Case Analysis
• Process Grouping 6. Resource Management
• Process Grouping 7. Documentation
• Process Grouping 8. Production
Phase III. Delivery
• Process Grouping 9. Marketing, Sales, and Delivery
• Process Grouping 10. After-Sales Services
• Process Grouping 11. Performance Analysis
• Process Grouping 12. Transformation

The Twelve Process Groupings

The following is a high-level view of the 3 phases and 12 process groupings that make up the innovative process:

- Phase I. Creation. This phase covers all the activities required to recognize potential improvement opportunities and problems, to creating a potential solution, and validating that the potential solution will address the opportunities and problems.

  Process Grouping 1. Opportunity Identification. This is where an individual or group view the same old situation and see it in a different light than before. It's where an individual or group states, "We should be able to do it differently bringing additional value to the organization." At this point the individual or group usually do not know how to make the improvement, but they are committed to come up with an innovative and creative solution. Frequently this ends up with the organization approving a mission statement.

  Process Grouping 2. Opportunity Development. During this activity, the organization identifies, analyses, and prioritizes several potential problem solutions and/or opportunity improvement approaches. Also, during this activity, the organization takes steps to protect intellectual capital (patent new and unique concepts and/or check to see that there are no patent infringements).

  Process Grouping 3. Value Proposition. During this activity, the organization will calculate the return-on-investment for the high-priority changes. It is important that the organization defines and analyses both the positive and negative impacts that the individual change would have on the organization. They need to take time to develop, refine, implement, and maintain then compare this to the value-added content that the changes will bring about. Based upon this analysis, the organization will prioritize the changes that have the biggest impact, both real and imaginary, on the organization. For a more thorough understanding of developing a value proposition, I recommend reading the book entitled *Maximizing Value Propositions to Increase Project Success Rate* published by CRC Press in 2014.

  Process Grouping 4. Concept Validation. During this activity, the organization models the proposed change allowing the collection of new performance data. The organization can accomplish modeling by building an engineering model of the change and submitting it to several conditions (for example, temperature, humidity, vibration, electronic delays, and so on). The organization can use the results to project failure rates and/or reliability. Also, they frequently use simulation models to validate the engineering and financial estimates.

- Phase II. Preparation and Production. During this phase, the organization analyzes the proposed changes to determine if they should include them as part of the organization's portfolio of active projects. After the change becomes part of the organization's portfolio of projects, the organization sets aside resources to support the change process, to create the necessary engineering and manufacturing documentation, to validate the acceptability of the production outputs through a series of manufacturing process model evaluations, and to start shipping to an external customer/consumer.

  Process Grouping 5. Business Case Analysis. During this activity, the organization conducts an independent analysis to estimate the value-added content that the project would have and compares it to other active and proposed opportunities to determine how they should best utilize the organization's resources. Approved projects should have detailed project management packages prepared for them. The organization usually funds a project that successfully complete this analysis through first customer ship and it becomes part of the organization's portfolio of active projects. To get a better understanding of the business plan analysis activity, I recommend reading *Effective Portfolio Management Systems* published by CRC Press in 2015.

  Process Grouping 6. Resource Management. During this activity, the organization puts in place the resources required for the approved project. In small and start-up companies, financing usually becomes a major problem. Initially, individuals use personal funding, then family funding, angel funding, and borrowing from banks as legitimate sources of funding.

  People resources also present a problem for both the small and large companies. Although there are enough people out of work today to fill all the available jobs, there's big shortage in fields like product engineering, programming, and manufacturing engineering.

Finding the right suppliers at the right price that can produce the correct item and do it on schedule in small lots is another problem that an organization faces during this activity. The last major item addressed in this activity is facilities. Not having the right equipment and/or the floor space required to support the output is a problem stressed during this activity.

Process Grouping 7. Documentation. During this activity, the organization prepares the engineering documentation, maintenance manuals, production routings, and job instructions and trains operators. The organization evaluates packaging and shipping containers to ensure that they provide adequate protection for the product. They define and put in place the information collection system. The project management data system generates frequent status reports to keep the management team aware of the status and to point out activities for management involvement.

Process Grouping 8. Production. As soon as the organization approves the product for shipment to the customer or consumer, they open the manufacturing floodgate. The documentation and estimates are put under stress to meet the initial output demands that occur at start. The organization initializes the information collection system and generates status reports.

• Phase III. Delivery. During this phase, the organization transforms the output from the process from items into dollars and cents. It also includes a performance analysis to compare actual results to projected value-added stakeholders.

Process Grouping 9. Marketing, Sales, and Delivery. Here the organization enters a different world. Somehow, the sales and marketing activities and culture is uniquely different than the culture in other parts of the organization. During this activity, the organization develops and implements promotional and advertising campaigns. They prepare sales strategy and quote approaches and design the motivational compensation packages.

Process Grouping 10. After-Sales Services. After-sales service includes individuals that man the control center, handle customer complaints, customer questions, and provide a line interface between the organization and its clientele. Another key part of after-sales service is a repair center. These two areas must have the "patience of

Job" since they continuously face unhappy customers who just need someone to be mad at. Empowerment is the most useful weapon the organization can give these people.

Process Grouping 11. Performance Analysis. During this activity, the organization collects data to determine if the results meet or exceed the commitments at the business plan analysis stage. They should conduct a postmortem before they close out the project. This postmortem will provide input both positive and negative into the knowledge management system to help optimize future projects. Usually, based upon this analysis, the organization rewards or recognizes individuals doing outstanding work.

Process Grouping 12. Transformation. Usually, the organization disbands the project team after they complete "Process Grouping 11. Performance Analysis," but that's only the beginning of the project story. The real test of the project occurs over the next year or two when the organization often resets the approaches to the original habit patterns. For successful innovative projects, changes must become part of the organization's culture and habit patterns. This is where the organization evaluates the real impact of the project.

ISC Summary

The ISC is a continuous flow activity with several loops to take advantage of additional data that becomes available. Treat it like a process and it will behave well; treat it like a lot of little pieces and it will bite you every time. Like any process, it must have a start and finish. The starting point for the ISC is the search for an opportunity to apply your creative powers to bring about a new and unique answer to a previously unanswered situation. It ends when output from the process delights the projected user.

TYPICAL DEFINITIONS

I debated long and hard if definitions should be given in Chapter 1 of this book or listed in its Appendix. I finally decided to put them in both places because how you define an innovator greatly impacts the certification process. Can an idea be innovative if the organization does not implement it or if it's just creative or inventive? If you are part of an established organization, the innovator must only be effective at handling a small part of one of the activities. If you're in a start-up company, the innovator will need to know and understand each of the 12 activities otherwise he or she probably will not be successful.

When I decided to certify people as innovation specialists, I chose to adhere to the most stringent requirements, rather than adjusting it to their present specific assignments. Often organizations call upon innovators to step away from the structured environment of an established organization to take on the excitement of building their personal brand. Based upon this, now is the time to establish a common understanding of the key terms I used throughout this book.

- **Innovation:** Innovation is a new or unique idea or concept that adds value to the organization and its customers. Innovation is the act of taking new unique and creative ideas developed, funded, produced, and distributed to external customers that result in creating value to both the organization and the consumer or customer.
- **Creative:** Using the ability of people to make or think of new things involving the process by which people create new ideas, stories, products, and so on.
- **Create:** Make something: to bring something into existence.
- **Entrepreneur:** An entrepreneur is a person who organizes and manages any enterprise, especially a business, usually with considerable initiative and risk. He or she does not have to create the idea or concept.
- **Innovative idea:** An innovative idea is one that adds greater value to the customer and the organization then it cost to produce it.
- **Innovation Systems Cycle (ISC):** The way a typical project for products would progress through the innovative activities from identifying opportunities to measuring the value-added to the stakeholders.
- **Innovator:** An individual who can create value-added for the organization and its customers by being capable of taking new and unique ideas or concepts all the way through the ISC from recognizing an opportunity to evaluating the value added.

Note: The definition of innovator greatly varies from company to company and consultant to consultant. At one end of the spectrum, an innovator is defined as anyone who creates a value-added idea or concept. It does not have to be unique or original nor does it need to be marketable. An extreme example is an employee who tells his manager that the filing cabinet needs to be bolted to the wall, so it won't fall over and hurt someone.

At the other end of the spectrum, an innovator is a person who generates a unique and original idea or concept for some portion of the product or service that adds value to both the organization and the external customer (for example, defining a new unbreakable material that is less expensive than the present material that can be used on the face of an iPad).

A third definition of an innovator is an individual who defines a new and unique idea that has potential value to the organization and the consumer and then is responsible for managing it through the total ISC. Due to the smokestack organizational structure in most large companies it is difficult, if not impossible, for any one individual to lead the innovative project throughout its entire cycle. In each of the major functions (research and development, project management, production control, purchasing, manufacturing, quality, personnel, sales and marketing, and so on), there are individuals who are experts in specific parts of the ISC and they must be creative in the way they conduct these activities. With this definition there is no employee or manager who is innovative although they may all be very creative. The organization itself may provide output that is very innovative.

- **Intrapreneur:** An employee of a large corporation who is given freedom and financial support to create new products, services, systems, and so on, and does not have to follow the corporation's usual routines or protocols.
- **Natural Work Teams:** A natural work team is any group of individuals who report to the same individual. It could be employees who report to the first-line manager or first-line managers who report to a second-line manager, and so on.
- **Organization:** A company, corporation, firm, enterprise, or association of any part thereof, whether it is incorporated or not, public or private, that has its own function and administration.

(Source: ISO 8402–1994). It can be as small as a first-line department and as large as the government in United States.

- **Organizational culture:** The values and behaviors that contribute to the unique social and psychological environment of an organization. Organizational culture includes an organization's expectations, experiences, philosophy, and values that hold it together, and is expressed in its self-image, inner workings, interactions with the outside world, and future expectations. It is based on shared attitudes, beliefs, customs, and written and unwritten rules developed over time and considered valid. Also called corporate culture, it's shown in:

  1. The ways the organization conducts its business, treats its employees, customers, and the wider community.
  2. The extent to which freedom is allowed in decision making, developing new ideas, and personal expression.
  3. How power and information flow through its hierarchy down the rest of the organization.
  4. How committed employees are towards collective objectives (Business Dictionary).

- **Organizational structure:** It is a system used to define a hierarchy within an organization. It identifies each job, its function and where it reports to within the organization. The development of this structure establishes how an organization operates and assists an organization in obtaining its goals to allow for future growth. The structure is illustrated using an organizational chart.
- **S-curve:** A mathematical model also known as the logistic curve, describes the growth of one variable in terms of another variable over time. S-curves are found in fields from biology and physics to business and technology. In business, the S-curve is used to describe, and sometimes predict, the performance of a company or a product over time.
- **Structure:** The arrangement of and relations between the parts or elements of something complex.

The company's weakness is the inflexibility of its management structure.

H. James Harrington

Notes

- **Innovative versus Creative:** The output from an innovative process must create added value while the output from the creative process does not have to be valued.
- **Innovator versus Entrepreneur:** The entrepreneur does not have to originate the idea or concept. An innovator needs to have created new and unique concepts that is value-added to the organization and the external customer. To be considered successful, they both must produce an output that is value-added to someone other than themselves.
- **Innovation versus Invention:** Innovation differs from invention in that innovation refers to the use of a better and, as a result, novel idea or method, whereas invention refers more directly to the creation of the idea or method.
- **Innovation versus Improvement:** Innovation differs from improvement in that innovation refers to the doing something different rather than doing the same thing better.

WHO DRIVES THE ISC?

Basically, there are four types of people who interact and drive the ISC (Figure P.6). Each of these interact in a slightly different part of the total cycle:

1. **The inventor:** The inventor is the individual who comes up with a unique creative solution to a potential opportunity. His or her primary drive is to see his or her idea come to market. After the organization validates the concept and issues the associated patents, the inventor's enthusiasm fades and he or she heads back to the lab hoping that they can invent something bigger and better than their present invention.
2. **The entrepreneur:** The entrepreneur is always looking for a new idea that has marketing potential. He or she is not concerned with who originated the idea. These are usually extroverts who get a great deal of satisfaction out of making things happen. Their major objective is to get the concept out to market where they can make some money for the organization.
3. **The innovator:** The innovator is a combination of the inventor and the entrepreneur. The innovator comes up with the new release that

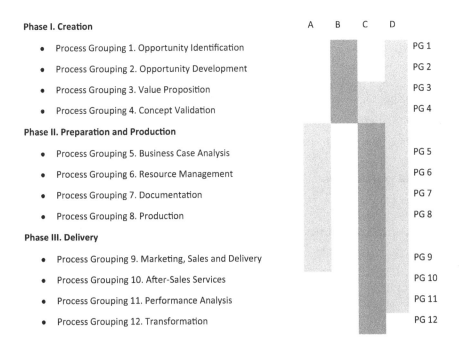

FIGURE P.6
A view of how each of the 4 types of work assignments relate to the 12 Process Groupings that make up the ISC.

is unique and different and has the capabilities to process through the ISC. The innovator is involved in driving the cycle starting with "Process Grouping 1. Opportunity Identification" to "Process Grouping 11. Performance Analysis."

4. **The project manager:** The organization assigns the project manager to a project during the business process analysis. On occasion, the organization could assign the project manager as early as when the organization approves the value proposition. His or her primary responsibility is to ensure implementation of the project on time, within budget, and ensure it is performing as required. He or she is held accountable for overseeing the project up until the time that delivery of the output starts to the external customer.

You will note there is considerable overlap particularly in Phase 1 and Phase 2. Basically, the innovator and entrepreneur activities are overlapping work assignments. Innovation is made up of a combination of invention (creation) and entrepreneurship. Take away either one of these two activities and you do not have innovation. As a result, the organization needs to schedule only one of the overlapping types of work assignments for an individual project. The exception to this would be when an inventor develops the project concepts and an entrepreneur picks up the project to develop the market. I will be discussing this type of interface in more detail throughout this book.

SUMMARY

In this preface, I introduced the reader to the 3 phases and 12 Process Groupings that make up the ISC. This is a process layout that I will use throughout this book. Each of the following chapters will discuss one of the 12 Process Groupings.

The 12 Process Groupings that make up an ISC provide an excellent model for a specific project or program. For many organizations, there is a need to improve the creativity and innovation levels for the total organization. In these cases, the organization needs a cultural change to obtain the desired impact.

In Chapter 1 I will immediately start to lead the reader through "Phase I. Process Grouping 1. Opportunity Identification."

Acknowledgment

I would like to acknowledge the support and assistance from all the individuals who have co-authored a book with me.

- Charles Mignosa
- Frank Voehl
- Christopher Voehl
- William Ruggles
- Brett Trusko
- Ken Lomax
- Thomas McNellis
- Bob Reid
- Daryl Conner
- Nicholas Horney
- Neil Kuhn

Author

Dr. H. James Harrington,
Chief Executive Officer
Harrington Management Systems

In the book, *Tech Trending*, Dr. Harrington was referred to as "the quintessential tech trender." The *New York Times* referred to him as having a "...knack for synthesis and an open mind about packaging his knowledge and experience in new ways—characteristics that may matter more as prerequisites for new-economy success than technical wizardry....". The author, Tom Peters, stated, "I fervently hope that Harrington's readers will not only benefit from the thoroughness of his effort but will also 'smell' the fundamental nature of the challenge for change that he mounts." William Clinton, former President of the United States, appointed Dr. Harrington to serve as an Ambassador of Good Will. It has been said about him, "He writes the books that other consultants use."

Heartbeat of America, which focuses on outstanding small businesses that make America strong, featured Harrington Management Systems (formerly Harrington Institute) on a half-hour television program. The host, William Shatner, stated: "You (Dr. Harrington) manage an entrepreneurial company that moves America forward. You are obviously successful."

PRESENT RESPONSIBILITIES

Dr. H. James Harrington now serves as the Chief Executive Officer for the Harrington Management Systems. He also serves as the Chairman of the Board for several businesses.

Dr. Harrington is recognized as one of the world leaders in applying performance improvement methodologies to business processes. He has an excellent record of coming into an organization, working as its CEO or COO, and initiating a major improvement in its financial and quality performance.

PREVIOUS EXPERIENCE

In February 2002, Dr. Harrington retired as the COO of Systemcorp A.L.G., the leading supplier of knowledge management and project management software solutions when IBM purchased Systemcorp. Before this, he served as a Principal and one of the leaders in the Process Innovation Group at Ernst & Young; he retired from Ernst & Young when Cap Gemini purchased it. Dr. Harrington joined Ernst & Young when Ernst & Young purchased Harrington, Hurd & Rieker, a consulting firm that Dr. Harrington started. Before that Dr. Harrington was with IBM for over 40 years as a Senior Engineer and Project Manager.

Dr. Harrington is past Chairman and past President of the prestigious International Academy for Quality and of the American Society for Quality Control. He is also an active member of the Global Knowledge Economics Council.

CREDENTIALS

H. James Harrington was elected to the honorary level of the International Academy for Quality, which is the highest level of recognition in the quality profession.

H. James Harrington is a government-registered Quality Engineer, a Certified Quality and Reliability Engineer by the American Society for Quality Control, and a Permanent Certified Professional Manager by the Institute of Certified Professional Managers. He is a certified Master Six Sigma Black Belt and received the title of Six Sigma Grand Master. H. James Harrington has an MBA and Ph.D. in Engineering Management and a BS in Electrical Engineering. Additionally, in 2013 Harrington received an Honorary Degree of Doctor of Philosophy (Ph.D.) from the Sudan Academy of Sciences.

H. James Harrington's contributions to performance improvement around the world have brought him many honors. He was appointed the honorary advisor to the China Quality Control Association and was elected to the Singapore Productivity Hall of Fame in 1990. He was named life-time honorary President of the Asia-Pacific Quality Control Organization and honorary Director of the Association Chilean de Control de Calidad. In 2006, Dr. Harrington accepted the Honorary Chairman position of Quality Technology Park of Iran.

H. James Harrington was elected a Fellow of the British Quality Control Organization and the American Society for Quality Control. In 2008, he was elected to be an Honorary Fellow of the Iran Quality Association and Azerbaijan Quality Association. He was also elected an honorary member of the quality societies in Taiwan, Argentina, Brazil, Colombia, and Singapore. He is also listed in the "Who's-Who Worldwide" and "Men of Distinction Worldwide." He has presented hundreds of papers on performance improvement and organizational management structure at the local, state, national, and international levels.

RECOGNITION

- The Harrington/Ishikawa Medal, presented yearly by the Asian Pacific Quality Organization, was named after H. James Harrington to recognize his many contributions to the region.
- The Harrington/Neron Medal was named after H. James Harrington in 1997 for his many contributions to the quality movement in Canada.
- Harrington Best TQM Thesis Award was established in 2004 and named after H. James Harrington by the European Universities Network and e-TQM College.

- Harrington Chair in Performance Excellence was established in 2005 at the Sudan University.
- Harrington Excellence Medal was established in 2007 to recognize an individual who uses the quality tools in a superior manner.
- H. James Harrington Scholarship was established in 2011 by the ASQ Inspection Division.

H. James Harrington has received many awards, among them the Benjamin L. Lubelsky Award, the John Delbert Award, the Administrative Applications Division Silver Anniversary Award, and the Inspection Division Gold Medal Award. In 1996, he received the ASQC's Lancaster Award in recognition of his international activities. In 2001, he received the Magnolia Award in recognition for the many contributions he has made in improving quality in China. In 2002, H. James Harrington was selected by the European Literati Club to receive a lifetime achievement award at the Literati Award for Excellence ceremony in London. The award was given to honor his excellent literature contributions to the advancement of quality and organizational performance. Also, in 2002, H. James Harrington was awarded the International Academy of Quality President's Award in recognition for outstanding global leadership in quality and competitiveness, and contributions to IAQ as Nominations Committee Chair, Vice President, and Chairman. In 2003, H. James Harrington received the Edwards Medal from the American Society for Quality (ASQ). The Edwards Medal is presented to an individual who has demonstrated the most outstanding leadership in the application of modern quality control methods, especially through the organization and administration of such work. In 2004, he received the Distinguished Service Award which is ASQ's highest award for service granted by the Society. In 2008, Dr. Harrington was awarded the Sheikh Khalifa Excellence Award (UAE) in recognition of his superior performance as an original Quality and Excellence Guru who helped shape modern quality thinking. In 2009, Harrington was selected as the Professional of the Year (2009). Also, in 2009, he received the Hamdan Bin Mohammed e-University Medal. In 2010, the Asian Pacific Quality Association (APQO) awarded Harrington the APQO President's Award for his "exemplary leadership." The Australian Organization of Quality NSW's Board recognized Harrington as "the Global Leader in Performance Improvement Initiatives" in 2010. In 2011, he was honored to receive the Shanghai Magnolia Special Contributions Award from the Shanghai Association for Quality in recognition of his 25 years of contributing to the advancement of quality in China. This was the first time that this award was given out. In 2012, Harrington received the ASQ Ishikawa Medal for his many contributions in promoting the understanding of process improvement and employee involvement on the human aspects of quality at the local, national, and international levels. Also, in 2012, he was awarded the Jack Grayson Award. This award recognizes individuals who have demonstrated outstanding leadership in the application of quality philosophy, methods, and tools in education, healthcare, public service and not-for-profit organizations. Harrington also received the A.C. Rosander Award in 2012. This is ASQ Service Quality Division's highest honor. It is given in recognition of outstanding long-term service and leadership resulting in substantial progress toward the fulfillment of the Division's programs and goals. Additionally, in 2012, Harrington was honored by the Asia Pacific Quality Organization by being awarded the Armand V. Feigenbaum Lifetime Achievement Medal. This award is given annually to an individual whose relentless pursuit of performance improvement over a minimum of 25 years has distinguished himself or herself for the candidate's work in promoting the use of quality methodologies and principles within and outside of the organization he or she is part of.

CONTACT INFORMATION

Dr. Harrington is a very prolific author, publishing hundreds of technical reports and magazine articles. For the past 8 years he has published a monthly column in *Quality Digest Magazine* and is syndicated in five other publications. He has authored 40 books and 10 software packages.

You may contact Dr. Harrington at the following:

Address: 15559 Union Avenue #187, Los Gatos, California, 95032.
Phone: (408) 358-2476
Email: hjh@svinet.com

1

Phase I. Creation—Process Grouping 1: Opportunity Identification

INTRODUCTION TO OPPORTUNITY IDENTIFICATION

The Innovation System Cycle (ISC) starts with identifying a problem or an improvement opportunity. Sometimes the opportunities are defined for you or assigned to you to take the proper action. An innovative individual never waits for someone else to identify an improvement opportunity. He or she takes pride in discovering opportunities which others are blind to or too lazy to take advantage of. It is much more challenging and enjoyable to identify and select the improvement opportunities you would like to work on. An improvement opportunity seeker is the individual who believes he or she can make things better rather than complain about how bad things are (example of the "dictated by management" improvement opportunity: your manager tells you to reduce the process cycle time).

Many of the improvement opportunities that the innovator identifies are beyond his or her scope to change. There's no use talking about these opportunities unless you find someone who has the responsibility to make the required changes. Talking about them is just a waste of time and you get a reputation as a complainer rather than a doer (for example, you identify that it would be an improvement to have four cup holders in the front seat rather than two and you get the four cup holder design approved and installed in the next year's cars).

Some improvement opportunities have a negative impact on one stakeholder and a positive impact on another stakeholder. An improvement opportunity is when the combined impact on all stakeholders is in the positive direction (for example, combining three activities together will increase productivity by 30 percent; this increase will allow the organization to get rid of one employee).

Some improvement opportunities relate to your personal lives and others relate to the organization you work for. Usually innovation refers to things that impact the organization you work for (a business example: automating the welding operation.) Some improvement opportunities may conflict with your values or the organization's values. In this case the individual's values hopefully will drive the final decision (for example, the woman next door is younger and prettier than your wife; should you pursue the woman next door?). Answer no; it's a lost opportunity.

INNOVATION BY THE NUMBERS

The 11 Opportunity Sources

You can identify improvement opportunities from many different sources. Most of them are defined by the 11 opportunity sources in the following list. Can you define one more making it an even dozen?

1. Customers
2. Friends
3. Surroundings
4. Experiences
5. Observations
6. Work
7. Play
8. Children
9. Research
10. Family
11. Mistakes

The 12 Wow Questions

How do you know if something is an opportunity source? If you answer "yes" to any one of the following 11 plus Wow questions, it is an opportunity candidate for innovation.

1. Wow! Can you make it go faster?
2. Wow! Can you build it faster?

3. Wow! Can you make it do what I want?
4. Wow! Can you reduce the cost?
5. Wow! Can you fix it so it won't break?
6. Wow! Can you make it do more?
7. Wow! Can you make it with fewer parts?
8. Wow! Can you make more customer friendly?
9. Wow! Can you make it work better?
10. Wow! Can you do it easier?
11. Wow! Can you reduce its weight?
12. Wow! Can you make it smaller?
13. Wow!????????????
14. Wow!????????????
15. Wow!????????????

The preceding list gives 12 good examples of what you might thinking when you recognize a potential opportunity. Can you think of three more examples making it an even 15? Look around where you are right now. Can you see anything that you could improve? The typical answer to this question is, "Yes, I see a number of things that I could improve." Let me give you a personal example of some of the things that are opportunities within 5 feet of where I'm sitting.

- My wastebasket has a contract in it. I threw it away because I signed it in the wrong place. Wouldn't it be nice if I had erasable ink?
- My desk is cluttered with paper, books, telephones, pen holders, paper-clips, a television, incoming and outgoing mail, my glasses and their holders, a cup of coffee, the picture of my wife, several reports that I must read and sign before they can go out, etc. Wow! It would be so much better if I just had the work on my desk that I am using now!
- My office is too small to keep a copy of all the books that I have written. In addition, I need books that I use for reference that someone else wrote. My reference library has over 300 books in it and I have written over 50 books. Wow! It would be nice if I could automatically go to the pages in these books that I want to work with without getting up from my desk or going to the library downstairs. Every time I get up from my desk and go down to the library I seem to find reasons to stop in the kitchen to get something to drink or eat, to stop by the bathroom for a quick break, or to stop and gossip with Candy, my office manager, for a little while. The trip that should have

taken 15 minutes often takes up 1 to 1.5 hours of my workday. Wow! Wouldn't it be great if I could store all that information automatically in my knowledge management system?

- I just broke my fingernail trying to open a 3-ring binder so I could put something in it. Wow! It would be nice if I could open the binder by touching a button on it rather than by the clumsy way they open today. For that matter why is poking holes in a piece of paper the best way to keep the information together?

- Hay! Why do I have to process all this paper? What happened to the paperless office?

- Wow! Why can't I scan and file a 50-page report without taking my time or my associate's time?

- Wow! Why isn't the paper size the same for European and American business?

- I have mountains of paper work, reports, manuscripts, and forms to read and make decisions related to them. After 2 or 3 hours just studying the papers that come into my office, my eyes are so tired that I am not able to finish the task. Wow! Why do I have to use my eyes to transform the information from the paper to my mind?

- I see a glass of Diet Coke sitting here in my desk and it reminded me that it stains my teeth. I am now trying to cut back on it. Wow! If you want to make $1 billion quickly, just find a way to create a soft drink that whitens your teeth rather than staining them.

I could go on and on for these are just a couple of the opportunities all within my personal view from my desk. I identified them purely by observation using the 12+ Wow approach.

The 8 T's for Prioritization

By now you should have identified several opportunities available to you. Your next assignment is to prioritize the opportunities. To accomplish this, first drop from your list all the opportunities that are obviously wrong for you to work on. The remainder of opportunities should be evaluated each using the "8 T's." For each of the opportunities, rate it for each of the eight statements using a scale of 1 to 10 (Note: a rating of 1 is given if the statement is totally false and a rating of 10 indicates the statement is absolutely true).

1. Taking advantage of this opportunity will have a major positive impact upon the customer and consumer.
2. Taking advantage of this opportunity will have a significant impact upon reducing output productions costs.
3. Taking advantage of this opportunity will have a significant impact upon reducing cycle time and stock.
4. Taking advantage of this opportunity will provide a competitive advantage.
5. Taking advantage of this opportunity is in line with the organization's culture.
6. Taking advantage of this opportunity will improve morale.
7. Taking advantage of this opportunity will require few resources.
8. Taking advantage of this opportunity will create more jobs for our employees.

Sum up the rating for each of the 8 T's (minimum rating of 0, maximum rating of 80). Let the total sum's value be an indicator but not as the final selection process. This number needs to be considered along with experienced management judgment. I recommend that you include between 3 and 10 improvement opportunities in this evaluation. Of course, if there is one opportunity that stands out above all the others, this evaluation is not necessary. You should make the final selection based upon engineering and management knowledge and priorities.

New Ideas and Concepts

> The things that get done are the things that are easy to do and where the rewards are the highest.
>
> **H. J. Harrington**

New ideas and concepts are the life blood of most organizations today. The value proposition approach primes the pumps that move the most important and relevant ideas and concepts through an organization's business cycles. No matter how good the pump is, if you don't have an abundance of subject matter, the system soon runs dry and the organization becomes obsolete. The challenge that many organizations face is how to turn all employees into entrepreneurs who are actively searching for ideas and concepts that will add value to the organization. In most organizations, employees are not challenged or motivated to challenge the status quo to find better ways of doing things. Literally billions of dollars are lost due to the lack of ability of those employees closest to the problems to adequately document the ideas they have. Even when these employees do have the ability, many are reluctant to take the time to document the problem and suggest improvements. In most cases, first-level employees face many improvement opportunities and problems every day that are not brought to anyone's attention. As a result, the organization considers that many of troublesome processes are functioning effectively even though they really have the potential of functioning far more efficiently.

Suggestion Programs

With today's national focus on increased innovation, organizations are searching for ways to help their employees become more creative and innovative. In the 20th century, suggestion programs were an extremely active approach to stimulate creativity within the workforce. However, today these programs have lost favor, not because of the programs themselves, but because of the way many organizations implemented them. Following are a few of the major problems:

1. The long cycle time between when an employee turned in a suggestion and when the organization completed the suggestion cycle.
2. Many professionals felt that line people who didn't have the relevant professional education were telling them what to do. In addition, managers tended to ask the engineers why they didn't think of this if an unskilled worker could figure it out.
3. In many cases it is difficult to determine if the idea was eligible as suggestion or if it was part of the employee's job responsibilities. In the former case, employees get paid for the suggestion and in the latter case, they do not. I personally know of one case in which an engineer had one of the line workers turn in one of his ideas as a suggestion with the agreement that they would split the money awarded for the suggestion.

The suggestion program is an American institution started in 1896 by the National Cash Register Company. The suggestion program offers the opportunity to suggest improvements to the person closest to the work activity. This opportunity often results in more effective utilization of assets, increased productivity, waste reduction, product costs reduction, and improved quality.

For the employee, the suggestion program offers an additional extra income, a means for self-expression, a path towards achievement, recognition, and a feeling of contribution. Paul Petermann, past Manager of Field Suggestions at IBM Corporation, stated, Ideas are the life blood of the company and the suggestion plan is a way to get these ideas marketed. Suggestion programs save organizations around the world billions of dollars each year and allow the organizations to share these savings with the employees.

> Listen to your employees' ideas and help them to implement them to build trust and loyalty throughout the organization.
>
> **H. J. Harrington**

How does the Suggestion Program Work?

Normally, employees document their ideas for improvement and submit them to a central suggestion department. The suggestion department chooses the area within the organization that is best suited to evaluate and implement the suggestion. If the evaluation area accepts the suggestion, the evaluator will determine what tangible savings will result from implementing the idea. In some cases, the evaluation area will accept suggestions even though the savings are intangible: These ideas have benefit to the organization, but organization cannot measure the savings or estimate it in precise dollar-and-cents terms.

The evaluation area returns the accepted and rejected suggestions to the suggestion department to review them for for completeness and accuracy. The suggestion department sends a letter to the employee's manager that describes the action taken on the suggestion. For accepted suggestions, a check usually accompanies the letter. The manager reviews each suggestion with the employee. When the accepted suggestion results in a major cash award, the managers will usually call a department meeting to present the award to the employee. This meeting provides recognition for the employee and sends a message to other members of the department to participate in the suggestion program.

The Opportunity Center

To stimulate the creativity and innovation movement within their organizations, many of the more advanced U.S. organizations are now establishing or replacing their suggestion departments with a new organization called "Opportunity Centers." These Opportunity Centers play a key role in stimulating creativity and innovation in all areas of the organization. However, in most cases the Opportunity Center was the outcome of the evolutionary growth of the suggestion system. Some organizations also have delegated the Innovation Center and the Knowledge Management System responsibilities to the Opportunity Center. Often the Opportunity Center will be the champion for an idea presented to them. Employees who believe they have a good idea will often go to the Opportunity Centers where professionals help them clarify and document their ideas. For some ideas the Opportunity Center will schedule meetings with key executives and assess the employee in presenting their concept including the projected value added.

A typical mission statement for an Opportunity Center could read as follows.

> The Opportunity Center is responsible for stimulating and activating the creative and innovative activities for all the organization's employees. The Opportunity Center accomplishes these activities by providing training on problem solving, creativity, and innovation. The Opportunity Center personnel provide one-on-one and group mentoring with the objective of helping employees clarify and develop their ideas. They then provide guidance and help the employees and the organization to transform these concepts into tangible results.

Typical services provided by an Opportunity Center are:

- Review suggestions to identify ones that have a high potential payback and putting them on a fast track to get them implemented.
- Review suggestions to identify ones that need additional clarification. Then sit down with the employee who made the suggestion to help the employee document his or her ideas.
- Serve as a resource that will work with an employee who is having difficulties in expressing and documenting his or her ideas.
- Help employees prepare value propositions used to evaluate conceptual ideas.
- Provide training on various problem-solving tools, innovation approaches, and knowledge management methodologies.
- Serve as the ombudsman for employees or teams who are presenting ideas and concepts to the management.
- Help employees or groups to find executive sponsors for ideas that have significant merit.

- Help employees develop their high potential ideas into documented value propositions to present to management.
- Provide mentors for teams or groups who are holding brainstorming or problem-solving meetings.

Typically, an employee who is having problems in clarifying and documenting a concept he or she has developed will schedule a meeting with a member from the Opportunity Center. Often these meetings focus on getting a better understanding of the difficulties in implementing his or her concept and calculating potential benefits, costs, and risks related to the implementation of the concept. The Opportunity Center personnel are responsible for helping the employee clarify and refine his or her concept. The outcome of this activity can result in the concept being discarded or the preparation of a value proposition for presentation to the management team. On occasion, what results from this meeting is a decision that the concept is not in line with the mission of the organization. When this is the case, in the more advanced organizations, the Opportunity Center personnel will help the employee to determine if it is a marketable idea. Some organizations even encourage the employee who has a marketable idea not related to the organization's mission to become an entrepreneur. In these cases, the personnel in the Opportunity Center will inform the employee of the risk, benefits, and activities required to form his or her own corporation or to market the idea to an organization outside of the one that presently employs them. These are organizations that are concerned about its employees and realize that small business is the heartbeat of the American economy. These are organizations that look beyond their own bottom line, thereby encouraging innovation and entrepreneurship throughout the organization.

Typical Objectives of the Opportunity Center

The following is a list of typical objectives that an organization could set when establishing an Opportunity Center:

- Obtain 100 percent of all employees submitting ways to improve how they perform their assigned task each year. This includes everyone from the Chief Executive Officer (CEO) down through the organization chain.
- Obtain an average of two implemented suggestions per month per employee related to how he or she performs his or her assigned tasks.

- Obtain from each major function in the organization at least one major improvement concept every year that will generate revenue or define operating savings equal to the operating cost of that function over the following 2 years.
- Obtain from each function, creative concepts that will improve their productivity by a minimum of 5 percent per year. The organization will measure this improvement by the function being able to increase its output by a minimum of 5 percent using the same resources or by producing the same quantity of output using less resources by 5 percent or more.
- Help the organization generate 35 percent of its revenue each year from products and services that the organization did not offer 3 years earlier.
- Provide training to 100 percent of the employees to help improve their problem-solving ability and their creativity.
- Conduct the closing postmortem related to successful and unsuccessful projects. The results of these postmortems are entered into the knowledge database.
- Establish and maintain an online database of best practices and proven applied approaches that the organization used and that the organization may use to create new solutions and products.

You may wonder why an organization would include their knowledge management system as part of the Opportunity Center. More and more today's improvements are based upon an evolution, rather than revolution, of concepts. A good knowledge management system collects information related to how the organization solved problems in the past and groups them in a format so that the organization can readily apply experience to existing problems. Reapplying proven concepts, slightly modified to correct a current problem, often is the less risky path to take in your continuous improvement. Techniques like TRIZ, with good examples of how the organization applied each of the 40 principles in other innovative applications, provide an excellent idea-generating platform that can lead as breakthroughs in creativity and innovation (see Figure 1.1). One very effective approach used is that each time the organization defines a new concept or solves a problem, the organization classifies the approach used into one of the 40 TRIZ principles. This classification soon results in a large database of the organization's related examples grouped in line with the 40 TRIZ principles. This database is then used to help define future solutions.

Altshuller's 40 TRIZ Principles for Conflict Resolution

1	Segmentation	21	Rushing through
2	Extraction	22	Convert a harm into a benefit
3	Local conditions	23	Feedback
4	Asymmetry	24	Mediator
5	Combining	25	Self-service
6	Universality	26	Copying
7	Nesting	27	Disposable object
8	Anti-weight	28	Replacement of a mechanical system
9	Prior counter-action	29	Use a pneumatic or hydraulic construction
10	Prior Action	30	Flexible film or thin membranes
11	Cushion in advance	31	Use of porous material
12	Equipotentiality	32	Changing the color
13	Inversion	33	Homogeneity
14	Spheroidality	34	Rejecting and regenerating parts
15	Dynamicity	35	Transformation of physical and chemical states
16	Partial-excessive action	36	Phase transition
17	Shift to a new dimension	37	Thermal expansion
18	Mechanical vibration	38	Use strong oxidizers
19	Periodic action	39	Inert environment
20	Continuity of a useful action	40	Composite materials

FIGURE 1.1
Altshuller's 40 TRIZ principles for conflict resolution.

Capturing and maintaining data related to best practices and problem-solving approaches previously used by the organization and having it readily available in a database provides a competitive advantage that is often a necessity in today's fast-moving very competitive environment. An effective knowledge management database is an essential part of any organization's creativity and innovation processes.

Reinforcing the Opportunity Environment

To help create and reinforce an environment where all employees can be creative and innovative, the Opportunity Center often conducts the following activities:

- Coordinates the monthly functional opportunity-recognition luncheons. Each month the employee who submits the most creative implemented idea in each function (Product Engineering, Finance, Production Control, Sales and Marketing, Quality Assurance, Procurement, Human

Resources, etc.) receives an invitation to have lunch with the CEO and the COO of the organization. It is important to note that the organization selects the winning ideas based upon their originality and how creative the ideas are, not upon how much money they save the organization. Focusing the selection on creativity allows all employees within the functions to compete on an equal playing field. During these luncheons, the participants discuss the winning ideas and each employee receives a small gift.

- Initiates the Opportunity Coin Program. The intent of the Opportunity Coin Program is to recognize employees who come up with creative ideas. Each month the head of each function will personally distribute tokens of recognition to the three employees in his or her function who were runners-up to the employee recognized at the monthly functional opportunity-recognition luncheon. Typically, the employee may exchange these tokens for a free lunch at the organization's cafeteria or at a local restaurant. Our experience indicates that employees rarely cash in these tokens, but cherished them as tokens of personal recognition. The head of each function is required to personally visit the winners in his or her work area and present the tokens to them in their personal work environment.
- Yearly Opportunity Awards Dinner. The Opportunity Center will coordinate the Yearly Opportunity Award Dinner. At this dinner typical awards presented are:

1. Most creative idea by function.
2. Most creative idea from the clerical support staff.
3. Most creative idea related to the new products.
4. Most creative marketing idea.
5. Most creative sales idea.
6. Most creative production operations related idea.
7. Employee submitting the most implemented ideas.
8. Employee submitting the idea that saved the most money.
9. Team that created the most creative idea
10. Recognition of employees who received patent approval during the year.

This is a dinner that the organization invites the award winners, their spouses or significant other, and their children to attend. One of the best ways to develop employee loyalty and personal satisfaction related to an employee's job is to make employees look good in front of the people who are most important to them—their family. The employee may not have a very responsible job at work, but at home they are king or queen. When one of the family is recognized for being the best at something, it is a golden day for the whole family. The CEO of the organization hosts the award dinner.

PROJECT CHARTER

Now that you have defined the priority opportunity, you are ready to prepare a project charter. At this point in the ISC, you should prepare a project charter with the understanding that it probably will undergo significant changes before you finalize it. You should include the following information in the project charter at this point in the cycle:

- The name on the project.
- A description of the opportunity.
- An estimate of what the value added over the first year of implementation would be to the organization.
- An estimate of what is value added over the first year of implementation to the customer or consumer.
- An estimate of the time required to define the action necessary to take advantage of this opportunity (Time before Process Grouping 4: Concept Validation).
- An estimate of the amount of resources required to develop an approach to take advantage of the opportunity and preparing a value proposition.
- Estimated probability of finding an acceptable improvement approach.
- Defined checkpoints during the cycle.

My customers frequently ask me why I have them prepare a charter when they have identified the improvement opportunity but have not created an approach to take advantage of the opportunity. The reason to do it before starting the creative part of the process is that I want the creative team to have a good understanding of what the expected outcome from their activities is. Usually the employees who identify the opportunity will prepare the charter and then his or her manager will review it prior to assigning a team to determine how the organization can take advantage of the opportunity.

The charter helps the creative team to better understand the present status, root causes, potential roadblocks, and required conclusions.

It is understood that these estimates are based upon the employee's or the team's best estimates. Usually these estimates are accurate to ± 30 percent. The creative team will accumulate a great deal more knowledge before they prepare the value proposition. The creative team should greatly reduce the errors by the time they prepare and present the value proposition to management. Of course, the employees should present this preliminary charter to management and, if necessary, the organization should set aside separate budget funds to collect resource usage data when the organization calculates the return on investment for the value proposition.

Innovation Maturity Analysis for Your Organization

We strongly believe that any new improvement initiative should not be started until there is a good understanding of the organization's strengths and weaknesses related to the type of improvement. Your impression of the organization's innovation performance is very important to you and your organization. As a result, we have developed a very short online survey that provides a snapshot view of how you believe the innovation activities within the organization are functioning. In addition, it will provide your impression of the strengths and weaknesses of the major innovation drivers within your organization.

Although your impression of the organization's ability to be innovative is very important and may or may not reflect the organization's actual performance, to have sufficient confidence in any survey a much larger sample needs to be analyzed and has to be a homogeneous sample of the population being surveyed. As a result, we recommend that this analysis be used primarily as a weathervane to determine if improving the innovative systems within the organization will result in significant bottom-line improvement.

You can get to the survey using the following link.

http://www.hjharringtonassociates.com/

When you get to this website, just click on breaking news. After you take the survey, the computer will analyze your inputs and provide a free customized report back to you within several minutes.

I hope you will find this report useful. Please let me know what you think of it.

H James Harrington HYPERLINK "mailto:hjh@svinet.com" hjh@svinet.com

2

Process Grouping 2: Opportunity Development

INTRODUCTION TO OPPORTUNITY DEVELOPMENT

I debated for several weeks trying to define what this process would be called. It could be a correction to a problem, which in this case should be called "corrective action." It could be developing some new and unique product, which in this case is truly the creativity process or a research project. I considered calling it "Improvement Process" which covers problem-solving and the highest percentage of the new design approaches, but it did not cover new paradigms for major discovery processes. I thought about calling it corrective and innovative activities which goes on during this part of the cycle but I eventually went with **Process Grouping** because both discovery and corrective activities are the processes where something is created. An example of creation comes from the most read book in the world—the Bible. Genesis 1–11 stated: "In the beginning God created heavens and the earth; and the earth was without form and empty, and darkness on the face of the deep; and the Spirit of God was brooding on the face of the waters."

Appendix B lists the tools and methodologies used to define potential improvement approaches. As a result, I will not repeat them here. I will only point out that our old stable friend, Brainstorming, in one form or combined with other tools and methodologies, often plays an important role. Brainstorming combined with other tools and methodologies is very effective with problem-solving or creating new and different products and services.

TEAM BUILDING AND DEVELOPMENT

The creation cycle starts with the forming of a group of people assigned with the responsibility for initiating a positive change in an opportunity the organization is facing.

Dancing with a Bear

Team building and team development can be compared to "Dancing with a Bear" (see Figure 2.1). The story goes like this. You can select the bear, the music, the time, the place, and the very moment of embrace. But then, the bear determines the pace, the power of the embrace, how long you dance, and your final condition. The moral is: "Be prepared when you decide to dance with a bear." The lesson to remember is to be prepared when you embark upon the journey to build a team.

Teams are naturals at problem solving. The employees are also the experts at their work. It is the right thing to do to encourage employees to be the problem solvers. The dance begins with problem solving that

FIGURE 2.1
Dancing with a bear.

leads the team to decision making. The team must live with the choices they make. It is only right to involve the team members in making the team decisions. The dance continues. Decision making prepares the team for goal setting by opening new horizons. It is their future. It is only right to allow employees to participate in goal setting for the team. The dance continues. Goal setting teaches the team to embrace change. Change is part of the human condition that drives all of us toward continuous improvement. Change is a thirst and a hunger that can be temporarily satisfied. I liken it to eating Chinese food. The meal fills you up but in a short time you're hungry again.

Keys to Teamwork

The keys to teamwork include concepts, strategies, and tactics. These keys are most effective when used together, and each is essential to unlocking the team's potential. The following are eight keys that open the door to teamwork:

1. Chemistry. The "magic" happens when individuals unite to achieve something totally beyond the reach of any single person.
2. Recruiting. Selecting people with specific knowledge, skills, education, and experience needed to excel in each role on the team.
3. Attitude. The state of mind and feeling to achieve goals with other people. Attitude more than aptitude determines a team's final altitude.
4. Diversity. Create and sustain an environment that values all individuals on the team and enables them to reach their full potential. The team benefits from exposure to other learning styles, social backgrounds, and so on, thus making them more innovative with their ideas and approaches to problem resolution.
5. Role Acceptance. Being fully committed to a specific role and the accompanying responsibilities and accountabilities that go with the functions and tasks of that role.
6. Environment. The total combination of the conditions surrounding the team including the physical, social, and cultural things which affect the team defines its environment. The environment provides direction and support. Alignment and integration with the environment provides point-of-view, energy, and safety for the team members.

7. Mission. Knowing what the organization expects of the team.
8. Vision. The desired future state. A compelling vision which can be communicated in under 10 seconds can change the world.

The Seven Teamwork Drivers

Team building is achieved through stages. It begins with a collection of people who form an awkward group lacking purpose. The group progresses and over time transforms it into a well-organized, committed, and highly involved team of people striving to reach a shared goal. Teams and teamwork don't simply happen. The following seven teamwork drivers will create teamwork momentum:

1. Foster team ownership of the team goals
2. Increase members' feelings of controlling team destiny
3. Enhance members' self-direction, self-development, and self-management
4. Satisfy members' needs for a sense of dignity, self-esteem, and self-actualization
5. Support member communications which are true, fair, and necessary
6. Involve members in team leadership with timely and appropriate delegation
7. Unite members through team decisions

Qualities of Team Players

I frequently compare teams to a hummingbird. A hummingbird hovers in front of the flower to capture its nectar that gives it energy and life. When the work is done, it darts away faster than a speeding bullet to the next opportunity. As the hummingbird hovers in front of the flower, its rapidly beating wings create the humming sound that gave it its name. Recruiting quality members is key to making teams hum. The qualities of members on the teams that hum are not unique to humming teams. What is unique is the level to which these teams raise these qualities. It is rare that the leader gets to recruit all the members for the team. It is also rare that the members get to be on a team with the leader and members exactly the way the member would choose. Team building requires taking the team from where it is and developing it to become what it could be.

The Six Team Member Personality Traits

These are the six team member personality traits to consider in recruiting a team member:

1. Unselfishness. The quality to climb onto another person's bandwagon and cheer that person on when the wagon is not going in your direction.
2. Discipline. The quality to stay on task until the lights are turned off, the work is finished, and the force is spent.
3. Determination. The quality of identifying the right thing to do and then staying committed to do the right thing when the risks are high and the probability of reward is low.
4. Dedication. The quality to stay on a chosen course of action or thought when others have evidence that it can't be done.
5. Confidence. The inner quality of being able to enhance personal self-assurance when only you are certain of your destiny.
6. Enthusiasm. The quality of eagerness for a subject or a cause when the going is uphill through the mud and muck with the wind and chilling rain in your face.

So remember, when recruiting and selecting prospective members, provide them with opportunities to describe actual situations, actions taken, and results achieved as a direct result of their actions.

Selecting Innovation Project Members

The selection of the Innovation Team (INT) members is a most crucial step in the total project. Selecting the wrong INT members will cause the project to fail. Being a member of an INT is hard work and often conflicts with the normal work activities to which the individual is assigned. The INT members need to be free thinkers who will speak out, be creative, and make things happen.

The INT leader should determine which departments play key roles in the process and ensure the representation of each of these departments on the INT. These representatives will communicate and coordinate activities between the INT and the department managers.

The INT member will facilitate implementation of the necessary changes to the department's process. To ensure that the correct people are assigned to the INT, and to obtain an initial assessment of the process, the INT leader should meet with the manager of each key department to discuss the following items:

- The INT's purpose
- The INT's objectives
- The amount of involvement that the manager's representative will need to devote to the project
- The INT members' responsibilities
- Problems the manager is experiencing with the process
- Improvement suggestions for the process
- The names of department representatives

Do not underestimate the importance of these meetings. If well managed, they will provide the INT leader with important information about the process that he or she will find extremely valuable as the improvement efforts progress. They may even lead to new process boundary definitions. Most companies have never really studied their business processes, so it usually is difficult to initially determine their exact focus and scope. Participants should consider these meetings as means of furthering the problem definition.

The 10 Department Representative Credentials

The INT leader should point out to the manager that the department's representative to the INT should be an "expert" in his or her knowledge and understanding of the detailed activities performed in that area of the process. It is extremely important that the very best person be assigned. The INT leader should be sure that the department manager understands the role that the department representative plays and the amount of time required. It is a good idea to give him or her a copy of the job description for the INT members. In most cases he or she will select the employee who will represent his area considering the time limitations, lack of detailed knowledge of the process, or because an individual is best suited to be a team member. The selected department representative should have the following ten department representative credentials:

1. The authority to commit the department resources
2. The time to participate on the INT
3. The time to follow up on assignments given during the INT meeting
4. Practical and actual process knowledge

5. Credibility with the other INT members
6. A desire to be part of the innovation activities
7. A belief that the organization can improve
8. The willingness to embrace and lead change
9. A vested interest in the problem
10. Trained in team dynamics and problem-solving

When a team member is named, the INT leader should be sure that the individual's manager has assigned part of the individual's work to another person. I cannot emphasize enough the importance of assigning part of the individuals' present workload to someone else. Failure to do so indicates that the manager believes the individual is not giving a fair day's work for a fair day's pay. At least 25 percent of the individual's time will be required for working on the assigned project. The biggest reason for innovation failures is a conflict in assignments.

If for some reason a department that should have a representative on the INT will not assign a representative, the issue should be escalated immediately to the executive sponsor for that project or the innovation champion.

I believe that every team should have an executive sponsor. This executive has the responsibility to monitor the team's performance and progress. Often the executive sponsor is the manager who had the power to legitimize the project. His team's responsibility is to periodically present to the executive sponsor the status of the project and to request help with the project if it is not progressing according to the plan.

In many cases, a customer of the process is also a member of the INT. This relation helps keep the INT focused on the customer. Frequently, the process suppliers are also members of the INT and play a very important role. I have found that most effective teams include representatives of their suppliers and customers as part-time members.

Innovation Team Orientation

After identification of INT members, you need to prepare them for this important assignment. Prior to the first meeting, the INT leader should send the INT members the following:

- The project goals and assumptions
- A list of the INT members' addresses and phone numbers
- Copies of this book

- Copies of the INT member's job description
- The agenda for the first meeting and training session

I have found it effective to bring together two INTs for their first meeting and training session. This session provides an effective way of introducing the INTs to the innovation technology while working on their assigned processes. This jump start will provide the team with the needed understanding of the innovation methodology and help them to develop their charter and project plan.

THE SUGGESTED ACTION (SOLUTION)

There are almost as many ways to take advantage of an opportunity as there are opportunities to be taken advantage of.

H. James Harrington

The very first thing that the INT should do is to gain an agreed-to project charter. It is very important that everyone understands the team's objectives and what management is expecting from them. Management does not need to approve minor changes but does need to approve the major ones.

Although there are many ways, tools, techniques, and methodologies to define ways to take advantage of the identified opportunities, I find that after there is a common understanding relating to the project charter, it is usually advantageous to start the INT off by doing a simple brainstorming exercise. Appendix B in this book presents several options that you can use to develop an approach to take advantage of the opportunity. Due to the extremely large number of approaches that you can use, I will not try to cover them in this chapter. The INT training should already identify frequently used approaches and provide training on how to use them.

Alternative Solutions—"What if" Ground Rules

One of the major problems that face INTs is a tendency to latch onto a potential solution and then spend most of the time trying to justify using that solution. I prefer to change some of the ground rules and search for a second, third, or even fourth alternative solutions. The following are examples of five typical "What if" ground rules changes that could be considered:

- What if you had to get the change installed in the next 30 days?
- What if you had a maximum budget of $20,000?
- What if you needed to cut the cycle time by 50 percent?
- What if your competition's product was twice as fast as yours?
- What if you had lost 30 percent of the market in the last 6 months?

Often the "What If" alternatives end up as an additional approach that combines the best thought patterns together into a solution that is much better than any of the previous solutions. I recommend that your value proposition contain a minimum of 2 to 3 options. The team should present the pluses and minuses related to each option and point out the option that they determine is best.

3

Process Grouping 3: Value Proposition

INTRODUCTION TO VALUE PROPOSITION

The best time to stop a project that will add little or no value to the organization is before it is started. Effectively prepared value propositions will help you make the better decisions.

H. James Harrington

Definition of value proposition: A document that defines the benefits and negative impacts that will result from the implementation of the change or the use of output as viewed by one or more of the organization's stakeholders. A value proposition can apply to an entire organization, parts of the organization, customer accounts, product, service, or internal process.

Why would anyone write a book on value propositions? Why should you take time to read it? I suggest that you read the book entitled *Maximizing Value Propositions to Increase Project Success Rates* published by CRC Press in 2014. Well, value propositions are the first step in the process of transforming an idea or concept into tangible results. The value proposition is the document that an organization should use to drive all the significant change, growth, and improvement. I have worked with many organizations to help them define, document, and improve their major business processes. We are continuously surprised when we are asked by an organization to make a list of their major business processes and they do not include the process of transforming a concept/idea into a business initiative. In most organizations the initiation of a new business concept or initiative is unstructured. It happens by random occurrence enhancements, almost accidentally, rather than by design. Sure, there are processes for new product development, performing market studies, ordering capital equipment, suggestion programs, approving new projects, assigning resources, and so on. But when I ask the question, "What is the process for ensuring you are investing in the programs and initiatives that will give you the best long and short range results?," I find that they relied customer inputs but mainly on management experience. Probably one of the most important processes within an organization is a process that collects all the possible product and performance improvement ideas and concepts, and then evaluates them to see which they should be include in the organization's portfolio of approved projects, programs, and products.

THE NINE CHANGE DRIVERS THAT DRIVE PROJECT AND PRODUCT APPROVAL

Many different inputs drive change to the organization's processes, products, and concepts. Following is a list of nine change drivers:

1. *Market studies.* Market studies usually result in defining new or modified products and/or services within the organization that customers are interested in procuring. They are also used to define changes to marketing strategy.
2. *Problems.* Daily problems arise everywhere, and everyone is impacted because of them. As a result, everyone within the organization should be providing input to solutions for these problems. Because problems can vary from very minor to major, the impact that solving the problem has on the organization varies greatly. This high degree of variation requires that the organization design mechanisms into the system to ensure that they address minor problems in a different manner than the major problems.
3. *Observed opportunities.* There are many opportunities for improvement in most organizations. These opportunities include things that are not recognized as problems but have the potential to be better than they are, and things that are good as they are that with a little modification could be outstanding. For example, the organization is machining a part now but they could cast it. By changing the design slightly, the organization reduces the assembly time by an hour. By streamlining the process, the organization improves efficiency and

effectiveness by 30 percent. By loading the truck based upon the delivery schedule, the truck can service 20 percent more customers than before. Providing a fixture to hold an assembly improved the assembly operators' productivity by 20 percent. Putting finished goods inventories online resulted in 10 percent productivity improvement for the sales team and a 5 percent increase in sales. In almost every department in every organization there are many opportunities for improvement. Some of them are minor and some of them can have a major impact upon the organization's total performance.

There's no debating the fact that by addressing these observed opportunities, organizations could make major improvements to the organization's total performance. It is not just a matter of an organization opening its eyes and recognizing these opportunities; the organization must go further and establish processes that will allow it to take advantage of the value-added opportunities.

4. *Personal Experience.* From the day an individual is born to the last breath an individual takes, he or she is gaining knowledge based upon the surroundings and activities with which he or she is involved. It is a well-known fact that the best way to learn something is to do it. Doing something is over 50 percent more effective than being lectured about how to do it. Every individual in your organization has a wealth of experience based upon the activities he or she has been involved in both outside and inside of the organization. In many cases, an employee has worked for other organizations whose processes differ from the processes within his or her present organization. In the employee's mind, he or she is continuously doing a gap analysis that compares the effectiveness and efficiency of the processes with which he or she is involved today to the processes with which he or she was involved in the past. Often this experience provides the employee with some excellent insight into how to improve the processes in his or her current organization. For example, an assembly worker may have worked for another organization that effectively implemented a 5S system (the 5S's in the 5S system are Sort, Set in order, Shine/Sweeping, Standardize and Sustain) that improves their previous efficiency and effectiveness. Typically, a conscientious, involved employee would want to recommend to his or her current organization that they should also implement a 5S system. (A 5S system is an approach developed in Japan directed at organizing the workplace to make it more efficient, effective, and adaptable.)

Another example would be a new salesperson may have previously worked in a company that had an effective Customer Relations Management software system in place that greatly increased the level of customer satisfaction while reducing the workload of the individual salesperson.

Although these two examples demonstrate experiences of individuals while working for another organization, much of the experience that an individual brings to his or her organization is the experience that he or she gained in the non-working environments that he or she can apply to the activities going on within his or her current organization.

5. *Benchmarking studies.* One of the biggest mistakes an organization can make is to think that they have the sole passport on creativity. I continuously hear organizations complain that although they are improving their quality and productivity, they're still losing market share. The truth of the matter is that improving quality and productivity will only gain market share if it's at a greater rate than the competition. Too many organizations set improvement target rates at X percent when they should be at 3X percent. It is imperative that you know how efficiently and effectively other organizations are performing similar activities to evaluate how much improvement your organization needs. When other organizations' processes are performing better than your processes, studying them often provides you with good and sound proven ideas on how to bring about major performance improvements within your organization.

6. *Research studies.* The sole purpose of research studies within any organization is to creatively develop new or improved products, processes, and/or concepts that are relevant to the organization's basic mission statement. These research studies should be a rich source of new ideas, concepts, and products that are crucial to the organization's future financial successes.

7. *Customer complaints/recommendation.* There is a lot of discussion today about listening to the voice of the customer. When a customer comes in contact with your product, they have predefined expectations about how it will impact their environment. When these expectations are not fulfilled, the customer will turn to your competition

to fulfill their future needs. Unfortunately, it is estimated that only 1 in 25 people whose expectations are not fulfilled will complain about the inadequacies. As a result, the organization loses 24 customers because they have not been given the chance to satisfy them. I consider every complaint a golden treasure as it allows the organization to improve and thereby stop losing future customers. The organization must offset this lack of open dissatisfaction communication from the customers with a proactive approach to gaining insight into the customer experience. For example, if a customer thought the soup was too cold, but when asked, "Is everything all right?," their tendency is to say yes. But what they're really thinking is, "When I want soup, I am going someplace else." The correct way to ask for input about your services is to say, "Do you have any recommendations on how we can do better?" This puts the customer in a position of being knowledgeable, experienced, and helpful by giving advice and recommendations rather than complaining. Of course, there are many effective tools to gain understanding of the voice of the customer. Many organizations use tools like focus groups and survey effectively.

8. *Conferences, books, and magazine data sources.* Some of the most effective ways to quickly acquire new ideas and concepts that you can apply to your present organization is by reading relevant books and magazines and attending relevant conferences. This exposure provides a continuous flow of state-of-the-art knowledge and insight into how other organizations are managing their companies and initiating change within their organizations. Any conference that you attend and don't come back with a minimum of two new ideas to implement within your organization you should consider a waste of your time and your organization's money.

9. *The Internet.* Today the internet has proven to be one of the most effective ways to identify performance improvement initiatives that you can apply to individual organizations. Discussion groups actively exchange ideas defining their problems and sharing solutions for most of the critical processes throughout an organization. Organizations openly share successes and failures on the internet as never before. Millions of dollars of free consulting services are given away every day based upon questions proposed in internet

discussion groups. Unfortunately, the validity of the information on the internet is highly questionable in many cases. It is recommended that organizations verify carefully the information and concepts acquired on the internet and define the risk involved before they implement them within their organization.

WORLDWIDE COMPETITIVE ENVIRONMENT

In today's fast-moving electronic age, the number of information sources available to an organization is continuously increasing. To effectively compete in a worldwide competitive environment, organizations need to consider all the sources of new and creative ideas. No organization can rely on individual departments within the organization as a sole source of valuable creative ideas and concepts. The workforce within an organization today in most cases are highly educated knowledge workers each of which has the capability of generating that next multimillion dollar idea. As a result, organizations need to put a system in place that provides everyone in the organization with the ability and opportunity to have his or her business-related creative ideas fairly considered for implementation. In truly creative organizations today best practices calls for each individual to generate an average of two new ideas related to improving their work environment per month. In this highly creative environment, most of these ideas are small steps forward in the organization's performance, but a few of them have the potential of becoming major projects within the organization. The organization can implement most of these ideas within the already established budget with no additional human resource requirements. A few of these ideas and concepts, due to their financial, resource, cultural impact, and/ or potential of value to the organization considerations, are so extensive that the individual or team needs to prepare a formal value proposition for approval by higher-level management. After management approves the value proposition and validates the ideas for proof of concept, the organization considers it a candidate for comprehensive business case development in support of it becoming an approved organizational project and/or product.

OBJECTIVES OF THE VALUE PROPOSITION

There are several objectives of a value proposition:

- To quantify the value-added content and resource requirements of the proposed project.
- To obtain management approval on resources (human, equipment, time, space, and materials) to complete "Process Grouping 4: Concept Validation" and "Process Grouping 5: Business Case Analysis."

The organization will make the decision to include a project in the organization's portfolio of active projects during "Process Grouping 5: Business Case Analysis." Based upon this decision, the estimates resulting from "Process Grouping 4: Concept Validation" and "Process Grouping 5: Business Case Analysis" should be very accurate. There are some projects that require little or no resources to perform concept validation. In these cases, the organization drops the preparing a value proposition and the "Process Grouping 5: Business Case Analysis" (prepare Business Case Analysis). To accomplish this, the organization combines the activities performed in a value proposition and business plan analysis, thus reducing cycle time and work effort. Combining value proposition and business case analysis is based upon the degree of risk that management is willing to take. I advise dropping the value proposition and only doing a business case analysis only in very rare occasions as the risks usually are greater than the savings.

WHO SHOULD PREPARE THE VALUE PROPOSITION?

> A value proposition should evaluate a new proposal separating the winners from the losers, and the moneymakers from the money losers.
>
> **H. James Harrington**

A value proposition is an extremely important document as it will determine the life or death of a unique creative idea. The individual or group who was assigned to develop the potential innovative project usually prepares it. A second life or death situation for the innovative project will occur when more information and experience is available during the Business Case Analysis. I strongly advise that you involve other functions in making the projected estimates. For example, in an established organization you could involve the following groups in making projections related to their area of responsibility:

- Sales and marketing should provide input related to quantity of sales and price point. They also should provide performance requirements as seen by the customer.
- Finance should provide information related to employee hourly cost divided by fixed and variable costs. The only costs that are legitimate to use in projecting cost-saving is the variable cost. The combined fixed and variable costs are used in calculating project cost.
- Purchasing should provide information related to software purchase price, software installation price, and major equipment purchase price.
- Industrial engineering should provide information related to floor layout cost.

Involving these organizations in preparing the value proposition has the advantage of getting a much more accurate estimate and helps to prepare them for their activities during "Phase I. Process Grouping 4: Concept Validation." It also has the advantage of each of the functions having a committed minimum improvement goal related to the project.

In evaluating a specific proposed project, I generally add 20 percent to all invalidated costs and subtract 20 percent from all invalidated projected savings. My experience indicates that organizations in most cases estimate cost related to the project low and projected value added high for most value propositions. These estimations result in a much better return on investment than the organization will receive.

PREPARING THE VALUE PROPOSITION DOCUMENT

As a result of the activities that are in "Process Grouping 2: Opportunity Development" and "Process Grouping 3: Value Proposition," you will be able to define a list of questions that the executive team might ask or to provide information related to the proposed project. In "Process Grouping 3: Value Proposition," you will establish a data collection plan, collect the necessary information, and validate that the information was accurate. Now you are ready to analyze this data and put it into the formal value proposition document. Much of the data analysis activities that will take part are in parallel with "Process Grouping 2: Opportunity Development" as you will analyse the data as you collect it. Too often teams are interested in saving a few minutes so they put off looking at data until all the data is available. This delay can often be a major mistake. Not only does reviewing the data as you collect it save cycle time in completing a project, but it also allows the team to validate the usefulness of the data and often identify fallacies in some of the assumptions they made. This immediate review of data will allow the team to determine early in the cycle if they need to revisit the data collection plan before they implement it completely.

Value Proposition Table of Contents

As the Innovation Team (INT) starts to prepare the value proposition document, it needs to first prepare an outline of what the document will look like (table of contents). The table of contents serves as an outline for the report. It provides the storyline that the INT will present to the executive team. Although the basic tendency is to make the value proposition as comprehensive as possible, the excellence of the report is not based upon its volume; it is based upon how well it presents an unbiased view of the AS/IS situation and how it will function after implementation of the proposed idea or concept. I recommend that the INT develop a standard format for the organization that defines the basic structure and content of the value proposition document. Having a common structure for all value propositions helps the management team to understand and analyze the specific recommendation so they can make better decisions faster. The following is a typical example of what a value proposition document table of contents might look like:

- Title and the names of the originators of the proposed change
- Table of contents
- Executive overview
    1. Description of the proposed change
    2. Description of the AS/IS state
    3. Value added content that the proposed change would bring about

4. Overall cost and time frame to implement the change
5. Other solutions that were considered and why they were not chosen
6. Risk and obstacles related to the change
7. Recommendations
8. List of the key people associated with the value proposition (executive sponsor, individuals recommending the change, individuals who created the value proposition)
9. Financial calculations
10. Details related to other value-added results (for example, cycle time reduction, stock reduction, improved customer satisfaction, reduced defect levels, increase market share, etc.)
11. List of assumptions
12. Implementation plan
13. Three-year projection of the situation if the organization does not approve proposed change
14. The Net Value-Added when the Cost (Money and Other Resources) related to installation of the change is subtracted from the value-added content
15. References

A major mistake that many INTs make when they are preparing a value proposition is spending too much time collecting information. It is important to remember that if this is a major improvement in the organization's activities, it will still cycle through additional screening activities before the organization includes it in its portfolio of active projects. An independent team will prepare a business case for the project and the organization will conduct another executive analysis before it will include the project in its portfolio of active projects. This process may seem like an excessive amount of checks and balances, but the organization must be extremely careful in defining what goes into the portfolio of active projects that they are processing at the same time within the organization. Why? These projects are the ones that define the future of the organization and with an estimated project failure rate running as high as 80 percent, responsible executives are asking for a high degree of assurance that the project will yield the benefits that it is projecting.

I've seen time after time organizations or teams define a course of action and spend all their effort in trying to justify that course of effort rather than looking at the alternatives that may or may not be a better answer for the total organization. The big advantage in having a separate independent group prepare the business case is they can challenge some of the decisions that were made by the INT and suggest alternative answers. This process requires that the independent group have an excellent understanding of the situation so they can make legitimate and fact-based suggestions related to alternative approaches that the INT making the proposed change recommendation documented in the value proposition did not consider. At this point in the ideas or concept approval cycle, it is better to take the time to be creative rather than to accept the simplest and most obvious answer. It's more important to take the time to define the very best alternative than it is to use that time collecting information to justify a less than optimal solution to a situation.

> When Thomas Edison set out to invent the light bulb, he didn't start by trying to improve the candle.
>
> **H. James Harrington**

INTRODUCTION TO APPROVAL OF A VALUE PROPOSITION

After you come to this point in the project, the value proposition is nearly completed. Of course, the approval or rejection, or another reaction, of the value proposition is the most critical part of the project. However, if you perform all steps in the interim correctly and thoroughly, this part can also be the least difficult step in the process. Of course, this data can also be frustrating if there are parts of the project that the INT left incomplete or did not clarify adequately. Keys to this part of the project are an honest assessment of the status, a reconciliation to the private knowledge base, assembly of the value proposition, review of the value proposition, obtaining management approval of the organization's value proposition, and finally publishing the value proposition.

Present the Value Proposition to Management

There are two parts to this activity: assembling the value proposition and reviewing the value proposition with management.

Assemble the Value Proposition

How you assemble the final value proposition varies from organization to organization. Some may be expecting a Microsoft PowerPoint presentation, others may be expecting a full text document, including executive summaries and formalized layout. You should be careful however, that the fully assembled value proposition completely supports the recommendations and changes. If the organization does not ask for a complete proposition, it is at least incumbent upon you to have a well-organized and coherent package in case you need to support the proposition later. Therefore, you should document well the finalized package and presentation medias including page layouts, graphics, tabs, binders, their volume estimates, their distribution requirements, and delivery dates and, at a minimum, have a computer and paper file.

As previously mentioned, the contents of the package may vary widely from organization to organization. Even if your package may be more comprehensive than those required by your organization, you will still want to confirm the contents. This process might mean that you will need to confirm that the deliverables table of contents aligns with the deliverable content originally described in the project charter. Fonts, table format, pagination, and so on may be important and you should be prepared to explain any variances in report format including variations in change requests or issue resolutions that resulted in new or deleted sections in the final deliverable. Since many managers have specific sections that they like to review, be sure to explain any variations from the corporate norm.

Also, as mentioned previously, be sure to understand the presentation's quality objectives and perform final refinement edits to ensure that the deliverable meets those objectives. Organizations reject many projects because of poo- quality photos, the wrong font, sections out of order, or any number of variations that indicate to management and sponsors that you did not conduct the project with due diligence. It is always a shame when an organization rejects a project that is well done because of a failure to pay attention to the details in the report. Many managers view such things as misspelled words as an indication of the quality of the entire project.

Finally, assemble the deliverables into the final delivery format and review the final packaging. Once again, pay particular attention to the details which, if incorrect, can reflect poorly on the project and lead to rejection.

Review of Value Proposition with Management

Review of the deliverable is one of the most critical things to consider when scheduling a management review and approval sessions. You should schedule this meeting well in advance and provide a copy of the deliverable to each participant at least a week before the approval session. Although this can be difficult to accomplish, the important point is to give people enough time to put the meeting on their calendar. Holding the meeting without a key decision-maker can mean that you will need to reschedule the meeting and a high probability that the organization will not approve the project.

When holding this meeting, consider those that need to be in attendance and be sure that they are available. Confirm that they're available and do not hesitate to postpone the meeting as long as it takes to have the right people available. At a minimum, this review meeting should include the project sponsor and the executive sponsor. Of course, however, there may be other members of management and the control structure who wish to be involved in the review. Determine whether you will require or invite one or more of the work project reviewers to attend the sessions. In a highly technical process, it may also be advantageous to have a technical expert in attendance who can explain highly technical details about statistics, chemistry, software, and other technical issues.

When scheduling the review, confirm the availability of the participants before scheduling the review session. Reconfirm the meeting 1 or 2 days prior to the scheduled date to ensure that key people will still be available. Distribute copies of the deliverable before the review. Point out to the participants that the review is a forum for discussion; therefore, the participant should read and review the deliverable prior to the session. The participants need to answer the following key questions and agree to the answers during this meeting:

- Does the deliverable meet the overall organization's needs?
- Does the deliverable meet the needs of the target area of the business
- Has the project met the quality assurance requirements?
- Is a project already included in the present allotted budgets?
- How long will it take and how much will cost?
- What type of resources would be required?
- Why do you think it should be done now?
- Is the concept a new and original idea?

As best you can, find out in advance if there are any major open issues to discuss. Also, consider whether the sponsor's priorities have changed. If so, modify the project appropriately. The decision to include a project in the organization's portfolio of active projects will be made during business case analysis. Based upon this, the estimates resulting from the process validation and business case analysis should be very accurate. There are some projects that require little or no resources to perform concept validation. In these cases, the project flows directly from "Process Grouping 2: Opportunity Development" directly to "Process Grouping 4: Concept Validation." To accomplish this, the activities performed in a value proposition and business case analysis are combined, thus reducing cycle time and work effort but increasing the risk of failure. Combining value proposition and business case analysis is based upon the degree of risk that management is willing to take.

> Generally, 50 percent of the meeting attendees have already made a decision related to the proposed project before they come to the meeting; the other 50 percent have no idea why they are coming to the meeting.
>
> **H. James Harrington**

After you have come to this point in the project, it is a "*to continue or to stop*" situation. Of course, the presentation of the value proposition is one of the most critical parts of the project as a negative response can terminate the project. However, if you perform all the preparation activities correctly, there will be no surprises during this presentation because the results will speak for themselves. Too often the attitude by the INT team is to sell the concept or they are a failure. Management attitude is to reject the concept so they don't have to change their focus. The attitude that both parties should have is to use the value proposition to help define how they can assign the limited resources to get maximum value-added to the organization and its customers. Certainly, the value proposition is the first major checkpoint in the Innovation System Cycle (ISC). The most critical analysis in the business case analysis occurs later when the proposed change initiative is competing for resources with the other activities of the organization. It is not unusual for a potentially innovative product not make it through the business case analysis because there are other projects that provide a greater value-added to the stakeholders.

If management accepts the value proposition, it should result in getting budget approval for the project through "Process Grouping 5: Business Case Analysis." Usually there is a very diligent evaluation scheduled later on when the business case is presented to management

Outcome of the Management Review

At this point in the process, the object is to get management's decision related to the soundness of the value proposition figures and to estimate if the risk of failure is low enough to justify investing additional resources to validate the proposal potential meeting its projections. Typically, the organization funds the project to go through the process validation and business case analysis that will determine if the organization will include the project in the organization's list of active portfolio project.

During the business case analysis, you ask management to decide between the value-added content of the proposed project and the other priorities and opportunities that the organization is considering. The INT team should not assume that the management team will approve the proposed project. In some cases, management may reject the proposed project and cancel future activity on the project. Obtaining management's positive and negative determinations related to the project is not something you should expect entirely at the formal meeting. In fact, the INT team should have a very good impression of management's attitude towards the project based upon their many contacts with management as they prepared the value proposition in the business case analysis. In some ways, gaining approval for a project deliverable is like lobbying politicians for passage of government legislation. The project manager should take a piecemeal approach to gain insight into the position the project sponsor and other key decision-makers will take at the formal meeting. Keep the stakeholders in touch with day-to-day activities, major decisions, and issues of the project. This way they will witness each work product and the deliverable as it is created and the INT will be aware of the major issues long before final review time. If this preliminary preparation is successful, it will minimize or avoid any surprises at the final review meeting.

Prior to the final meeting, discuss the deliverable with the executive sponsor, product sponsor, and other participants to obtain their comments. This preliminary preparation will allow you to address any concerns prior to the meeting. These opportunities to check-in should proceed an opportunity to provide a project status update and some public relations work for the project. After receiving the comments, you will need to determine the impact of their comments. If the participants raise critical issues, add them to the issue log and assign them for immediate resolution. Reiterate any tasks required to finalize the deliverable.

Developing an excellent deliverable and determining how you will manage the meeting is an extremely important part of making a good presentation. I strongly recommend that the individual or team that created the idea or concept attend the meeting and be involved in presenting the project. Depending upon the individual's delivery capabilities, he or she may give the entire presentation. Keep the focus of the presentation on the idea or concept that was evaluated rather than on the evaluation itself. Be sure to allow 30 to 40 percent of the time for discussion. I have seen many meetings where the presenter gave an excellent value proposition, but he or she did not allow time for the executive team to accept the concepts. Completing a presentation and turning the floor over to the executive team members to discuss the project is absolutely crucial. If the executive team members don't feel comfortable with the project or if they don't understand how it will impact the organization, there's a high probability that they will either put the project on hold or completely reject it.

The purpose of this meeting is to obtain the necessary, formal approval for the project sponsor. Use a management approval signoff form for this purpose. If your organization does not have this form available, you should develop one and add it to the knowledge database. Remember to keep a signed copy of each deliverable's approval in the project's control file.

Also, before the meeting, follow up on any changes and issues with the reviewers. Ensure that you handle each issue and change to the satisfaction of the reviewer who suggested it.

Publish the Value Proposition

The final task in your project will be to publish the deliverable. Remember, you can publish the deliverable in many ways. For example, many deliverables do not lend themselves to publication in more traditional, paper-based sense. These days, you can publish deliverables in many ways:

- On paper as formal reports
- Electronically as online documentation

- By reference to populated knowledge bases
- By producing summary documentation which references populated knowledge bases as websites

When publishing a deliverable, consider all of these in addition to the typical format of your organization. Do not become obsessed with the need to produce paper-based materials if the type of deliverable does not warrant it. In some cases, the development of a new product will lend itself better to a different presentation format.

Make copies of the deliverable or the deliverables for each of the project's stakeholders and anyone else who requires a copy. Keep a record of the distribution list in the project control file. Additionally, if you choose to publish electronically or via a website, be sure you have a system in place that requires registration or login before download. Alternatively, having the document only viewable is a viable alternative.

POTENTIAL OUTCOME OF THE MANAGEMENT REVIEW

The objective of the executive meeting is to provide the executive team with enough information so they can take a position on the future status of the proposed change. Typically, there are three different positions they can take:

- Alternative 1—Approved project to perform process validation and business case analysis
- Alternative 2—Rejected/project dropped
- Alternative 3—Implement using current resource

The meeting is a success if the executive team selects alternative 1 or 3. The meeting is a failure if the executive team states that they have not received enough information to make a firm decision and thus require the project team to go back and collect additional information or if the executive team states that they will decide at a later date. When this pushback occurs, it is an indication that the project team did a poor job in preparing the value proposition.

Alternative 1—Approved Project to Perform Process Validation and Business Case Analysis

The best outcome from the management value proposition review is approval of the project contingent on it passing process validation and the business case analysis. This outcome is an indication that the executive team believes that the proposed change project will bring real value-added to the organization and/or selected stakeholders. As such, the executive team will approve the value proposition and authorize it to go into the next stage where you will prepare a business case for the change project. The business case builds upon the information included in the value proposition, but now the focus is a great deal more on refining the accuracy of the projections and documenting how the change will impact other projects planned for or underway within the organization. After you prepare the business case and the executive team approves it, they will analyze the change project to determine if they should include it in the organization's portfolio of active projects.

If the executive team believes that the proposed change project will bring real value-added to the organization and/or selected stakeholders, they will approve the value proposition and authorize INT to start the next two activities—proof of concept (often you will build and test a pilot process or project) and the business case analysis. The business case builds upon the information included in the value proposition, but you will base the analysis upon a greatly expanded database including the other projects underway within the organization. This analysis includes results of the concept validation, refining the accuracy of the projections, and documenting how the change will impact other projects planned for or underway within the organization. On occasion, the executive team will not approve the value-added projections because, from a business standpoint, there are other ways that are more attractive for investment of the discretionary resources or because the organization does not have the required skills to implement the project. After you prepare the business case, the executive team will analyse the change project to determine if they should include it in the organization's portfolio of active projects.

Alternative 2—Rejected/Project Dropped

Just because the executive team decides not to approve the change project, it does not mean that it is a bad idea or concept. It only means that from their point of view, there are other projects that add more value to the organization and/or its stakeholders than the one that you prepared the value proposition for. It is extremely important if the executive team rejects the project that you document the reason for the rejection well. You will need to provide this information to the individuals who created the idea or concept in a manner that they can understand. It is important that they feel that the organization evaluated their idea fairly and that the INT understands why the executive team did not approve it. Failure to consider the emotional impact for an individual whose idea the management team did not accept can have a great impact upon his or her future contributions to the organization. An individual's ideas are a very special part of the individual's emotions so it is important that you are very considerate in the way you reject his or her ideas. You must be a lot more tactful when you're saying "no" than when you're saying "yes."

Alternative 3—Implement Using Current Resources

Sometimes the executive team decides that the change project should continue and that they have covered it under the already-approved budget and resources. In this case, the executive team determines that there isn't a need currently for initiation of a special project and that the organization should complete the project with the already-approved budget and resources. In these cases, the executive team will assign the value proposition to a specific function within the organization. This function will then prepare a work plan to complete the project. These are usually small to mid-range projects that are part of the normal continuous improvement activities that the individual functions include in their annual budgets.

IS THE CONCEPT A NEW AND ORIGINAL IDEA?

Although some of the things I have pointed out in this section of the book are relevant to me, they may not be applicable to your specific assignments or products. But, I would be remiss if I didn't discuss the patent considerations at this point in the ISC. Most entrepreneurs, inventors, and innovators have very limited knowledge about the patent process. There are two points that you need to consider:

1. Infringement on somebody else's patent
2. Protecting your organization's knowledge capital

If either of these two conditions exist, start to work on protecting you and your organization from legal action related to infringement on someone else's patent or on protecting the organization's knowledge capital through the patent process (the patent process will be discussed in detail later in this book).

GOOD AND BAD DECISIONS

Basically, the purpose for preparing a value proposition is to analyze a potential project to determine the degree of value that would be added if the organization implements it. The last step in the value proposition process is a meeting with management where they make a final decision. The objective of the executive meeting is to provide the executive team with enough information so they can take a position on the future status of the proposed change and to approve the resources required to complete Process Grouping 4: Concept Validation and Process Grouping 5: Business Case Analysis.

It is the INT's responsibility to provide management with enough information so that they can make an informed decision. Unfortunately, management is only human and at times makes bad decisions. Sometimes they base those decisions upon having inadequate data and other times upon their own personality. The following are some typical examples of bad business decisions:

- "We don't like their sound—guitar music is on the way out." —Decca Recording Company on declining to sign the Beatles (1962)
- "This telephone has too many shortcomings to be seriously considered as a means of communications. The device is inherently of no value to us." —Western Union internal memo (1876)

- "I think there is a world market for maybe five computers." —Thomas Watson, chairman of IBM (1943)
- "X-rays will prove to be a hoax." —Lord Kelvin, president of the Royal Society (1883)
- "Everyone acquainted with the subject will recognize it was a conspicuous failure." —Henry Morton, President of the Stevens Institute of Technology on Edison light bulb (1880)
- "The horse is here to stay but the automobile is only a novelty—a fad." —The president of the Michigan Savings Bank advising Henry Ford's lawyer not to invest in the Ford Motor Company (1903)
- "Television will last because people will soon get tired of staring at a plywood box every night." —Darryl Zanuck, movie producer, 20th Century Fox (1946)
- "There is no reason for any individual to have a computer and in his home." —Olson, present and chairman and founder of Digital Equipment Corporation in a talk given to a 1977 World Future Society meeting in Boston (1977)
- "If excessive smoking actually plays a role in the production of one cancer, it seems to be a minor one." —W. C. Halleuper, National Cancer Institute (1954)
- "No, it will make war impossible." —Hiram Maxim, the inventor of the machine gun, in response to the question "Will this make war more terrible?" (1893)
- "The wireless music box has no imaginable commercial value. Who would pay for a message sent to no one in particular?" —Associate on David Sarnoff responding to letters for investment in the radio (1921)
- "How, sir, would you make a ship sailing against the wind and currents by lighting a bonfire under her deck? I pray you, excuse me, I have not the time to listen to such nonsense." —Napoleon Bonaparte, when told of Robert Fulton's steamboat (1880s)
- "The idea that cavalry will be replaced by the iron coaches is absurd. It is little short of treasonous." —Comments made by an aid to Field Marshall Haig at a tank demonstration (1916)

SUMMARY OF VALUE PROPOSITION

Value proposition, an old concept, is taking on a new significance in today's innovation-driven environment. Business focus has shifted from developing many creative ideas to developing only those that will successfully flow through the ISC and fulfill any customers' needs. The old approach resulted in as little as 10 percent success rate for concepts that started through the cycle; organizations today cannot tolerate this low success rate. The value proposition discussed here outlined a systematic approach to making an early evaluation of potential projects and programs so you can determine if it can add real value to your organization and/or its customers. This approach could potentially save an organization millions of dollars and months of valuable time.

Through the effective use of value propositions, it is completely possible for your organization to increase the number of new products or services it offers to its customers by over 100 percent. It is not unusual for this to result in more than a 40 percent increase in profit per year. Adapting the approaches presented here can save your organization millions of dollars and much time. What can be better than reducing costs while increasing sales?

The value proposition document includes key points from the data collected and the best judgment of the INT. This document includes a view of the present conditions and a review of old and new data collected. It is understood that this is a first assessment of the validity of the proposed change and that you will prepare a much more detailed and accurate document for the business case analysis. The INT and the part of the organization responsible for the activity should prepare estimates jointly. Value proposition estimates error value by as much as plus or minus 30 percent. In most organizations approved proposals for new product should at a minimum break even within the first 2 years. Approved proposals for new or updated processes, services, and software should at a minimum break even after 12 months.

4

Process Grouping 4: Concept Validation

Concept validation could be called transforming dreams into reality.

H. James Harrington

INTRODUCTION TO CONCEPT VALIDATION

Our experience indicates that organizations can improve the current process significantly just based upon the additional attention the AS/IS activity is getting. I observed on several occasions where the present process is outperforming the proposed process because of the additional attention that made it function better. Without running the parallel system, you would never know if you've got a winner or loser. Be sure you run a large enough sample to get statistically sound comparison data. One of the biggest problems I have seen related to validation is the use of too small of a sample to obtain statistically sound data. I have seen several major financial commitments made using data that had a 50 percent chance of providing good information and a 50 percent chance of providing bad information.

The concept validation report document generated includes key points from the data collected and the best judgment of the INT. This document includes a view of the present conditions and a review of the proposed change based upon the new data collected and the INT's best judgment. It is understood that this is a first assessment of the validity of the proposed change and that you will prepare a much more detailed and accurate document for the business case analysis. The INT and the part of the organization responsible for measuring value-added should prepare estimates jointly. Value proposition estimates vary as much as plus or minus

30 percent. In most organizations approved proposals for new products should at a minimum break even within the first 2 years. Approved proposals for new or updated processes, services, and software should at a minimum break even after 12 months.

At the end of "Phase I. Process Grouping 3," the product should have developed to the point that it is ready to have a model constructed to validate the concept and to compare its function to the AS/IS conditions and the organization has approved the budget for the activities necessary to support "Phase I. Process Grouping 4. Concept Validation" and "Phase II. Process Grouping 5. Business Case Analysis."

Often the INT grows to accomplish the tasks assigned in a minimum amount of time. It is understandable that if you have a truly unique idea, you want to get it to the market in an expeditious manner. Work on preparing the concept validation should take priority, but you need to also start collecting statistically good data related to the AS/IS conditions for use during the "Process Grouping 5. Business Case Analysis."

> The definition of concept validation (proof of concept) is a realization of a certain method or idea to demonstrate its feasibility, or a demonstration in principle, with the aim of verifying that some concept or theory has practical potential. INTs use concept validation to validate the performance of the activities defined in the value proposition. Concept validation and proof of concept are often used interchangeably. The major difference between the two is that concept validation requires a complete analysis of compliance whereas the proof of concept can be directed at just a few features in the proposed change and/or product. The concept validation purpose is to demonstrate that the proposed project can meet its documented goals and objectives usually from a technical standpoint. It provides an insight into how the project will add value to the organization and customer.

My experience indicates that the current (AS/IS) process will significantly improve based upon the additional attention it receives. I observed on several occasions where the present process is outperforming the proposed process because it got additional attention that made it function better. Without running the parallel system you never know if you've got a winner or loser.

Be sure you run a large enough sample to get statistically sound comparison data. The biggest problems I have seen related to validation is the use of too small of a sample to obtain statistically sound data. I see several major financial commitments made using data that had a 50/50 chance of being right or wrong based upon the data. Often setting up a pilot facility that can produce sufficient output to make a statistically sound comparison to the AS/IS process is not practical due to the cost in constructing the pilot facilities and the amount of time required to collect a statistically sound sample. As a result, management frequently finds it necessary to accept the risk of using data that has potential errors associated with it in making the decisions.

> The definition of proof of concept is a realization of a certain method or idea to demonstrate its feasibility, or a demonstration of whose purpose is to verify that some concept or theory has the potential of being used. A proof of concept is usually small and may or may not be complete. Demonstrations for start-up companies or new products often use the proof of concept approach to show how the concept will perform out in the real world.

You should take great care in designing the value proposition process because it will play a major role in getting the innovative concept/product approved to become part of the organization's project portfolio. On many occasions excellent value-added projects have not passed the business case analysis due to a poorly designed concept validation design and/or inadequate, sloppy implementation of the concept validation design.

A question that is frequently asked is, "Why not do the concept validation prior to preparing and presenting the value proposition?" That's a good question. In some projects, typically continuous improvement projects, organizations complete "Process Grouping 4. Concept Validation" quickly with little or no interruption to the present product and relatively low-cost service processes. The validation can become very expensive when the organization needs to prepare models, which is very time-consuming. I've been involved in a cleaning solution for use in hospitals to kill contagious bacteria where the proof of concept activities took more than a year to complete. In many cases, "Process Grouping 3. Value Proposition" resulted in the organization dropping the project or greatly modifying it in scope. If the organization drops the project, then they lose all the money and effort devoted to the project. If the organization makes a major change in the project scope, then they will have to redesign and re-evaluate the proof of concept. For many of the continuous-improvement type changes, the concept validation activity can take place during "Process Grouping 2. Opportunity Development".

In these cases, the organization sometimes combines the value proposition and the business case analysis together depending upon the risk that management is willing to take. When this combination occurs, management has little or no impact in defining the performance parameters related to the change until the INT conducts the business case analysis. Changes at this stage in the cycle can be very expensive and time delaying.

Note: I decided to write this book in a very comprehensive manner that will allow the individual INTs to drop portions of Innovation System Cycle (ISC) based upon the specific project requirements.

Frequently, the concept validation activities will require a prototype model to show that the idea or device will be capable of performing to expectations. An organization also may use these models to convince the financial investors that they should invest in the organization.

THE FOURTEEN CONCEPT VALIDATION TASKS

Concept validation for new or updated products consist of 14 tasks:

1. Manage the potentially innovative process
2. Prepare preliminary specifications, prints, and drawings necessary to prepare pilot products (model outputs)
3. Review paperwork to determine if there are any patent infringements or items for which the organization should obtain a patent and take action to protect the organization's knowledge base
4. Review the design to ensure that the organization defines and qualifies all relevant functional and nonfunctional parameters that would be important to the stakeholders
5. Develop a concept validation plan
6. Construct pilot products (for some products, this requires setting up a pilot facility)
7. Characterize the pilot product and compare it to functional and nonfunctional parameters defined in Step 4 and the customer-input requirements prepared by sales and marketing (be sure you have a big enough sample to get statistically sound data)
8. Use the product internally if there is an application
9. Ship to key customers for performance feedback

10. Conduct environmental and reliability test as it is related to the product

11. Compare test results to customer performance requirements as defined by marketing and sales and the requirements defined in Step 4

12. Review to determine the design for:
    - Safety
    - Reliability
    - Testability
    - Manufacturability
    - Environment
    - Serviceability
    - Ergonomics
    - Aesthetics
    - Packaging
    - Feature additions
    - Time to market

13. Analyze results to determine how much value-added the product will be to the company and the customer/consumer

14. Make a list of the risk related to the project

CONCEPT VALIDATION FOR NEW OR UPDATES PROCESSES, SERVICES, AND/OR SOFTWARE

Concept evaluation for new or updated processes and/or services is a much more direct and simple task to perform. It consists of the following seven tasks:

1. Prepare a detailed flow diagram of the present processes, services and/or the software activities

2. Draw flow diagram of the proposed improvement process, service, and or software

3. Take action to protect the organization's knowledge base

4. Prepare preliminary paperwork related to the new flow diagrams

5. Set up a parallel pilot process, service or software (do not disturb the present process, service, or software)

6. Ensure that measurement systems are in place to collect both costs and value-added information for both the present and new flow diagrams

7. Operate the two processes in parallel collecting information from both processes
8. Estimate the cost of installing the future state solution
9. Compare the AS/IS to the future state solution
10. Estimate based upon the information collected in the estimates made by the INT to come up with a positive or negative impact to each of the stakeholders if the organization implements the future state solution

Concept Validation Preparation

With successful completion of the value proposition, the change initiative has a much higher probability of being included in the organization's portfolio of projects. At this point in the cycle, the project has an approved budget for "Process Grouping 4. Concept Validation" and "Process Grouping 5. Business Case Analysis." Now is the time to start managing the change activities as a legitimate project. All key players involved should now be keeping an engineering notebook that is adequate to support a patent application and/or a dispute over patent infringements.

The concept validation is used in many different areas including research and development, software development, process refinements, production facilities, major organizational structure changes, and even in art. It is particularly useful in innovative products or services directed to an external customer. The entrepreneur uses it to convince potential investors that the proposed item is financially valid. It doesn't matter if it is a long-term, established, and large organization or a young start-up firm because the proof of concept is a powerful tool used to acquire additional resources to develop and produce the desired output.

The Nine Approaches to Concept Validation

1. Short animations or films to prove that a concept is *viable*
2. Laboratory testing that simulates the item's performance
3. 3D printing to rapidly produce simulated models
4. Detailed research papers and reports to prove a business model

5. Run a controlled experiment on a client's facilities
6. Build a mockup model of the output (for example, clay models of automobiles)
7. Environmental testing (for example, wind tunnel, higher low temperature, vibration, humidity, etc.)
8. Simulated process flow experiments
9. Mathematical models to accurately produce projected outputs (for example, design of experiments)

Designing the Concept Validation

The concept validation is the first and only functional analysis made prior to announcing the product to your customers in most cases. Usually there is no additional testing performed until the executive team has approved the output during its business case analysis. The concept validation analysis frequently is the only test of the technical capability of the system and experienced laboratory technicians conduct it. The concept validation testing usually takes place in the organization's laboratory under the guidance of experienced development engineers, programmers, and system specialists. The testing usually does not provide an opportunity for the production-line employees to gain practical experience related to the solution. It is for these reasons that it is extremely important for the INT to design the concept validation evaluation carefully. The concept validation evaluation uses a more comprehensive evaluation plan. Prerequisites to starting a concept validation activity are:

- Obtain input from all the stakeholders, executives, customers, engineers, and employees to establish the criteria used for the proof of concept activities
- Define in writing the purpose, goals, objectives, and scope of the proof of concept activities
- Define acceptable and rejected criteria for the activity
- Define the benefits of conducting the concept validation and the risk if proof of concept activities not performed
- Establish an administrative infrastructure assigned to assist in completing the concept validation activities

Measurement—The Foundation of Concept Validation

> Write it down. Written goals have a way of transforming wishes into wants, wants into dos, dos into plans and plans into reality. Don't just think—ink it.
>
> **Mr. Rahul Revne**

It is easy for the executive team to take exception to individual's estimates, but it is very difficult to take exception to a statement based upon statistically sound data no matter what your culture is. A good measurement system that collects the right kind of data in sufficient quantities to statistically measure its accuracy is a key ingredient in most concept validations. I am not indicating that you can always process a big enough sample to get data that's accurate to plus or minus 15 percent. Your real obligation is that for every measurement, you define the accuracy of the data that's being presented even though the potential error is as high as plus or minus 50 percent. There's an old saying, "Measure twice and cut once."

> When it comes to concept validation, the rule is "5 minutes of well-analyzed, statistically sound data is worth more than 4 hours of debate."
>
> **H. James Harrington**

The Eleven Measurement W's

There are 11 W questions that an organization should answer to develop a comprehensive measurement plan:

1. Why should you measure?
2. Where should you measure?
3. What should you measure?
4. When should you measure?
5. Who should be measured?
6. Who should do the measuring?
7. Who should provide feedback?
8. Who should audit?
9. Who should set the targets?
10. What will you do with the data?
11. Who will analyze the data and prepare the report?

DATA COLLECTION FORMS

Designing data collection forms is an art. The forms designer must design the forms to serve the person who is recording the data, time, and reducing input errors and for how it is best to enter the data into the computer. The designer must design the forms for the user and then use the software to arrange the data so that the software package can use it.

Does a good form make a difference? When the British Government agencies focused their attention on form design, errors plummeted, and productivity soared. For example:

- The British Department of Defense revised its travel expense form. The new forms reduced errors by 50 percent, the time required to fill it out by 10 percent, and processing time by 15 percent
- By redesigning the application form for legal aid, the British Department of Social Services.

Excessive handling—the Internet has greatly reduced the time required for the distribution of information, but it has also caused a lot of needless. Too often we use distribution lists rather than selecting the individuals who need to read the information. This is very costly for people who don't need or even want the information.

The Ten Steps to a Measurement Family

The group of people who are involved in the following 10 step process are the best ones to formulate the process for developing a family of measurements:

1. Review the project's goals. Management and the group should have some fairly specific goals in mind. This insight comes from the vision, strategy, business plan, and objectives developed by management, with input from their employees. This insight is typically what the group turns in at the management review meeting to validate that the solution will perform as required. The measurement plan should relate directly to those objectives.

2. Carefully define the way the group measures the change to ensure the type of measurements used will provide the desired analysis.
3. Conduct a brainstorming session. The INT should brainstorm to define the types of measurements that are necessary. After the free expression phase and combining phase, the group should rank the measurement.
4. Discussion and debate. The team should discuss the relative merit of each proposed measurement and weed out those which are redundant and/or of little value.
5. Reorder the ranked list of potential measurements to management. The management team should then agree on the final measurement plan.
6. Define the data collection methods (often requiring new recording forms).
7. Train the employees involved in making the measurements and/or recording the data to ensure the validity of the data collected.
8. The INT then develops a plan to collect, track, and review the measurement data. Don't wait until the end of the evaluation cycle to collect the data. Collect the data very soon after employees record information so that the INT can correct misunderstandings and errors prior to the completion of the data collection cycle.
9. Develop a baseline. The team should take baseline values and calculate the performance index, if appropriate.
10. Ongoing measurements. Take measurements periodically to check out how the proposed change will react under the day-to-day, hour-by-hour variation as seen when becoming part of the organization's general operating culture.

When performing a concept validation analysis, it is extremely important that the person collecting the data understand how to do it in a way that the INT can effectively utilize the information. In addition, it is extremely important that someone from the INT periodically observe the way the person is collecting the data to ensure that the INT use quality data in the analysis. We all know the old saying, "Garbage in, garbage out."

The Five Simple Statistical Approaches

Don't let the word statistics frighten you. It is not as difficult as you think it is. Some statistics are as simple as brainstorming and the more complex statistical methods are computerized so that all you must do is enter the data and know how to use the output. To measure the effectiveness of a solution, or how it is meeting requirements, it is necessary very often to use statistical methods. The following are five very simple statistical approaches:

1. Sampling. A method used to obtain information from a portion of a larger population when it is too expensive or time-consuming to measure the total population.
2. Data collection.
   a. A method that has three purposes:
      - analyze performance
      - measure variation
      - except or reject solutions
   b. Two types of data are used:
      - Attributes to identify "yes/no," "go/no—goal," "accept/reject" usually related to units or parts that the INT can use related to concept validation.
      - Variables to identify variations between measurements. After data collection, one or more of the following techniques is used to analyze information and identify problem areas
3. Stratification. A special sampling technique utilizing information from subgroups of larger population. Used in conjunction with histograms that indicate an abnormal distribution.
4. Frequency distribution (arrangement). Used to measure the analysis variation between items produced by a process.
5. Scatter diagrams. Used to display the relationship between two different variables

Measuring Concept Validation

The problem that the INT faces is how to use the data to maximize its benefits to the project and the organization. Essentially measurement data can be used for these very purposes:

1. Process Control
2. Engineering Solution Analysis
3. Management Reporting

There are several easy- to-use methods for identifying, measuring, and displaying data. Some of the more simple ones are:

1. Check sheets. Used for data collection and analysis.
2. Graphs. Used to display data. There are several types of graphs, including line graphs, bar graphs, and pie charts.
3. Histograms. A type of bar graph used to display distributions of whatever is being measured.
4. Pareto diagrams. Another type of bar graphs showing data classifications in the descending order from left to right.

THE EIGHT DATA COLLECTION PITFALLS

As you begin to collect data, avoid the common data collection pitfalls:

1. Lots of planning, no action.
2. Data collection assigned to a small community; the rest of the team does not get involved.
3. Insufficient resources are applied to collection, analysis, and reporting the data.
4. Too much data; no analysis and no assessment.
5. Too much analysis; never satisfied with the analysis. Parenthesis "just one more comment on the data."
6. Incompatible data are collected. ("apples" and "oranges" are counted as the same).
7. Sample sizes too small to make a legitimate conclusion.
8. You should not compare past performance using historical data to performance of the change that uses data collected during the concept validation. With additional attention to project management you could have significant improvement in the current process activities for products because outside attendance is directed to them. You need to run a control sample in parallel with the concept validation of the proposed change. This increased performance related to the AS/IS activities can be greater than 20 percent improvement. If you're going to compare past performance to projected future performance, they both should be measured the same way in parallel with

each other. I have seen situations where comparing historical data to data collected in a design experiment indicated that the solution was much better than the current activities. When both sets of data were collected using the same experimental design, the data indicated that the current method was better than the proposed method.

CONCEPT VALIDATION SUMMARY

The concept validation activities are some of the most important activities in the ISC because the results will determine if the organization will refine, implement, or drop the concept. The concept validation activities often are more difficult and costlier than "Process Grouping 2. Opportunity Development." It requires a great deal of skill in developing the concept validation plan and implementing it. Often it drives major changes in the original concepts for the solution to meet required performance levels. Often people are very creative in coming up with a solution to an opportunity, but have little or no skills in how to validate its concepts. Validating requires a combination of specific engineering, knowledge, and preproduction concepts (making models, design of experiments, customer interviews, supplier capabilities, production methods, and understanding the various software methodologies). Don't take concept validation lightly. It serves a similar role as yeast does in making bread. You can mix all the other ingredients together in the right proportion, but until you add the yeast, you will never be able to deliver acceptable output.

> Don't go into something to test the water. Go into it to make waves (The Quotable coach, http://www.thequotablecoach.com/make-waves/).

5

Phase II. Preparation and Production. Process Grouping 5: Business Case Analysis

INTRODUCTION TO PHASE II. PREPARATION AND PRODUCTION

Phase II. Preparation and Production is a critical part of the Innovation System Cycle (ISC). It focuses on a large quantity of processes, systems, and tasks. Each of these need to function efficiently, effectively, and be designed to be adaptable. The organization will disband most of the creative and potentially innovative concepts not prepared for production before they produce any output. It is here where innovative concepts related to supporting software, robotics, automation, processes, and management style play a major role in the future success of the organization.

Many people feel that the creative or innovative cycle is over when they complete Phase I. Creation. This is far from the truth as the organization normally expends less than 20 percent of the total ISC cost during all of Phase I. All of Phase II is an investment in future that may or may not pay off. Phase I should have put the organization in a position where it has a high degree of confidence that continuing the project into Phase II will result in real value-added to the organization and/or the customer. Phase II consists of four process groupings:

- Process Grouping 5—Business Case Analysis
  This is where you get approval, financing, budget, performance specifications, human resources, schedules, and executive support to an individual project or concept. It is usually a go or no-go decision activity.

- Process Grouping 6—Resource Management
  This is where you get a budget covering money, people, facilities, and materials required to develop the concept so that it can be produced in large quantities. This is typically the point where the organization assigns an official project manager and adds additional staff to the Innovation Team (INT).
- Process Grouping 7—Documentation
  This is where the organization transforms the rough notes from the engineering notebook into engineering specifications released as product specifications and requirements. These product specs are then used to document the processes and procedures used to produce the output and control its efficiency and effectiveness.
- Process Grouping 8—Production
  This is where the manufacturing documentation (routings, training procedures, operating instructions, test procedures, build/subcontract, compliments decisions are made, equipment installed, data collecting systems are installed, and facilities set up. It includes training the people who will produce the output and the suppliers who provide input to the process to minimize the process cost and so that the external consumer receives output that meets and preferably exceeds their requirements at a price they consider reasonable. The object is to maximize the value-added for all the stakeholders.

As they say in the stock-car circuit, "This is where the rubber meets the road."

H. James Harrington

INTRODUCTION TO BUSINESS CASE ANALYSIS

I have too few resources and too many new projects. How can I possibly keep the present commitments that are being made by our sales force and still assign the resources required to support the new projects that are going to drive our future? I need to keep our delivery commitments to our present customers as my top priority or we won't have customers when the new projects are completed.

I hear this comment over and over and when we don't hear it, it is because they are thinking it but are afraid to say it. New projects are the lifeblood of most organizations. Without them the organization has little or no future.

BUSINESS CASE ANALYSIS OVERVIEW

Many people are confused between the two terms—value proposition and business case analysis (BCA)—so let me define them for you.

Definition of a Business Case Analysis. A BCA is an evaluation of the potential impact of correcting a problem or taking advantage of an opportunity on the organization to determine if it is worthwhile investing resources to correct the problem or take advantage of the opportunity. An example of the results of the BCA of a software upgrade could be that it will improve the software performance as stated in the value proposition, but (a) it would decrease overall customer satisfaction by an estimated 3 percentage points, (b) it would require 5 percent more processing time, and (c) reduce systems maintenance costs only $800 a year. As a result, the business case did not recommend including the project in the portfolio of active projects. Often an independent group prepares the business case thereby giving a fresh unbiased analysis of the benefits and costs related to completing the project or program. The BCA is a much more accurate and comprehensive analysis of the proposed project impacts both positive and negative. Successfully completing the BCA automatically puts the project in the organization's portfolio of active projects/programs.

Definition of a Value Proposition. A value proposition is a document that defines the benefits and negative impacts that will result from the implementation of the change or the use of output as viewed by one or more of the organization's stakeholders. A value proposition can apply to an entire organization, parts of the organization, customer accounts, product, service, or internal process.

The World Is Our Oyster

After you open up the world as your customers, you also open up organizations around the world as your competition. This process has resulted in highly competitive research activities that have extremely short product cycles. Many of our best-known and most productive organizations depend upon technology as their edge against competition. But in today's environment an organization can acquire and transfer technology around the world in a matter of hours resulting in very little competitive advantage. Where technology and the latest software applications used to be considered a competitive advantage, it now is a requirement to use to keep from becoming noncompetitive. As a result, there has been a great deal of pressure to reduce project cycle times and greatly improve the percentage of projects completed successfully. The organizations most successful today are the organizations that can create new concepts on demand, minimize the time from concept to delivery, and have a high percentage of successful projects.

Many people are promoting the idea that people learn from their failures. That's a good concept, but if it's the one you're using, let's hope you don't spend a significant portion of your resources learning instead of succeeding.

Now with the increased emphasis on innovation, organizations are introducing more projects into our systems with increased requirements for implementing these in shorter periods of time. The importance of effective management of these projects has become a key element for successful organizations. With this increased emphasis on shorter development cycles, increased, efficient, and effective project management activities have become a very important part of an organization's critical factors. The concept of Organizational Portfolio Management has become a key element in an organization's competencies. The purpose of this book is to identify and highlight effective, proven approaches to maximize the quantity and caliber of the innovative concepts that successfully complete the process from business plan to external positive results based upon the resource limitations within the organization. This approach requires a continuous focus upon optimizing the resources consumed by the organization.

Purpose of Business Case Analysis

Many managers question the need to do a BCA. It's often looked upon as increased bureaucracy with little or no value-added to the organization. This belief may or may not be justifiable; it all depends upon the way the organization conducts the BCA.

Many managers feel that if the value proposition indicates that a project will have a positive impact on the organization, then the organization should approve the project and assign the resources without delay. Unfortunately, there are many projects that could have a positive impact upon the organization, but organizations have a limited amount of discretionary money available to invest in projects. The whole purpose of the BCA is to maximize the probability that the organization will complete approved projects on scheduled, at or below projected cost, and provide significant value-added to the customer, the organization, and preferably to all the stakeholders. Although failure rates of typical projects run at 70 percent or more, it is worthwhile taking the additional time to do an independent analysis with the objective of identifying and prioritizing projects that have a high potential for success. Here is a personal example: One day my wife goes shopping and comes back with a carload full of packages bragging about how much money we saved because everything was on sale at 10 percent off. That may be good sound thinking, but most of what she bought are things that we will never use.

The best time to stop a project that fails is before it is started.

H. James Harrington

In order to eliminate any confusion, we are employing the following definition of key terms used. (Appendix A is a complete list of definitions and acronyms that are commonly used throughout this book.)

Important Definitions

- **Business Case:** A business case captures the reason for initializing a project or program. It is most often presented in a well-structured written document, but, in some cases, also may be in the form of a short verbal argument or presentation. The logic of the business case is that whenever resources, such as money or effort, are consumed, they should be in support of a specific business need or opportunity and be of more value to the organization than the ones that are not approved.
- **Manager:** A manager is an individual who accomplishes an assigned task using other individuals to whom the work is delegated.
- **Organizational:** Refers to those activities, projects, programs, processes, and systems that apply to the total organization, not just one or two departments or units.

- **Organizations:** Systematic arrangements of entities (people, departments, companies, divisions, teams, agencies, etc.) focused on accomplishing a purpose, which may or may not involve undertaking projects. They are often documented in an organization chart that shows the relationships of the individual organization to the total organization.
- **Process:** A series of interrelated actions and/or tasks performed to create a pre-specified product, service, or result. Each process is comprised of inputs, activity, outputs, tools, and techniques, with constraints (environmental factors), guidance, and criteria (organizational process assets) taken into consideration.
- **Program:** A group of related projects, subprograms, and program activities managed in a coordinated way to obtain benefits not available from managing them individually. They may include work outside the scope of projects. A program will always have projects contained within scope.
- **Program or Project Management:** The application of tasks, tools, and techniques along with skills and knowledge to meet program requirements and to obtain benefits and control not available from managing them individually. It is harmonizing projects and program components and controlling interdependencies to achieve benefits outlined in the business case and value proposition.
- **Project:** A temporary endeavor undertaken to create a unique product or service. Projects should always have a time related to them.
- **Project Manager:** A project manager is an organizational employee, representative, or consultant appointed to coordinate the project or program. This individual plans and organizes the resources required to complete a project or program, prior to, during, and upon closure of the project or program lifecycle. Note: Project manager is also the term used for individuals who are managing programs.
- **Project Portfolio:** A centralized collection of independent projects or programs that are grouped together to facilitate their prioritization, effective management, and resource optimization to meet strategic organizational objectives.
- **Project Team Manager:** A project team manager is an individual who is truly accountable for the success or failure of a specific project or program. They usually will have many, if not all, the people working on the project or program assigned directly to them. They will be responsible for getting people from other organizations to work on their project as needed. The project manager's job is to monitor

how is to provide guidance and leadership to the Business Process Analysis team or the INT while the project team manager is responsible for ensuring his team implements the performance plan and often provides day-to-day guidance to the members of the team. A project team manager manages projects that do not have project managers assigned to them.

SETTING THE STAGE FOR THE BUSINESS CASE ANALYSIS

Now, let's set the stage for a well-managed, progressive organization functioning in today's global work environment. Such organizations have realized that innovation is the key to a successful future. They have initiated communication and training systems to prepare their staff to be highly creative individuals who are prepared to take prudent risks to make the organization more successful. The organization is flooded with creative and innovative ideas from marketing, sales, product engineering, finance, information technology, product engineering, manufacturing engineering, and research, and development. Each of the functional groups may have a number of creative ideas that they would like to see implemented. In support of each idea, a group from the function prepares a value proposition for each idea. As a first cut, the functional manager should review the value propositions prepared by his or her organization and screen out the ideas that do not provide acceptable value-added content to the organization. The functional manager will submit the creative ideas that made it through the first screening to the executive committee to approve or reject the idea. Those items that the executive committee approves will have a proof of concept prepared for each one. The data collected in the proof of concept activities will provide a major impact into the business case assessment. I recommend that you have the business case assessment documents prepared by an independent group. Some organizations refer to this as the BCA team. The independent analysis team provides additional insurance that the analysis truly reflects the impact the project will have on the organization and its customers. Many of them are short-term, easy-to-implement concepts that are refinements to the current activities. Others will require a long-term investment with the known risks associated with them. The ones that were successful in completing the BCA are already aligned with the organization's strategic plan, future visions, and the organization's values.

MAJOR CONSIDERATIONS IN SELECTING PROJECTS

There are several key factors to consider in selecting projects to include in an organization's portfolio of active projects:

- The organization's strategic plan and culture
- The five pillars of organizational excellence
- The value-added to the stakeholders
- Long-term impact on net favorable returns (profit)

The Organization's Strategic Plan and Culture

A total strategic planning process (business plan) has three main objectives where innovation needs to play a key role (see Figure 5.1).

There are eleven kinds of planning documents needed in a total, comprehensive strategic business plan:

- Mission Statement
- Value Statements
- Organization's Vision Statements
- Strategic Focus
- Critical Success Factors
- Objectives
- Goals
- Strategies
- Tactics
- Budgets
- Performance Plans

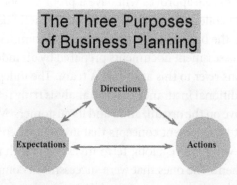

FIGURE 5.1
The three purposes of business planning.

In doing a BCA the INT and executive committee need to use these documents as a baseline in making its final selection.

The Five Pillars of Organizational Excellence

If the project successfully completes "Phase II. Process Grouping 5–Business Case Analysis," the INT team will need to consider each of the pillars in the five pillars of organization excellence. Organizational excellence is designed to permanently change the organization by focusing on managing the five key pillars that support the organization. Each of these five management pillars is not new by itself. The key to organizational excellence is combining and managing them together. We call the methodology that provides a holistic approach to improving the organization's performance organizational excellence which is supported by five pillars that must be managed simultaneously (see Figure 5.2):

- Pillar I: Process Management Excellence
- Pillar II: Project Management Excellence
- Pillar III: Change Management Excellence
- Pillar IV: Knowledge Management Excellence
- Pillar V: Resource Management Excellence

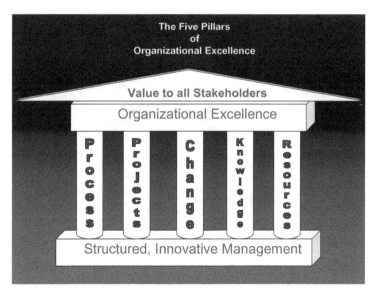

FIGURE 5.2
The five pillars of organizational excellence.

In preparing a BCA the team needs to consider the impact the potential project will have on each of the five pillars.

- You need to manage the **processes** and continuously improve them for they are the way you do business.
- You need to manage the **projects** for that is the way you obtain major improvements and breakthroughs in the outputs. Today, most organizations are doing a very poor job of project management as demonstrated by the high failure rate of projects.
- You need to manage the organization so that it is prepared for the chaos that it is being subjected to due to the magnitude and quantity of **changes** that they must implement to sustain their innovation.
- You need to manage the organization's **knowledge,** which is the organization's most valuable asset. (It is the organization's knowledge that gives an organization its innovation and competitive advantage, as technology can easily be reverse engineered and transferred to any place in the world almost overnight.)
- You need to manage the **resources** and assets for they drive the business results.

By effectively managing these five key pillars and leveraging their interdependencies and reactions, an organization can bring about a transformation within itself. An organization will emerge from its cocoon, which had been restricting its potential, and become a butterfly that will float on the winds of innovation, success, and organization-wide self-fulfillment.

These companies (excellent organizations) implement their results through effectiveness in developing and deploying management capital's intellectual, technical, human information, and other resources in creating an innovative organization.

Armand V. and Donald Feigenbaum
The Power of Management Capital

By focusing on the five pillars of organizational excellence an organization can bring about a new birth in innovation designed to permanently change an organization. Learning to manage them together is the key to success in the endless pursuit of innovation resulting in improved performance. To help you in this endeavor, I have assembled a series of five books on organizational excellence, each addressing one of the five pillars:

- Process Management Excellence: The Art of Excelling in Process Management
- Project Management Excellence: The Art of Excelling in Project Management
- Change Management Excellence: The Art of Excelling in Change Management
- Knowledge Management Excellence: The Art of Excelling in Knowledge Management
- Resource Management Excellence: The Art of Excelling in Resource Management

I believe that it is very important for you to understand that none of the five pillars can support organizational excellence alone as all of them must be equally strong to support the weight of innovation and excelling in the organization's interface with all its stakeholders. The challenge that all excellent organizations face today is how to maintain an innovative learning culture and still maintain the procedures and structure needed to ensure optimum performance with the required high levels of customer and investor satisfaction. I designed this series of books, *The Five Pillars of Organizational Excellence* (published by Paton Press), to help you to solve this dilemma.

Selecting the Priority Projects

The problem now rests with selecting the projects or programs that will provide the maximum value both short-range and long-range to the organization based upon the resources available to support the projects or programs. Although most of the projects or programs that successfully complete the BCA have the potential of providing an acceptable value-added value level to the organization, often the organization cannot approve all of them due to a limit on the money, staff, skills, and facilities. As a result, the organization needs to select an organizational portfolio that maximizes the values that they can create from the implementation of the projects and programs that make up the active projects and programs.

The Sixteen Reasons Potential Projects Fail

The activities that take place during this phase are some of the most difficult activities that the organization performs. This is the phase where it is very difficult to set up win-win scenarios for everyone involved. The organizations may need to drop some projects projected to add value to the organization that individuals may have been working on for months if not years in favor of other projects. Following are some of the typical reasons why organizations drop projects:

1. Miscalculations in the original justifications
2. Changes in the marketplace
3. Too many changes already taking place in the portion of the organization affected
4. Projected technology advances will render the project obsolete before realization of significant return on investment
5. Lack of available resources with the proper skills
6. Lack of sufficient financial resources
7. Lack of a legitimate sponsor
8. Risks associated with the project are too great compared to other projects available
9. Another project will accomplish the same results with fewer resources invested
10. Identification of potential patent infringements
11. Lack of a champion for the project
12. Project not in line with the short-term strategic goals
13. Project not in line with the organization's culture
14. A related dependency will not be in place in-time to support the project

15. Political disagreements between members of the executive team
16. Other activities that are going on that would eliminate the need for the project

Objective of the Business Case Analysis

The objective of the BCA is not to get a project approved, but to approve the projects that have a high probability of producing significant value-added to the organization and its external customers. Projects approved during this phase but not successful in adding significant value to the organization and its customers, represent a failure of the BCA team. Projects rejected during this analysis and implemented by a competitor producing a high level of value-added to the competitor's organization represent inadequate research values and poor judgment by the BCA team. It should be highlighted here that this committee activity is one of **analyzing** and selecting the best project alternatives for the organization, not **approving** the projects submitted for their review. Too often this committee is disappointed when the organization rejects a proposed innovative project. I will admit, it's harder to say *no* than it is to say *yes*. I always feel bad saying no to a proposed project, but it is better for everyone when you think about it because it prevents someone from failing. Have conviction enough to take a firm position so that the organization can continue to move those projects forward that have the highest potential of producing the desired results.

THE TWELVE BUSINESS CASE ANALYSIS PREPARATION ACTIVITIES

- Activity 1. Current Data—collect and analyze as much of the related data already recorded
- Activity 2. Personal Contact—meet with as many of the internal and external customers of the project output to determine first-hand:
  - What they must have
  - What they think they should have
  - What they would like to have
  - What is important for the assignment
  - What will be the impact if they don't have it

- • What will be the impact if they do have it
- • What are they getting out of it and how will they use it
- • Do they have any suggestions that would improve the project?
- Activity 3. Prepare a plan to conduct the BCA activity
- Activity 4. Collect additional information required to do the analysis and improve the accuracy of the estimates
- Activity 5. Define risks associated with the project and their organizational exposure
- Activity 6. Prepare the BCA report
- Activity 7. Review the report with the INT members and the executive sponsor to obtain their inputs (modify the report as appropriate)
- Activity 8. Present the report to the executive committee
- Activity 9. Executive committee compares the product resources required and projected value-added to decide whether to approve it
- Activity 10. Add the report to the knowledge management system
- Activity 11. Set up project management system
- Activity 12. The INT manager and finance establishes the project budget and a financial reporting system

---

PATENTS AND TRADEMARKS

Note: Christopher Voehl wrote this section of the chapter in a book we co-authored, *Making the Case for Change* (published by CRC Press).

Business case recommendations involving potential candidates for patents and/or trademarks are a data-driven approach which involves proactive action for the opportunities being pursued; yet, it cannot be treated as a stand-alone item. This is the point at which organizations need to investigate the use of patents and trademarks/copyrights to link the business plan recommendations with the organizational policies and management systems.

Starting the Patent or Copyright Process

If the proposed idea or concept proves that it is an original idea or concept which another organization has not registered, the BCA team will contact the originator of the idea or concept and recommend that he or she register it. If the originator makes the decision not to register the idea or concept, the BCA team should escalate the decision to the sponsor of the proposed project and record the results in their final report.

Learning how to avoid patent and trademark infringement is crucial to an inventor, entrepreneur, or any type of business case involving these items. It is best to spend a little time and money during the business case planning stage in order to avoiding patent infringement rather than defending a costly, time-consuming patent infringement lawsuit later. Considering that the concept of patent infringement can be complex and confusing to many, it is easy to understand why many business case developers choose to hide their heads in the sand rather than investigate the potential infringement issues up-front. This avoidance can be a path that can sometimes derail the best-developed business plan and even bankrupt the healthiest business. It is never too late to take the necessary steps to avoid patent infringement whether you are developing a product or have manufactured the product for many years and are attempting an upgrade.

Issues to Consider

Following are some possible issues to consider during your BCA to determine whether you have any patent infringement issues prior to producing a product (or continuing to produce a product).

- Possible Costly Lawsuit. A patent infringement lawsuit is extremely expensive compared to other types of lawsuits. A patent infringement lawsuit typically will cost $1 million or more in legal fees alone. It is not uncommon for even simple patent infringement lawsuits to end up costing a company millions of dollars. If you lose the lawsuit, you will then be responsible for paying damages to the patent owner along with the potential for the associated damages and attorneys' fees. The attorneys' fees alone can put many small businesses out of business when the business could have avoided the lawsuit by spending as little as $10,000–$15,000 to hire a patent attorney to review a patent for patent infringement issues. It is also important to note that many insurance policies do not cover patent infringement which requires that you to pay the legal fees and damages yourself.

- Possible Preliminary Injunction. A patent owner may be able to get a preliminary injunction early in a lawsuit that stops the manufacture and sale of the alleged infringing product. An injunction can be costly to defend against and the "unknown" of whether the injunction will be granted can be negative to your business planning (and your customers).
- May be Time Consuming. A patent infringement lawsuit requires the officers and technical people of the company to participate heavily in litigation decisions. Although one may believe that the lawyers will do most of the work, it is fair to say that the client's business developers will end up doing as much as 20 percent of the total work involved in a lawsuit.
- Your Customers May be Sued. Some patent owners may sue your clients, which can be very destructive for your continued business relationships. It can also be expensive for you since you may have an indemnification clause with your customer where you agree to pay their legal fees and any damages.
- May Be Able to Identify Non-Infringing Alternatives. By identifying potential infringement issues up-front, you can then determine how to best design your product to avoid infringing upon one or more patents. The longer you wait in the product development process, the harder it will be to redesign your product when you identify a patent infringement issue.

The Common Patent Mistakes Made

"We know about all the patents in our industry." One of the most common mistakes a BCA team makes is taking the attitude that they know all the products that exist and their related patents. This attitude fails to consider the technology that a competitor may develop that they haven't commercialized yet. It also fails to consider that a small company with limited geographic reach may have a patented product.

Another mistake made by some BCA teams is in believing a smaller company will not sue them. This view fails to consider that a small company may be very tenacious in defending its intellectual property. This view also fails to consider that the patent owner may later sell the patent rights to a larger company that can afford a patent infringement lawsuit. Finally, there has been an increase in the number of infringement attorneys willing to take patent infringement lawsuits on a contingency arrangement.

Steps to Avoid Patent Infringement

1. Start Early and Keep Your Diligence. Do not delay even 1 day your business case development efforts to avoid patent infringement. The best place to begin your infringement review is during the product concept stage (i.e., prior to developing a prototype) when you are busy characterizing the current state. This is the stage when usually more than one alternative exists. By identifying potential infringement issues at this stage, you can weed out product designs which carry a high risk of liability.
2. Keep Your Business Development Heads Above the Sand. Some people will intentionally avoid becoming aware of a competitor's patent believing this will help them later. The fact is, ignoring a patent will not help you later in litigation and it can potentially result in a judgment finding that you have intentionally infringed upon a patent. It is best to respect the intellectual property rights of others by becoming aware of and understanding their rights.
3. Find out about the Patent(s) You May Be Infringing Upon. Before a proposed project reaches the business case level, the individual who created the idea or concept should thoroughly analyze the possibility of patent infringement and the sponsor should validate the results. The BCA team cannot take for granted that all the possibilities have been thoroughly evaluated. As a result, the BCA team should identify what patent(s) exist that their project or initiative could possibly be infringing upon by doing the following activities or verify that someone else has already completed the following activities:
   - Online Patent Search. You can search for patents at the U.S. Patent Office (USPTO) or by using any type of software product such as Patent Hunter, which has a free 60-day trial. When doing your patent search, you will want to search for patents related to your technology using keywords describing your product and by also searching the assignee records for patents owned by specific competitors. Keep in mind that some smaller companies may not assign a patent to their company, so you will have to search by any known inventor names (e.g., often the owner of a small company will be an inventor on the patent). In addition, some larger

companies use separate intellectual property holding companies that own their patents so searching by company name may not result in finding a company's patent.

- Review the Competitor's Product. In addition to performing a patent search for patents related to your new product, you should also review all known competitor products for any patent notices. Most companies that have a patent on a product will conspicuously mark the product with the patent number (e.g., U.S. Patent No. 14,8253,547). If the competitor's product does not have a patent number directly on it, you can also check the packaging, marketing materials, and website for any patent notices. After you identify a patent number of interest, you can perform a patent number search to view the patent.

- Contact the Competitor Directly. If you have reason to believe that one of your competitors has a trademark or patent on a related product but you cannot find the patent through an online patent search of the competitor's product, you may want to consider contacting the competitor to see if they have a patent. Keep in mind that by contacting a competitor, you are immediately putting your company "on the radar" and they will diligently watch your future product developments (i.e., you should only contact them if you have a solid reason for believing they have a patent you cannot find). If they say the product is patented but refuse to provide you with a patent number, they are most likely not being truthful since patents are public knowledge and there is no reason to withhold such information if it is true.

- Preliminary Patent Infringement "Screening" of Patents by your BCA team. After you identify one or more patents related to your product, you will want to do a preliminary patent infringement "screening" before sending the patents to your patent lawyer for review. Sending all the patents you found can be very costly as a formal patent infringement review by a patent attorney can cost range from $10,000–$20,000 plus per patent reviewed.

Steps in Performing a Preliminary Screening of a Patent or Trademark

To perform a preliminary screening of a patent, you should perform the following steps:

Step 1. Determine if the patent term has expired.

In the United States, a utility patent automatically expires 20 years after the earliest effective filing date, while a design patent in most cases automatically expires 14 years after the issue date. To determine if a patent term has expired, you will need to determine the earliest effective filing date and then calculate the expiration date from there. You can use www. PatentCalculator.com to determine the expiration date for a patent.

Step 2. Determine if maintenance fees have been paid.

If the patent term has not expired, you will then want to check with the USPTO to see if the patent owner has paid the required maintenance fees. There are three maintenance fees due for utility patents (most design patents do not have maintenance fees: 3 years, 7 years and 11 years). If the patent owner has failed to pay a required maintenance fee, the patent is no longer valid and you can incorporate the patent or trademark without infringing upon the patent.

Step 3. Self-review of patent claims.

If the patent has not expired (see previous two steps), then you will want to review the patent claims which define the "meets and bounds" of the patent protection. The patent claims are located at the end of the patent and are consecutively numbered starting with 1 and continuing consecutively. It is important to note that while a patent may disclose Invention A, Invention B, and Invention C, if the patent claims only protect Invention B, you will not have to worry about infringement if your product relates only to Invention A or C. Reviewing patent claims can be difficult, but with the assistance of a patent attorney you should be able to grasp the concept of what to look for.

Attorney-Client Work Privileged

Business case developers need to keep in mind that any internal communications regarding the patent and the patent claims are most likely not covered by the attorney-client work privilege. This means that if a patent infringement lawsuit is filed, the patent owner will be able to discover all e-mails, notes, letters, and conversations relating to the patent not involving your patent attorney. Therefore, it is important to be extremely careful as to what is said within internal communications and preferably keep communications to a minimum. For example, while it may seem obvious, some people will make statements such as 'This patent looks very similar to our product' when in fact they do not truly know if the patent is close. When in doubt, it is always best to retain a patent attorney to assist you with the infringement review.

Business Case Analysis Team's Self-Review

If your BCA team's self-review of the patent indicates there may be some potential infringement issues, you should immediately contact your patent attorney who can help you determine if you do in fact have patent infringement issues. If the formal review by your patent attorney reveals that there may be patent infringement issues for your product, you will then want to determine if the patent is valid or not. Some patents are invalid because the technology was used or known years prior to the filing of the patent application. You will want to bring any known patents, products, or publications that existed prior to the patent owner filing their patent application which could help invalidate the patent.

When infringement on patents, copyrights, or trademarks are included in the proposed project, the BCA team will recommend to the originator of the proposed project that he or she withdraw the project from the BCA cycle until they have resolved the issues. If the originator of the proposed project decides not to withdraw the proposed project, the BCA team will escalate the decision to the sponsor. If the originator still does not withdraw the proposed project from the BCA cycle, then the BCA team will highlight the issues in the BCA final report.

SUMMARY OF PATENT AND TRADEMARK PROCESS

As important as protection for the organization's intellectual assets is, it is equally important not to infringe upon another organization's intellectual assets. This chapter covers how the BCA team should investigate if the idea or concept that was considered new and unique to determine if it infringes upon another organization's patents, trademarks, or copyrights. For those ideas or concepts that infringe upon another organization's intellectual assets, the BCA team brings these issues to the attention of the originator along with a suggestion that he or she withdraw the proposed project until the originator eliminates the issues. If the originator decides not to withdraw the proposed project, the BCA team escalates the issues to the sponsor. If sponsor does not withdraw the proposed project, then the BCA team will highlight it in the BCA final report. For those ideas or concepts that are candidates for copyright, trademark, or patent, the originator should act to get the concept or idea started through the registration process.

Special Note: The patent or trademark process activity should start as soon as the organization recognizes the potential patent or patent infringement. Often this activity starts in "Process Grouping 3. Value Proposition."

> Protect your innovative capital for it often is the only thing that separates an organization from its competitors.
>
> **H. James Harrington**

CYBERSECURITY

No discussion with potential innovators would be complete without mentioning cybersecurity. All indications are that online threats are going to get worse before they get better. Sophisticated cybercriminal networks are growing in quantity and capabilities. Significant threats are occurring from countries like North Korea, Russia, Iran, and China—all of which today have the capability to initiate destructive attacks on organizations and government everywhere. Criminal entities are developing software packages today to make it easier and easier for the cyber terrorist to perform their criminal deeds. A major exposure rests with our employees and our supply chain.

Ernst and Young's 20th Global Information Security Survey (GISS) captured the responses of 1,105 C-suite leaders and information security and information technology (IT) executives and managers representing most of the world's largest and most-recognized global companies across 60 countries and encompassing nearly all industries. This study confirmed that cybersecurity is a major problem for large and medium-size organizations. Here are some of the results of their survey:

1. 48 percent indicated that they do not have a security operations center
2. Only 12 percent indicated that they would likely detect a sophisticated cyber attack

3. Only 17 percent indicated they have sufficient knowledge of effective oversight for cyber risk
4. 64 percent indicated that malware attacks increased in 2017 compared to 52 percent in 2016
5. 87 percent said that they were going to increase their budget related to cybersecurity by more than 50 percent

In an interview for *Chief Executive Magazine* (February 2018), Lieutenant General Rhett A. Hernandez, a retired officer in the United States Army and the former commander of the United States Army Cyber Command, which is the Army's service component to U.S. Cyber Command, offered the following advice:

1. Lead from the top and keep it simple
2. Don't be overconfident
3. Collaborate and communicate
4. Know the technology is always changing
5. Recognizing threats are people
6. Compliance is not cybersecurity
7. Monitor the right metrics
8. Get a second opinion
9. Practice, Practice, Practice
10. Keep asking questions

You need to get a lot more information than I'm providing here is to safeguard your crown jewels. To get the process started, here are some suggestions:

1. Define how and why you could be attacked
2. Protect the information related to your core capabilities and competencies
3. Define your most significant risks and how you can minimize the impact if they are attacked
4. Train your people on how they can minimize the impact of a cyber breach
5. Focus on potential cyber-attack risk between you and your suppliers

If you have been given serious thought to the impact a cyber-attack would have on your organization, I recommend that you get started right away.

Most companies have some minor protection built into their data system, but most organization's defense strategy falls far short of being adequate. Following are two steps to get you started:

- Step One. Concentrate on the obvious and simple things first. Focus on where you store the data and who has access to it. Start using multi-authentication to strengthen password control as it relates to your system. Strengthen interface controls between members of the supply chain. Be sure that the people who have access to the organization's computing system have legitimate needs to receive all the data they can acquire. Train your employees in cybersecurity practices and on to ensure they are adhering to these cybersecurity practices.
- Step Two. Define organizational risk impact as a result of cyber-attacks. Don't be discouraged because you cannot eliminate all risks related to a cyber-attack. The best you can do is minimize the impact on the information that are the most important and valuable to you and your competition. I recommend that an organization starts out by focusing its cyber-attack protection on its core capabilities and competencies. The next thing is the organization's interface to its external customers and consumers.

PREPARE BUSINESS CASE ANALYSIS FOR AN INDIVIDUAL PROJECT'S DOCUMENT

As a result of the activities that you will complete in Phase I, you will define a list of questions that the executive team might ask or would want information related to. You establish a data collection plan, collect the necessary information, validate that the information is accurate and now you are ready to analyze this data and put it into the formal BCA document. Much of the data analysis activities will take place as you collect the data. Too often teams are interested in saving so they put off looking at data analysis activities until all the data is available. This often is a major mistake. Not only does looking at the data as you collect it save cycle time in completing a project, but it also allows the team to validate the usefulness of the data and often identify fallacies in some of the assumptions they made or the way they are collecting the data. Looking at the data as the team collects it will allow the team to readjust the data collection plan before they completely implement it.

Business Case Analysis Report Table of Contents

As the BCA team starts to prepare the BCA document, the team needs to first prepare an outline of what the document will look like (table of contents). The table of contents serves as an outline for the report. It provides the storyline that the BCA team will present to the executive team. Although the basic tendency is to make the BCA as comprehensive as possible, the excellence of the report is not based upon its volume; it is based upon how well it presents an unbiased view of the AS/IS situation and how it will reach the desired result if the organization implements the proposed idea or concept. I recommend that the BCA team develop a standard format for the organization that defines the basic structure and content of the BCA documentation. Having a common structure for all BCA reports helps the management team in understanding and analyzing the specific recommendations so they may make better decisions faster. The following is a typical example of what a BCA document table of contents might look like:

- Title and the names of the originators of the proposed change
- Table of contents
- Executive overview
  1. Description of the proposed change
  2. Review of data collection approaches used
  3. Description of the AS/IS state
  4. Value-added content that the proposed change would bring about
  5. Overall cost and time frame to implement the change
  6. Other solutions that the BCA team considered and why they were not chosen
  7. Comparison to the value proposition
  8. Risk and obstacles related to the change
  9. Recommendations
- List of the key people associated with the project and the analysis efforts (executive sponsor, individuals recommending the change, individuals who created the BCA)
- Financial calculations
- Details related to other value-added results (for example, cycle time reduction, stock reduction, improved customer satisfaction, reduced defect levels, increase market share, etc.)
- List of risks and exposures
- List of assumptions
- Implementation plan

- Three-year projection of the situation if the organization does not approve the proposed change
- The net value-added when subtracting the cost (money and other resources) related to installation of the change from the value-added content
- Detailed recommendations
- References

Business Case Analysis Major Preparation Mistake

A major mistake that many teams make when they are preparing a BCA is spending too much time collecting information. It must be realized that you will never get 100 percent accurate projections. Define the accuracy needed and then develop your plan so that statistically you meet the accuracy requirements for the estimates. The other side of the coin is successful completion of the BCA often leads to an organization's announcement of the new product. This announcement is a major commitment to their customers and can result in losing sales of the present product while customers are waiting for the new product to hit the market.

This process may seem like an excessive amount of checks and balances, but the organization must be extremely careful in defining what goes into the portfolio of active projects processed at the same time within the organization. Why? These projects are the ones that define the future of the organization and with estimates running as high as 80 percent of the projects failing, responsible executives are asking for a high degree of assurance that the project will yield the benefits added that it is projecting.

I've seen time after time when the organization or team defines a course of action, they spend all their effort in trying to justify that course of effort rather than looking at the alternatives that may or may not be a better answer for the total organization. The big advantage in having a separate independent group prepare the BCA is they can challenge some of the decisions that were made by the INT team and suggest alternative answers. This process requires that the independent group have an excellent understanding of the situation so they can make legitimate and fact-based suggestions related to alternative approaches that the INT making the proposed change recommendation did not consider. At this point in the ideas or concepts approval cycle, it is better to take the time to be creative rather than to accept the simplest and most obvious answer. It's more important to take the time to define the very best alternative than it is to use that time collecting information to justify a less than optimal solution for a situation.

———————

EXAMPLE OF A NEW PRODUCT BUSINESS CASE ANALYSIS

On the following pages is an example of an executive summary for setting up a new production facility at the Jonesville plant to produce solid state drives (SSD) devices. Because it is a new product line, the executive summary is much more extensive than usual. We also did not include the remainder of the report which was an appendix.

The Coyote Drive Company (CDC)
Business Plan Analysis Report

Date: February 2010
Project: Installing a Solid State Drives (SSD) Production Line at the Jonesville
     Facilities
Prepared by: Agues Filman

Executive Overview

Recent advances in storage capacity have shown that there is a clear advantage to solid state drives (SSD) in computers. The reasons include faster start up time, less energy consumption, and higher reliability. Until recently, SSDs have been prohibitively expensive for the average consumer with the price of a benchmark 500 gigabyte (Gb drive) at nearly $1,000. This cost resulted in slow sales and only to those who had a definite need for this type of product. We agree with the recommendation that we convert the Jonesville plant to an SSD-only production facility.

Description of Current State

Currently, we are seeing a shift in demand by the market to higher efficiency and more reliable products. Random access storage/hard disk drives (HDD) have been the staple of the industry for the last 30 years and have proven to be a reliable product. Our drives have been rated among the best for most, if not all HDD, of those years. At this point we have eight plants located in strategic locations throughout the world that have produced a consistently high-quality product, but at a shrinking margin as a greater number of competitors have entered the market. It has become increasingly difficult to maintain a margin in the last several years.

Value-Added of Proposed Change

By making a gradual shift over time, we can begin to reapply our core competency away from strictly hard disk drives to a diverse line of HDDs and SSDs. Since SSDs are able to command a higher price in the market, and they are destined to be the next generation of technology, it is critical that we start to move to this technology to secure our market position in the future.

Backup Data

Hard drive costs have been declining for several years. Partially this decline in cost is due to the declining costs of production, but there is also a decline in product differentiation and a growing number of low-priced competitors (see Figure 5.3). Realize that the sales price of an output is not based upon the cost to generate the output but what the market is willing to pay for the output. According to the following chart, the cost of a benchmark gigabyte of storage has been declining significantly with an estimated algorithm of:

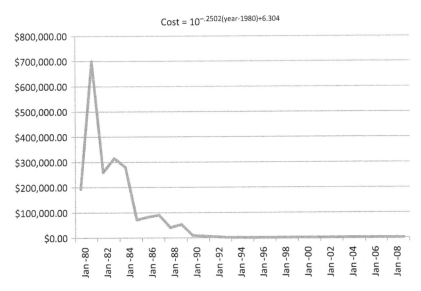

$$Cost = 10^{-.2502(year-1980)+6.304}$$

FIGURE 5.3
Benchmark for gigabyte of storage from 1980 to 2008.

The cost in the last 10 years follows:

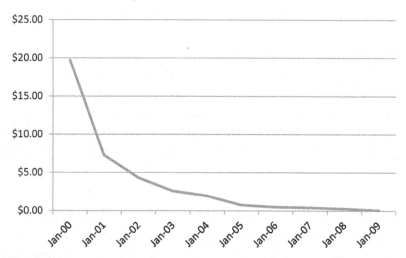

FIGURE 5.4
Cost for a megabyte of data stored on SSD.

This means that the current cost of a megabyte of data is below $.07, but seems to have stabilized, although disruption from the SSD space appears to be a significant risk (see Figure 5.4). Regardless, SSD prices have fallen from their high (see Figure 5.5).

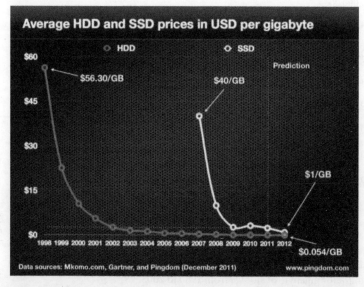

FIGURE 5.5
Average HDD and SSD prices in USD per gigabyte.

Two years ago, the organization approved a project to upgrade the line that produces HDD at the Jonesville facilities. Decreases since that date and projected future decreases in demand for HDD products indicate that this was a poor decision. This is the ideal time to establish our first SSD high-volume production line. Demand for SSD products is rising very rapidly. It is essential that our company establish itself as a major player in the SSD market. The customer HDD demands that Jonesville facility is presently servicing can be handled by creating a second shift at our Owego facilities. Re-machining the plant at Jonesville would require the following additional costs that are now already approved for upgrading the present HDD facilities at Jonesville:

1. Additional removal of disk drive equipment that is no longer needed $800,000. (total cost $1 million)
2. New equipment—$80 million[†] (total costs $83 million)
3. Additional construction costs $1 million[*] (total cost $2 million)
4. Additional $480,000 to cover salaries for people not productive for 80 working days (total cost $640,000)
5. Cost to establish and train people to operate the second shift Owego facilities—$200,000
6. Cost to prepare and release the engineering documents and the manufacturing documents—$2.3 million[†]
7. Cost to test product for reliability and to certify the production line—$700,000
8. Cost of repair and deliver new marketing and sales information— $1.4 million
9. The total estimated cost to bring up the new SSD facility is $91.24 million. We recommend that this value be increased by a little more than 20 percent due to several unknown factors or risks involved in establishing a new facility making the total budget $110 million

---

[*] Already budgeted for the upgrade of the Jonesville facility is $200,000 for removal of equipment, $3 million for new equipment, $1 million for refurbishing and installing new equipment, and $160,000 to cover the cost of 20 people that would be unproductive for 20 days while the upgrade was being installed.

[†] The research and development (R&D) group in conjunction with the Manufacturing Engineering function has already designed an SSD product and defined the production process that would be capable of producing the product and mass production quantities. This part of the project is already complete and no additional funding will be required.

Note: Based upon marketing's estimate of the share of the SSD market that our product would gain, the proposed production line working when shift would be able to handle it for 2011, 2012 and 2013. In 2014 is recommended that we establish a second shift and bring a second location online to provide backup in case of problems at the Jonesville facilities. Based upon the marketing forecasts and pricing considering the estimated production costs provided by manufacturing engineering, The Coyote Drive Company (CDC) will recoup its investment in SSD technology by June 2012 if the production facility is up and running by January 1, 2011.

Other Solutions Considered

Since we must begin to enter the SSD market to remain competitive, we had considered the possibility of outsourcing the manufacturing of the SSD to a foreign manufacturer. As we considered this more fully, we decided that there were several strategic considerations that needed to be discussed.

1. Outsourcing the process means failure to gain competency. Failure to gain competency in this space would mean that we would run the risk of not having the ability to perform R&D on our own product in the future. Retaining competency in hard drives, while losing it in SSD, is diametric to the strategy that should be pursued.
2. We could acquire an existing competitor, but this would mean that we would need to find one that does not recognize the shift in the market. This would probably result in us overpaying for the technology. Additionally, our engineers explain to us that they have the ability to design the new technology to fit our existing inventory of cases and connectors. This will result in tremendous savings as we can use much of the same technology in the SSD as we currently use in the hard drives.

Risks and Obstacles

We may be too late to get into the SSD market. While this is a real risk, we do not feel that the probability of failure is that high. The current makers of this technology are generally smaller-scale manufacturers and the high cost has been rationalized to be due to the small-scale production to date.

We may not be able to convince our customers to install SSD in their products due to the shift of PC usage to tablets (and modifying demand to a lower, rather than higher, priced product). We feel that since we will be able to offer hard drives to those that still need them, an SSD as a configurable option to consumers will actually improve the ability of the producer to sell products. Additionally, since one of the draws to the tablet is the instant on capability, consumers will expect this from their PCs eventually. This may mean the end of hard drives except in the case of massive storage. Even then, the amount of energy consumed by hard disk storage may push even server farms to the lower energy consumption of the SSD.

Recommendations

We will need to begin the conversion of the Jonesville plant as soon as possible to take advantage of the current shift in demand from hard drives to SSD. While it is not an inexpensive option, the SSD is still a high margin product that we need to be involved with to compete in storage in the future. Reliance on HDD could prove to be a disaster in the long-run, but acquiring a competitive advantage by moving aggressively into the space immediately makes sense for the company.

Comparison to the value proposition:
1. Our estimates of costs to make the cut over were about 12.3 percent higher than those used in the valve proposition.
2. Our estimate of the savings was 6 percent lower than the value propositions.
3. In spite of the differences in projected and estimated cost and revenue the end of value content is still very attractive and the project should be implemented in spite of the defined risk.

Key individuals:
- Executive Sponsor: Brett Pitt
- Lead: Ron McDonald
- Finance: Sandy Beach

Value proposition authors:
- Sam Iam
- Saul Train
- Niko Lasse
- Dom Inator
- Trey Moore

Assumptions:
1. Existing HDD equipment would have been replaced
2. SSD Equipment will be $80 million
3. Plant down time is already been committed to

4. Personnel idle time has already been committed
5. Training on the new equipment could be done during the remodel
6. The marketing planning cost estimates are correct to plus or minus 10 percent
7. The manufacturing engineering production cost estimates are correct to within plus or minus 15 percent
8. The Owego facilities will be able to establish a second shift
9. The reliability studies related to the SSD product produced on the new line will be positive
10. The new manufacturing facilities will be certified for producing customer shippable product by January 1, 2011
11. The personnel that are presently involved in manufacturing the HDD product are technically capable of producing the SSD product we just a minimum amount of training
12. The technology does not advance to the point that the product design for SSD is now been completed in R&D will not be obsolete until 2014

Other Value-Added Results

The relative efficiency and reliability of the SSD is superior to that of the HDD, so as the cost of the SSD comes down, we expect it to be the clear choice of most customers.

Risks and Exposures

If we do not act, we risk losing the window of opportunity. Based upon a number of assumptions, much of the demand in storage may shift from HDD to SDD in the next 10 years. This could potentially be a significant capital outlay to replace HDDs in server farms, desktop and laptop computers equal to billions of dollars in revenue. We are not currently positioned to take full advantage of this shift in demand, and have not acquired a significant amount of expertise to develop the larger drives.

Implementation Plan

Making a decision on the viability of modifying our product line to accommodate the addition of an SSD is not in doubt. The economic reality is that the HDD is producing a smaller and smaller margin as time goes on. Add to this the improved efficiency and there is a clear indication that HDD may become a relic of the past.

- Stage I will be to modify the existing remodel/retool process to accommodate the changes needed to manufacture the new line. Since the space requirements are approximately the same, we do not anticipate a major remodel and the existing footprint should be adequate.
- Stage II will require that we build the new equipment. While there are some proprietary methods in the manufacturing of this equipment, it's generally known to the market and we will be able to have the new line planned with the new equipment machined within 6 months. Since this is the approximate timeline for the existing remodeling plans, we feel that this will not be an issue. The additional cost for replacing equipment will be approximately $80 million.

The only significant cost above the equipment will be the retraining of the floor personnel. Since they will be on leave during the remodel, we will train them on the new equipment then.

Executive Summary

It would be a major error to continue with the plan to upgrade the Jonesville HDD production process as presently planned. This expenditure should be combined with the additional cost required to install a new SSD process line at the Jonesville plant. A total budget should be set aside for $110 million to cover this major new technology. It is strongly recommended that this project be given high priority so that the new facilities will be shipping customer ready product by January 1, 2011.

Note: This example was prepared by Christopher F. Voehl.

SUMMARY OF BUSINESS CASE ANALYSIS

During Process Grouping 5, the BCA team generated the BCA; it included the key points from the data that the BCA team collected and using their best judgment the BCA team considered data relevant to the proposed change. This document included a view of the present conditions and a view of how the conditions will change as a result of implementing the proposed change. The BCA team presented the BCA document to the executive team for their approval or rejection. Projects that the executive team approved became part of the organization's portfolio of active projects.

> In most companies more projects fail than are successful. The reputation of the INT and the BCA teams is based upon how good their projections are. Be sure the odds are in your favor.

H. J. Harrington

6

Process Grouping 6:
Resource Management

INTRODUCTION TO RESOURCE MANAGEMENT

In business, profits aren't the only thing, but it's hard to think of what is more important.

H. James Harrington

Nothing can be accomplished without resources. Resources are at the heart of everything you do—too little and we fail, too much and there is waste—making our organization noncompetitive. Too many organizations limit their thinking about resources to people and money. People and money are important, but they are only a small part of the resources that an organization needs to manage. *Resource Management Excellence—The Art of Excelling in Resource Management*, which is Book V in the series, *The Five Pillars of Organizational Excellence*, looks at all the resources that are available to an organization and how to manage them effectively.

Now, when I talk about resource management, I am talking about it in its broadest sense. It is all the resources and assets that are available to the organization. It includes stockholders, management, employees, money, suppliers, inventory, boards of directors, alliance partnerships, real estate, knowledge, customers, patents, investors, good will, and brick and mortar. It is easy to see that when you consider all of the resources that are available to the organization, effective resource management is one of the most critical, complex activities within any organization. As managers and employees, you need to examine your own performance to be sure you are the best you can be.

Jack Welch's Six Rules for Self-Examination

John Francis "Jack" Welch Jr. is an American and a retired business executive, author, and chemical engineer. He was chairman and CEO of General Electric between 1981 and 2001. In this role, he created the following "Six Rules for Self-Examination."

1. Face reality as it is, not as it was or as you wish it were.
2. Be candid with everyone.
3. Don't manage; lead.
4. Change before you have to.
5. If you don't have a competitive advantage, don't compete.
6. Control your own destiny, or someone else will.

An organization needs to manage each of these resources in its own special way to become an excellent organization. The big question is, "How do you pull all these different activities and improvement approaches together and prioritize them?" To solve this question, I will present a very thorough, total involvement approach to strategic planning—one that involves everyone from the chairman of the board to the janitor, from sales to personnel, from development engineering to maintenance. Yes, this is a total involvement approach to innovative strategic planning; it is both bottom up and top down.

Resource management cannot be an afterthought; all executive decisions must be based upon it. It requires a lot of planning, coordination, reporting, and continuous refining to do an excellent job at resource management. Too many organizations manage the operations by throwing more resources into the pot. They may be very successful with this approach as long as they have very little competition, but even the giants fail if they do not do an outstanding job of resource management. Just look at what happened to Big Blue.

We expect a lot—highly motivated people consciously choosing to do whatever is in their power to assure every customer is satisfied…and more. Every day. Without this concentrated effort, attempting a flawless service is really quite futile.

Fred Smith
Founder and CEO, Federal Express

TYPES OF RESOURCES

In Chapter 5, I discussed the importance of the five pillars of organizational excellence in selecting projects to be included in an organization's portfolio of active projects. Of the five pillars, resource management is most crucial in problem or start-up innovative organization and in all organizations focusing on providing innovative products and/or services. In the discussion related to organizational resources there are many subjects that could be discussed, such as:

- Human capital
- Financial
- Knowledge capital
- Equipment
- Facilities
- External customers
- Suppliers
- Staff
- Suppliers
- Alliance partnerships
- Technology development

Some books stress that human resources is the Number 1 issue and finance resourcing is the Number 2 issue. Another book stresses that financial resourcing is the Number 1 issue and human resources comes in as the second or third issue. Both are very important. The organization cannot exist without skilled human resources and adequate financial resources.

Due to the limited size of this book, I will discuss just four of the resources that most organizations depend upon:

1. Management of resources
2. Human resources
3. Financial resources
4. Knowledge resources

Successful organizations develop strategies that ensure they have sufficient resources to handle today's requirements and to invest into future development to provide a fair return on their stockholder's investment.

MANAGEMENT OF PROJECT RESOURCES

Often at meetings with my peers, we have debated which of the three major resource categories—financial resources, human resources, and management—is the most important resource. Several people stated that human resources should come first because it is an organization's most critical resource and it is the one thing that sets an organization apart from the competition. Some stated that financial resources should be first because without adequate financial resources, the other two would not exist. One person argued that management should come first because it is what drives the other two resources. It is human nature that the one who is listed first is the most important consideration. I was that one person who stated that management should be first and considering that I'm writing the book, I won the debate, at least as far as this book is concerned. I must admit the truth of the situation is the same as answering the question, "Which comes first—the chicken or the egg?"

DAILY WORK MANAGEMENT

A methodology called Agile recommends calling a meeting at the beginning of every day with your entire department to discuss daily work management. There are three levels of meetings to follow up on all standard work and discuss problems:

- Level I meetings take place every shift, in which a team leader discusses the last shift's performance with his or her group. The group also discusses the work that they need to accomplish during the up-and-coming shift. These meetings should be stand-up meetings and the tools to facilitate these meetings are part of the communication plan.
- Level II meetings are the daily meetings between group leaders, in which they discuss the top three problems of the different departments. They define improvement activities to prevent these problems from ever occurring again.

- Level III meetings are daily meetings between the group leader and the process owner, in which they discuss the escalated problems for the entire potential project.

PROJECT MANAGEMENT EXCELLENCE

When it comes to talking about managing projects, the drive is certainly to start discussing project management. Being a certified project manager has turned out to be a very lucrative and interesting career path. Project managers play a very important role in the most creative part of the Innovation System Cycle (ISC). Project management is one of the fastest-growing career fields in the United States. The Project Management Institute is the largest professional society in United States and is growing rapidly. If you want to catch several shooting stars, certainly project management is one of the best ones to grab hold of.

Why are over 70% of your improvement efforts unsuccessful?

According to the Chaos Report compiled by the Standish Group International,

- Only 26 percent of all projects are successful.
- 40 percent of all information technology (IT) projects fail or are canceled.

Processes define how organizations function and projects are the means by which organizations improve their processes or products. By definition, a project is a "temporary endeavor undertaken to create a unique product or service." Basically, you can classify potentially innovative projects into three categories:

1. Defining and implementing new or improved potentially innovative products and services project
2. Defining and implementing new or improvements to processes or systems
3. Defining and implementing new or improved managerial concepts and organizational structures

You will note that I left out continuous improvement projects and activities as they do not represent the level of creativity, enthusiasm, and excitement that naturally innovative concepts generate for the team.

There are endless numbers of examples of poor project management, such as:

- NASA's Space Station Freedom originally was budgeted for $8 billion; it is now up to $32 billion and climbing.
- The 2004 Olympic Games that were held in Greece were 300 percent over budget 1 year prior to the opening.

Successfully completing the Business Case Analysis (BCA) and obtaining management approval upgrades the status of the project from a temporary unfunded project to a committed project. Part of this successful upgrading is an operating budget to cover the project for each of the various functions participating. As a result, a team of individuals is assigned full-time or part-time to the project.

The Five Project-Related Managers

With the approval of a project team comes the need for five kinds of management related to the project:

1. Project Manager: Responsible for the project being completed on time, within budget, and capable of performing all the prescribed function
2. Project Risk Manager: Part of project management
3. Innovation Team (INT) Manager: Daily INT team
4. Daily work management: Daily management of the personnel in the affected areas
5. Executive sponsor: The individual that can approve variations to the project

Definitions of Project Management Roles

- Project manager: The project manager has the knowledge, skills, tools, and techniques to project activities to meet or exceed stakeholder's needs and expectations for the project. Frequently, a project manager will manage a portfolio of projects.

- Project risk management: Project risk management is a subset of project management that includes the project concerned with the identification, analyzing, reporting, and developing contingency plans. Project risk management prepares a list of things that could impact the project from being completed successfully and analyses each item to determine if it is a critical risk, a business major risk or a minor risk. All critical and major risks should have contingency plans prepared for them. Normally the contingency plans are not included in the budget but require a modification to the project plan and often to the budget in order to implement them. Normally the project risk management activities are assigned to the project manager.
- INT manager: The INT manager is responsible for the outcome of the project and people working on the project will report directly to the INT manager. He or she is responsible for the total success of the project and, as such, will make day-to-day decisions related to work priorities.
- Daily work management: Daily work management is managing the way the organization evaluates the change and phases it into the organization's current work environment without having a negative impact upon the output schedules. This management takes into consideration the collection of additional data, employee training, and special handling requirements.
- Executive sponsor: The executive sponsor is usually an executive within the organization who has been assigned or volunteered to work with the project team to help them overcome any difficulties the INT manager cannot handle. The executive sponsor is responsible for ensuring that the functions impacted by the project apply the required resources and have the proper skills and time available to perform in an excellent manner. The executive sponsor provides an organizational view of how the project is progressing and determines where additional executive involvement will ensure successful completion of the project. Depending on the project, the INT will get his or her approval at the key checkpoints from the executive sponsor without involving the total executive team.

Five different types of management involved in the individual project may seem like a lot of additional bureaucracy built into the process. I agree with you and for all but the large critical projects that require the involvement of many parts of the organization, you could reduce the project-related management to three, and for all but very small projects reduce to one INT manager.

The Five Things Required to Have a Successful Product or Process Cycle

Let's stop right here and define what makes up a successful innovative product or process cycle. The innovative cycle is successful when it is:

- Completed on or ahead of schedule
- Completed within budget
- The change performance is equal to or better than the marketing and engineering specifications
- Its return on investment is high enough to fairly compensate its employees, management, and its investors
- Output is seen as value-added by the customer in comparison to present conditions and/or performance

Project management has a direct impact on the first three requirements for a successful innovation cycle and a secondary impact on all five of them. In this case, I am suggesting that you implement project management methodologies and controls as soon as the organization approves the product to be part of the organization's portfolio or when the project risks are high and there is a high probability that the project will not successfully pass the BCA. A formal project management process may be started as early as preparation of the value proposition.

Projects in most organizations are mission-critical activities, and delivering quality products on time is non-negotiable. Even in IT projects, things have changed. The benchmark organizations are completing 90 percent of their projects within 10 percent of budget and schedule. Information systems organizations that establish standards for project management, including a project office, cut their major project cost overruns, delays, and cancellations by 50 percent.

Project Management Responsibility

Project management is the application of knowledge, skills, tools, and techniques to project activities in order to meet or exceed stakeholder's needs and expectations for the project. It includes the following:

- Project Integration Management
- Project Scope Management
- Project Team Management
- Project Financial/Cost Management

- Project Quality Management
- Project Resource Management
- Project Communications Management
- Project Risk Management
- Project Procurement Management
- Project Change Management
- Project Documentation and Consideration Management
- Project Planning and Estimating Management

Usually the organization defines how they will handle each of these 12 management responsibilities in the project plan for the individual project. The project plan is then used as the roadmap for developing and implementing the project.

> How can you compete when over 70 percent of your improvement efforts are unsuccessful?
>
> What would happen to your organization if 70 percent of your product were scrapped? You need engineering functions to be as capable and reliable as the manufacturing process.
>
> **H. James Harrington**

I liken project management to quality management; everyone thinks they know what quality is, so anyone can manage quality. This same thought pattern applies to project management, but just as a quality manager is a special type of professional with very special skills and training, so is a project manager. Project managers require skill, training, and effective leadership specifically related to project management.

Project Management Body of Knowledge 69 Tools (PMBOK)

The Project Management Body of Knowledge (PMBOK) defines 69 different tools that a project manager needs to master. Few of the project managers that I have known over the past 50 years have mastered all these tools. In today's complex world most organizations have numerous projects going on at the same time. Many of these projects are interlinked and others are interdependent. Their requirements and schedules are continuously changing, causing a chain reaction through the organization. As a result, the organization cannot afford to manage each project one at a time. They have to manage their portfolio of projects, making the proper trade-off of personnel and priorities.

Within any organization there usually are several projects for which the difficulty in implementation is low and the probability of successfully being approved during the BCA activities is relatively high. In these cases, the INT manager or leader will assume the roles of the project manager and be responsible for performing all the requirements for which a project manager would be responsible. Of course, the preferable organizational structure is to combine a group of projects into a single portfolio. In these cases, the organization will assign an experienced project manager to support all the projects assigned to the portfolio.

Project Management Excellence—The Art of Excelling in Project Management, which is Book II in the series, *The Five Pillars of Organizational Excellence,* focuses on how to use project management tools to effectively manage the organization's projects and to integrate them into the organization's total operations. This approach means the effective integration of projects, resources, and knowledge to obtain an effective, efficient, and adaptable business intelligence (see Figure 6.1).

> Processes define how organizations function and projects are the means by which organizations improve those processes.
>
> **H. James Harrington**

FIGURE 6.1
A view of how each of the three project success drivers interrelate.

Process redesign and process reengineering are two of the most important projects that organizations undertake. These types of projects have a failure rate estimated to be as high as 70 percent. There are two main causes for these high-cost failures: poor project management and poor change management. IBM launched 11 redesign projects that started from the way they manage internal information systems to the way they developed products and serve customers. IBM reported, "We have reduced IT spending by 31 percent for a total savings of more than $2 billion. Since 1993, cycle time for large systems development has been slashed from 56 months to 16 months. For low-end systems, it's seven months—down from two years."

The Five Reasons Projects Fail

Let's look at why projects fail.

- Failure to adhere to committed schedule caused by:
  - Variances
  - Exceptions
  - Poor planning
  - Delays
  - Scope Creep
- Poor resource utilization caused by:
  - Proper skills not available
  - Poor time utilization
  - Misalignment of skills and assignments
- The portfolio of projects was not managed correctly:
  - The wrong projects were selected
  - High risk projects were not identified
  - Poor control over interdependencies between projects
- Loss of intellectual capital and knowledge capital:
  - Lack of the means to transfer knowledge
  - People leave the organization
- Not preparing the people who will use the output from the project (change management)

Research confirms that as much as 60 percent of change initiatives and other projects fail as a direct result of a fundamental inability to manage their social implications.

Gartner Group

PROJECT CHANGE MANAGEMENT UNDERSTANDING

Change management is the process, tools, and techniques to manage the people side of change to achieve the required business outcomes. Change management incorporates the organizational tools that organizations can use to help individuals make successful personal transitions resulting in the adoption and realization of change. There are two basic approaches to organizational change management:

- Project Change Management. This methodology focuses on preparing a group of people to reduce resistance to a specific change and to accept the change as part of the routine life.
- Cultural Change Management. This methodology focuses upon changing the class culture throughout the organization to make it more resilient in the face of a continuous changing environment.

Everyone likes to think of themselves as change masters, but in truth, people are change bigots. Everyone in the management team is all for change. They want to see others change, but when it comes to the managers changing, they are reluctant to move away from their past experiences that have proven to be so successful for them. If the organization is going to change, top management has to be the first to change.

Change is inevitable and you must embrace it if you are going to be successful in this challenging world. In *Change Management Excellence—The Art of Excelling in Change Management*, which is Book III in the series, *The Five Pillars of Organizational Excellence*, I discuss the change management system that is made up of three distinct elements:

- Defining what will be changed
- Defining how to change
- Making the change happen

Most of the books written to date about change management have been theoretical in nature. They talked about black holes, cascading sponsorships, and burning platforms, but that is only the last phase of the change process. Most organizations do not understand or follow a comprehensive change management system. An effective change management system requires that the organization step back and define what it will change. By that, I am not talking about reducing stock levels, increasing customer satisfaction, or training people; I am talking about the very fundamentals. Which of the key business drivers does the organization need to change and how does the organization need to change them? That means that you need to develop very crisp vision statements that define how the organization will change key business drivers over time. This approach requires that the organization have an excellent understanding of what its business drivers are and how they are operating today. Then the organization must define exactly how it wants to change these key business drivers over a set period. After the organization has defined what it wants to change, then it can define how to change. During this stage the organization looks at the more than 1,100 different improvement tools that are available today, determines which tools will bring about the required changes to these key business drivers, and schedules the implementation of these tools and methodologies. This schedule makes up a key part of the organization's strategic business plan.

The last phase in the change management process is making the change happen. This is the area where behavioral scientists have developed several excellent approaches to break down resistance and build up resiliency throughout the organization. It is this phase that most change management books have concentrated on, but it is the last phase in the total change management system.

> We [Japan] will win and you [USA] will lose. You cannot do anything about it because your failure is an internal disease. Your companies are based on Taylor's principles. Worse, your heads are Taylorized, too. We have passed the Taylor stage. We are aware that business has become terribly complex. Survival is very uncertain in an environment filled with risk, the unexpected, and competition.
>
> **Konosuke Matsushita**
> *Founder, Matsushita Electric Industrial Company*

Project Risk Management

Project risk management is a subset of project management that includes the processes concerned with the identification, analyzing, reporting, and developing contingency plans.

During "Phase II. Process Grouping 5: Business Case Analysis," the team will need to consider application of the following:

1. Project Management
2. Change Management
3. Knowledge Management
4. Risk Management

HUMAN RESOURCES

Even the best ideas need resources to transform them into profit.

H. James Harrington

As far as human resources are concerned, you have three options:

1. You can hire people with the proper skills and experience.
2. You can train your people so that they have the proper skills and experience.
3. You can contract out to another organization that has the proper skills, equipment, and experience.

In business profits aren't the only thing, but it's hard to think of what is more important.

H. James Harrington

Building Human Relationships

All human beings have a tendency to live within a box they built for themselves. This is the way we brush our hair, put on our pants, what we eat for breakfast, the route we take to work, kiss our spouse as we go out the door to work, hold our golf club, the way our desk is laid out, the way we go to get that morning cup of coffee, how much sugar you put in to the coffee, the way we do our work assignments, and so on. Would you ask for help when you are park your car, when you read the newspaper, and so on? The box we live in is made up of habits, laws, work procedures, work associates, spouse's personality, personal needs, and your emotions. You walk into an elevator with a group of strangers and stagger like a wooden soldier never greeting them with a good morning. When Mary asks, "How are you today?" You always answer, "Okay!," no matter how bad or good you feel.

These boxes we make for ourselves limit our thinking, stifle our enthusiasm, and kill our innovation. The next time you step into elevator, greet each of the other riders with a cheery "Hello! It's too bad we can't say outside and enjoy the sun." Then step back and see the miracle that you created in their eyes. Sure, there will be some people who are irritated with you, but they are a small percentage of the people that ride on the elevator. Most of them will welcome the smile you give so freely and return it with an equal smile. Try not standing facing the elevator door, but stand facing the people in the elevator. Plan two or three options on the route you take to get to work and vary these options. On a nice sunny day choose the option that takes the longest so you can enjoy the ride more.

Human resources is the one thing that sets organizations apart from each other. Company A has employees that are very creative, Company B is an excellent sales force, Company C manages its finances in very effective ways, Company D has excellent technicians, Company E as excellent designers, Company F manufacturing engineers do an excellent job of using robotics, and so on. In each case, it is the people who set them apart. It's the people who add value to the organization, not the size of the office they work in.

It's unfortunate that organizations don't invest more of their discretionary spending in developing employees. Organizations in the United States should spend a great deal more than they are now are to develop employees and help them to establish a career path within the organization. There was a time when most people stayed with an employer throughout their working career. Now it is the exception, rather than the rule. If I suggested to your manager that he or she jointly develop a career plan for you, he or she might possibly just laugh at me. There was a time at IBM when every employee had the opportunity to work with his or her manager to develop his or her career plan. Now it's almost as though the organization and the individual are total separate entities and neither one depends upon the other.

For example, Michael Osanloo, Chief Executive Officer (CEO) of P.F. Chang, spends his time as follows:

- 60 percent on employees
- 20 percent on finance
- 10 percent on marketing
- 10 percent on IT

How Did It Get This Way?

Here is a simple explanation. Management paid low wages to maximize their profit. The employees started a union to represent them. Management treated the unions as adversaries. The union's only interest was in improving the employees' conditions and wages. Organizations started having large layoffs. Employees began to feel that they should leave the organization if they could get more money and better living conditions with another employer. Management cut back on employee development so the employees were not prepared to switch jobs.

The interface between management and employees has been a seesaw activity with each one focusing on his or her needs, rather than working together as a team. If you asked my father what he did for a living, he would say, "I worked for IBM." Today if you asked an IBM employee what he or she does for living, he or she would answer something like, "I am a project manager or I am the system analyst." In the past, an employee was proud of the organization he or she worked for. Today, the focus is on the type of work the employee does, rather than the company the employee works for. In an innovative organization this thought pattern has to turnaround so that the employee is proud of the organization he or she works for.

Our Human resources are very valuable assets, not liabilities. In innovative companies, human resources makeup the most valuable resources that the organization has. This means:

1. You need to be able to accurately project the skills that will be required 5 years now.
2. You have to consider future needs as well and present program needs.
3. You need to select new employees based upon their creativity rather than the labor that they perform.
4. You need to subcontract present activities that require a skill set that is not in keeping with the long-range strategy.
5. You need to identify those individuals who have the capability of developing new skills in line with future skills needs
6. You need to have an employee skill transformation strategy that will provide you with the skills you need when you need them.
7. You need to provide a reasonable level of job security for those individuals who have the desired skills or the ability to develop the skills.
8. You need to practice job rotation so that your organization challenges capable people in the job they're doing.

9. Management needs to work with the employees by developing career paths unique to the individual.
10. The organization needs to support the continuing educational needs of today's environment by paying for work-related training.
11. You need to have a rewards and recognition system that reinforces desired behaviors.

If you (management) create an expectation of continuous product or service improvement, but fail to deliver on that expectation, you will see a build-up of fear and negative forecasting.

Stephen R. Covey

FINANCIAL RESOURCE

Definitions

Financing is the acquisition of capital (money) and its management so that the organization can pay its bills, employee salaries, and its obligations to its stakeholders.

Resourcing is the acquisition of workspace, inventory, capital, equipment, software, and other facility.

In an established company, the executive team has taken on the responsibility for providing adequate financing for a specific time when they approved the value proposition and the related budget. The financing for existing organizations typically will come from the stockholders, existing product, or money borrowed from a lending organization. In some new product lines the acquisition of state-of-the-art components may be difficult, but the procurement and engineering organizations have the responsibility for overcoming these obstacles.

Financial Resources for Established Organizations

For an established organization, the executive team has usually assigned the managing of the financial resources to a finance function headed by the chief financial officer. The ideal way to support innovative projects is using discretionary profit to invest into future activities and improvement to current deliverables.

From the financial control and reporting aspect, established organizations will already have in place a computer system that tracks accounts payable and accounts receivable as well as internal operating costs. Typically the reporting system compares actual expenditures to approved budget. There are many software packages that prepare the financial reporting and control activities in keeping with good financial planning concept, so we will not discuss them in this book.

Financial Funding for Start-up and Small Organizations

There's no doubt about it—the probability of an innovator and/or entrepreneur making a lot of money is greater than for those individuals who are working for established organization in a low risk field. The innovator and/or entrepreneur also will have a lot more fun, self-satisfaction, and problems, but they also have a high risk of going bankrupt and losing everything they have invested. The old saying is true, "high risk activities pay big rewards."

From the start-up company standpoint financing is a very different story. Improving an organization's share of the market is much less difficult than raising the money. These small start-up organizations generally have serious difficulty to survive financially without external funding. Typical sources of money in the order start-up companies acquire it follows:

- The personal savings and life insurance of the individuals who are starting the new organization and that of their parents.
- Friends of the founders asked to invest.
- The founder's credit cards maxed out.
- The founders and parents homes mortgaged.
- Angel investors get a large percentage of the company for small investment.
- Throughout this process banks are regularly contacted requesting letters of credit and the founders will have little or no luck usually in getting the money.
- If they are lucky and their product is well accepted in the marketplace, the banks take a more supportive position related to loans.
- If things are going very well, the founders pursue a first round of pre-IPO funding.

Many problems plague the start-up organizations related to acquiring facilities. It's not unusual to see a start-up innovative organization in the garage, bedroom, or kitchen after acquiring used equipment and second-hand furniture to keep costs down. More start-up companies fail because of this activity than from poor product or service.

Small start-up organizations face a great deal of difficulty in surviving financially. I can remember the first business where I was the CEO. It was a start-up consulting firm that had a unique product called "Business Process Improvement." It took the start-up 4 months to get its act together which included getting all the space, travel, to the computers , and business cards, pulling together an advertising campaign and implementing it, hiring salespeople, office staff and consultants, developing the methodology, and trying to run the classes. The origins of money came from my retirement pay from IBM, and my partner's and my mother's savings. The start-up was overwhelmed with consulting opportunities, but the company couldn't hire people fast enough and train them in the methodology to meet our customers' requests. At the end of 6 months, I took the whole organization out for a steak and lobster dinner to celebrate the company's success. Life was good and the company had more contracts than our resources could handle with customers waiting for our services. After sipping the last glass of wine, I instructed our treasurer to write a check for the bill. She replied that she couldn't because the company had less than $200 in the bank. I couldn't believe my ears. She explained to me that she was worried because the company didn't have enough money to pay the employee salaries next week. I couldn't sleep that night and was in the office at 5 AM waiting for my treasurer to show up. I knew there had to be something wrong because the company was earning lots of money. When she showed up at 8:03 AM, I had a hot cup of coffee waiting for her and me. She pointed out that the company had a lot outstanding invoices, some of which were as much as 3 months old. She also pointed out that the company paid travel expenses even before employees took trips and the employees got their salary every week even if the company didn't collect money for the work they did that week. She pointed out to me that it was an accounts receivable problem. The situation is a way of life because that's the way accounts receivable operates in most organizations. Everyone wants to hold on to their money as long as possible. If a customer has 30 days before the payment is due, they try to schedule the payment so that the company receives it on the 29th day. If the company is doing business with the government, payment is always at least 3 months late. To help the cash flow problem, the company included in the contract a penalty clause if the bill was not paid within 90 days. Even with this clause in their contract, the company's accounts receivable was still running a 80-day average billing cycle.

How di the company recover? Everyone took a 50 percent cut in weekly salary for 2 months, my mother mortgaged her home, and I was acquiring additional funds necessary to keep the organization operating. Money may be the root of all evil, but a little evil is better than starvation.

The Financial Value of an Organization

It doesn't make any difference if you're a small or large organization. At this point in ISC, continuing the project is dependent upon obtaining financial resources from another source other than from the project under development. Of course, the best way to raise financial capital is to sell a product at a profit, but if the project is not developed to the point that you can deliver acceptable product to your customers, then this is not an answer. So, when you acquired everything you could from your friend, maxed out your credit cards, mortgaged your home, and borrowed money against your retirement and insurance, you have no other option but to borrow money from a bank or an angel funding organization. Banks are reluctant to lend money based upon futures. They want the loans they give out to be covered by organizations assets. (That's something I could never understand. If I had the assets, I wouldn't be borrowing money from the bank.)

Organizational assets are largely determined by the number and value of patents, inventory value, sales of other outputs, the amount of risks built into the business, and the reputation of the organization's Board of Directors. They certainly do take into consideration the amount of personal debt of key organizational leaders. Angel investors, on the other hand, are more likely to invest in excellent idea, but may require that the organization turn over a major portion of the ownership to them. I've been told that the average Angel has three failures out of five organizations they invest in. This means that the two organizations that are successful need to generate enough positive return on investment to cover the losses incurred because the angel investor invested in three organizations that failed and as well still provide the angel investor with a very significant profit.

FINANCIAL MANAGEMENT SUMMARY

The mighty dollar, yen, peso, frank, pound, or ruble—whatever you call it—has been the primary business driver since the beginning of time and rightly so. You go into business to make money—unless you're the government and you are spending someone else's money. People need it to buy food, clothing, medicine, shelter, books, and much more. People go to work and sell their lives, minute by minute, hour by hour. The people who invest their time and/or money into the organization have the right to make a fair return on their investment. Organizations that do a poor job of managing their financial operations cannot and should not stay in business. Bankruptcy laws should be changed to prevent organizations that do not meet their financial obligations from getting back into business until they have paid off the money they owe.

Every manager must be a good financial manager, spending each dollar as though it was his or her own. Each employee needs to be a miser about how they spend their time to be sure that the organization is getting its money's worth out of the progress that was made. Ask yourself, "Would you pay someone else what you are getting to do the job that you are performing?" If the answer is no, then look for ways for you personally to add more value to the organization. If your answer is yes, still go out and look for more ways that you personally can add additional value to the organization. Be sure you know what you are costing the organization. It is a lot more than your salary. Often the variable cost—insurance, benefits, equipment, space, direct support-related costs, and so on—is much more than the individual's salary.

This portion of the book just provides high level view of the problems related to managing resources. I could have written about how each manager needs training to understand how to control his or her financial obligations and how to prepare and manage a budget. I could have written about how to get financial help from venture capitalists to start an organization. I could have written about how to handle a bankruptcy. I could have written about the best way to use surplus money. I could have written about ways to reduce income taxes. Instead, I chose to look at only some of the highlights that are important to you if you are managing an innovative organization's finances and I did not try to make CPAs out of you. I recognize that this will disappoint some of you and make others as happy as a puppy with a big and juicy beef bone. If you are the latter one, you should buy a book on financial management. And if you are the former one, I know that you already have the book that the "happy" reader should be reading.

> Money is the root of all evil,
> unless you are cold, hungry, or sick;
> then it is the beginning of hope and happiness.

H. James Harrington

KNOWLEDGE MANAGEMENT EXCELLENCE

When a person dies, a library is lost.

H. James Harrington

Today, more than ever before, knowledge is the key to organizational success. To fulfill this need, the internet and other information technologies have provided more information than anyone can ever consume. Instead of having one or two sources of information, the internet provides people with hundreds, if not thousands, of inputs, all of which you need to research to ensure that you have not missed a key nugget of information. People are overwhelmed with so much information that they don't have time to absorb it.

To make matters worse, most organization still do not document most of their knowledge; it rests in the minds and experiences of the people doing the job. This knowledge disappears from the organization's knowledge base whenever an individual leaves an assignment. In *Knowledge Management Excellence—The Art of Excelling in Knowledge Management*, which is Book IV in the series, *The Five Pillars of Organizational Excellence*, I define how to establish a knowledge management system designed to sort out unneeded and/or false information and capture the "soft" knowledge needed to run the organization.

With the almost endless amount of information that fills up our computers, desks, and minds, the organization need to design a knowledge management system around the organization's key capabilities and competencies.

What is Knowledge?

Definition: Knowledge is defined as a mixture of experiences, practices, traditions, values, contextual information, expert insight, and a sound intuition that provides an environment and framework for evaluation and incorporating new experiences and information.

There are two types of knowledge: explicit and tacit.

Definition: Explicit knowledge is defined as knowledge that is stored in a semi-structured content such as documents, e-mail, voicemail, or video media. I call this *hard or tangible knowledge.* It is conveyed from one person to another in a systematic way.

Definition: Tacit knowledge is defined as knowledge that is formed around intangible factors embedded in an individual's experience. It is personal, content-specific knowledge that resides in an individual. It is knowledge that an individual gains from experience or skills that he or she develops. It often takes the form of beliefs, values, principles, and morals. It guides the individual's actions. I call this *soft knowledge.* It is embedded in the individual's ideas, insights, values, and judgment. It is only accessible through the direct corroboration and communication with the individual who has the knowledge.

Definition: Knowledge management is defined as a proactive, systematic process by which the organization generates value from intellectual or knowledge-based assets and disseminates it to the stakeholders.

The Six Phases of a Knowledge Management System

There are six phases required to implement an effective knowledge management system (KMS):

- Phase I: Requirements Definition (7 activities)
- Phase II: Infrastructure Evaluation (16 activities)
- Phase III: Knowledge Management System Design and Development (12 activities)
- Phase IV: Pilot (15 activities)
- Phase V: Deployment (10 activities)
- Phase VI: Continuous Improvement (1 activity)

One of the biggest challenges related to implementing a KMS is transferring knowledge held by individuals, including processes and behavioral knowledge, into a consistent format that employees can easily share within the organization.

Knowledge takes us from chance to choice.

H. James Harrington

The true standard of success for knowledge management is the number of people who access and implement ideas from the knowledge networks. These networks bring state-of-the-art ideas and/or best practices into the workplace. This process allows the organization to develop areas of critical mass that implement standards that work and provides access to all employees so that they can make comments to improve those standards. Even the newest novice to the organization can look at the materials and make recommendations based upon personal insight, creativity, and experience.

A big challenge related to implementing a KMS is in transforming knowledge held by individuals, including process and behavioral knowledge, into a consistent technology format that the organization can easily share with the organization's stakeholders. But the biggest challenge is changing the organization's culture from knowledge-hoarding to a knowledge-sharing.

OUTSIDE RESOURCES SUMMARY

The way an organization uses resources has changed. In the 1920s, Ford owned everything needed to produce the Model T—starting from the mills that dug the iron ore out of the mountain, to the smelter, to the machine shop, to the subassembly, and final assembly. Today's organizations have realized that they need to concentrate on what they do best and build a set of alliance partners and suppliers who can do the other jobs better, faster, and cheaper than they can. This approach from complete control to indirect control has greatly increased the need for fast, effective communication among suppliers, alliance partners, and organizations. Methodologies like supply chain management and other IT enablers have stepped up to meet this challenge, thus minimizing the total risk.

At the end of the supply chain is the external customer. Now, you may not think of the external customer as one of your organization's resources, but

I am sure you will agree, it is one of the organization's assets. Throughout this book, I have been considering resources and assets as I discussed each item. Management around the world has now realized that it is much less expensive to keep the customer they have than to go out and find replacement customer by a factor of 10 to 1. This realization has changed the way our organizations interface with their present customers. They are looking at the lifetime value of the customer, not just the transactional value. Customer survey results have come to be as important as profit and loss statements. Fast, effective corrective action on customer problems is now a requirement to keep your customers buying your services and products. Empowering your first-line service employees with a means to handle unhappy customers is a must. The level of customer dissatisfaction doubles each time a customer must speak to another individual to get his or her problem resolved. If a food store customer brings a quart of milk back claiming that it is sour, why would you question it? Why would your employee smell it or taste it? That's telling the customer that you don't believe he or she is truthful. For the sake of \$1.35, you are putting at risk your customer's future business, which is worth about \$1.35 per week, times 52 weeks, times 35 years, or \$245,700.

Marketing strategy needs to address keeping your present customer base, then consider attracting potential new customers.

A customer in the hand is worth five on the to-call list.

H. James Harrington

The essence of competitiveness is liberated when we make people believe that what they think and do is important—and then get out of their way while they do it.

Jack Welch
Past CEO, General Electric

7

Process Grouping 7: Documentation

INTRODUCTION TO DOCUMENTATION

I have a paperless office but that's only because I used up all the paper in the printer.

H. James Harrington

"Process Grouping (PG) 7: Documentation" is often approached with a high degree of reluctance. It is an activity that's just hard work. Up until now the first six process groupings (PG's) were almost like a game where you won or lost. Now that game has to be wrapped up so that anybody can play it and be able to win. Despite all of this, it is one of the most time-consuming activities in the innovative system and its outcome is extremely critical to the success of the project. This is the time where you clarify all requirements so that you can measure and control them in the manufacturing process. Designer views pick apart your work often with very minor changes that have little or no impact upon the end product. After this review, the product goes from engineering tooling to hard tooling and then to the manufacturing floor. It is a huge step and as such each process should undergo a certification activity. I personally really enjoy the challenges of taking advantage of an opportunity and coming up with a new and unique approach that often is patentable. I hate writing specifications, drawings blueprints, setting up databases, preparing routings, and so on. In a typical organization, there are many functions that have the responsibility to generate documentation in support of an innovative output. Some of them are:

- Project Management
- Project Engineering
- Industrial Engineering
- Production Control

- Human Resources
- Quality Assurance
- Manufacturing Engineering
- Marketing and Sales
- Information Systems
- Financial Controls

To add to that the confusion, most of these documents will go through a change review process where product engineering, manufacturing engineering, sales, and marketing will also review them to search for mistakes that the originator made or better ways of accomplishing the same objective. They do not target these reviews for majority approval; they require a consensus approval in these cases which allows one function to take exception to the document and thus bring activities to a halt.

To add to the difficulties of documentation for truly innovative projects, the organization bases the documentation largely upon experience and has never validated the actual usage of the documentation. This situation leads to many problems and it is a hotbed of corrective action.

For major innovative projects or products that have a great deal of risk associated with them, the organization should assign professional project managers. For the projects that do not fall within this classification, the project leader will have the responsibility to prepare a project management plan. There are two key documents for every approved project:

1. An Approved Financial Plan. The approved financial plan must include the 12 Process Groupings (PG) that make up the Innovation System Cycle (ISC). This plan is subdivided into the budgets for the individual natural work team. In an established organization, usually the organization's financial controller will coordinate the financial plan. An executive who the organization holds accountable for completing the project within projected financial resources always approves this plan.

   This financial cycle starts with the approved financial support of the project approved during the Business Case Analysis. You usually divide it into small segments that take the project through the next checkpoint. Then you usually divide this approved financial amount between the functioning natural work teams. This typically leads to a squabble over how the organization will divide the money. When this occurs, the project manager or the INT leader will negotiate hopefully a win-win situation for both parties. When it does not occur, it results in a negative situation that the organization needs to qualify and to eliminate uncertainties.

2. Activity Timeline Chart. This chart is often called a Gantt chart and defines what each of the natural work teams are going to do, when they're going to do it, and who is the customer for each of these activities. This is often called simply the "project plan." Usually a formal project manager or INT manager coordinates it. In these cases, the project manager serves primarily as a coordinator and status reporter who warns management whenever there is a probability that could incur costs or a schedule that could be negatively impacted.

Project activity plans are divided up into 10 separate independent knowledge areas, which are coordinated plans based upon the Project Management Body Knowledge (PMBOK) definitions. I added three more knowledge areas that I feel are important parts as major focus areas (the three additions I added are the ones printed in bold letters).

- Project Integration Management. Responsible area: Project manager or the INT leader
- Project Scope Management. Responsible area: INT leader or project manager
- Project Schedule Management. Responsible area: INT leader or project manager
- Project Financial and Cost Management. Responsible area: Finance
- Project Quality Management. Responsible area: Quality Assurance
- Project Resource Management. Responsible area: Personnel (Human Resources)
- Project Communications Management. Responsible area: Project manager
- Project Risk Management. Responsible area: INT leader
- Project Procurement Management. Responsible area: Purchasing and Production Control
- Project Statement Stakeholders Management. Responsible area: Project manager or INT leader
- **Project Change Management. Responsible area: Project manager or INT leader**
- **Project Documentation and Consideration Management. Responsible area: Information systems**
- **Project Planning and Estimating Management: Project manager or INT leader**

The individual organization responsible must take these planning activities very seriously as their budgets are based upon the individual plans. If using PMBOK as your project specification, the responsible area for each of these activities could be the project manager. Based upon my personal experience, the project manager usually is covering more than one project and he or she is busy so organizations will transfer this documentation activity to the INT leader. This transfer greatly increases the INT leader's roles and responsibilities. Typically, you will integrate these various project plans using a Gantt chart.

The Individual Innovation Plan Chart is typically a Gantt chart that lists the activities that each of the involved natural work teams need to complete for the project to meet its objectives (see Figure 7.1).

The flowchart in Figure 7.2 is a typical example of work in progress. The INT members use sticky tabs for the major activities and processes. After they identify the major activities, the individual members of the INT define their contribution to the activities as well as the required inputs and projected output. Today organizations tie the combined plans together usually using a computer program to connect the inputs and outputs.

Individual Innovation Plan
Key Performance Drivers: Management Support/Leadership

Activity #	ACTIVITY	MONTH												QUARTER							Person Responsible
		1	2	3	4	5	6	7	8	9	10	11	12	1	2	3	4	1	2	3	4	
1.0	Teams																					
1.1	Establish Task Teams																					EIT
1.2	Develop Training Plan & Budget for EIT																					Task Team
1.3	Implement Training Plan																					Division President
2.0	Start Departmental Improvement Teams																					Department Manager
3.0	Develop Strategic Direction																					Sam K.
3.1	Communicate to Management																					
3.2	Communicate to Employees																					
4.0	Performance Planning and Appraisal																					
4.1	New Appraisal Process																					Joe B.
4.2	Communicate Plan to Management																					Joe B.
4.3	Communicate Plan to Employees																					Division President
4.4	Implement Plan																					Management
5.0	Measurement/Feedback																					
5.1	MBWA																					Division President
5.2	Employee Opinion Survey																					H.I.
5.3	Feedback Results																					H.I.
5.4	Re-survey																					H.I.
6.0	Suggestion System																					
6.1	Establish Task Team																					Sam K.

= Action
= Ongoing Activity

FIGURE 7.1
Typical project chart for an individual natural work team.

Project Flow Charts

FIGURE 7.2
Typical flowchart used to combine three individual project plans.

This flowchart takes on some unique characteristics since it includes the amount of time to perform the task and the estimated processing cycle time for each block in the flowchart. The organization pays careful attention to connecting interrelationships and dependencies. Also, the flowchart identifies the individual or function responsible for that specific activity. This flowchart allows identification of the processing time critical path and the human resource critical path. By working on streamlining the processing and/or human resource critical plan, the organization can greatly reduce the time it takes to complete the project. It is important to note that whenever you address a critical path and bring it into line with the rest of the project, a new critical path arises like the Phoenix out of the ashes. This flowchart turns out to be the heart of the innovative program as it completely controls all the product cycle through the organization. One of the major jobs the project manager has is attacking worst-case conditions thereby minimizing total processing time for the project.

Typically, the Gantt chart will indicate any interdependencies that a specific activity has and where the outputs from the activity are used. Each activity will have a start and end date and the name of the person or organization responsible for meeting the specific commitment.

I have already discussed the duties and makeup of a project manager. If you still would like more detail, I suggest you read the book entitled *Project Management for Performance Improvement Teams* published by CRC Press in 2018. The book includes all the pertinent information related to the revision of the PMBOK that came out in 2018.

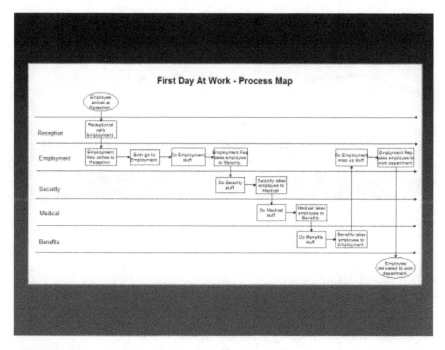

FIGURE 7.3
Swim lane flowchart of the process to which an organization subjects a new employee on their first day on the job.

Figure 7.3 is a Swim Lane flowchart for a project to reduce cycle time to process a new employee. This is not the flowchart that drives the project. It is the flowchart of what the project is trying to improve.

Definition of work breakdown structure

A work breakdown structure (WBS) in project management and systems engineering is a deliverable-oriented breakdown of a project into smaller components. A work breakdown structure is a key project deliverable that organizes the team's work into manageable sections.

There are many excellent software packages that will produce the desired flowcharts and project management work breakdown structures in activity tracking reports. Basically, a work breakdown structure is a list of activities or tasks that organizations need to be perform often late related to a projects (see Figure 7.4). Following each activity is a time sequence for the projected processing time and schedule to complete that specific activity. Activities that are interrelated are connected to show the dependencies.

Figures 7.5 and 7.6 are typical work breakdown structures generated by software packages.

Work Breakdown Structure Outline
(task numbering optional)

Project Management Improvement Project – Phase 1

1	**Initiate Project**
1.1	**Develop Project Charter**
1.1.1	Define Scope
1.1.2	Define Requirements
1.1.3	Identify High-Level Roles
1.1.4	Develop High-Level Budget
1.1.5	Identify High-Level Control Strategies
1.1.6	Finalize Charter and Gain Approvals
1.1.6.1	Consolidate and Publish Project Charter
1.1.6.2	Hold Review Meeting
1.1.6.3	Revise Project charter
1.1.6.4	Gain approvals
2	**Plan Project**
2.1	**Develop Work Plan**
2.1.1	Develop Work Breakdown Structure
2.1.2	Develop Project Staffing Plan
2.1.3	Develop Project Schedule
2.1.4	Develop Project Budget

FIGURE 7.4
Typical list of activities that would drive a project breakdown structure.

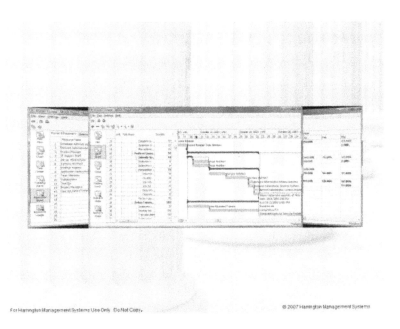

For Harrington Management Systems Use Only Do Not Copy.   © 2007 Harrington Management Systems

FIGURE 7.5
Typical computer-generated breakdown structure.

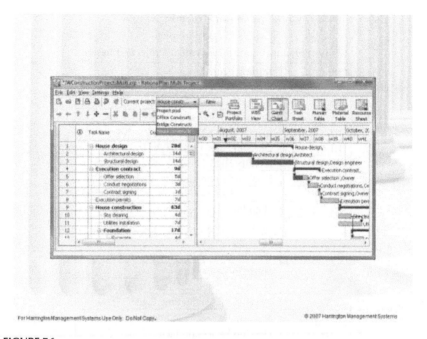

FIGURE 7.6
Typical computer-generated work breakdown structure.

MANUFACTURING ENGINEERING ACTIVITIES DURING PHASE II

The manufacturing engineer is a key player in Phase II as he or she converts the many product engineering documents and production procedures along with setting up the production process. Some of the activities that product engineering is responsible for are:

- Routings
- Training programs
- Workmanship standards
- Determining which activities to subcontract (the department in house will be responsible for the house activities)
- Breaking down complex activity into small building blocks that assembly operators can produced
- Defining workflow throughout the organization and the equipment used to produce a specific device in conjunction with the industrial engineering group

- Designing tools and fixtures that are unique to an individual product
- In many organizations also defining the work standards for the individual activities
- Identifying problems that occur in the manufacturing process and correcting them
- Developing repair procedures for product that otherwise the organization would scrap
- Using automation mechanization and robotics (becoming the tools of the trade for manufacturing engineers)

One of the biggest commercial contracts ever issued went to China because the United States did not have enough manufacturing engineers to support the activities.

Definitions

Automation is the technique, method, or system of operating or controlling a process by highly *automatic* means, as by electronic devices, reducing human intervention to a minimum. It can be mechanical device, operated electronically, that functions automatically, without continuous input from an operator.

Robotic is a mechanical device that sometimes resembles a human and can perform a variety of often complex human tasks on command or by programming in advance. It can operate automatically or by remote control.

Organizations are turning over more and more manual operations like welding, painting, and environmentally hazardous activities to automation and robots. Even the floors in your home are being cleaned by an automatic vacuum cleaner. Now computers write, talk, and even think for you. You must question how long it will be before there is no need for humans. Organizations are getting closer and closer to the fulfilling the old joke where one man runs the production facilities and turns the facility on and off once a day. A dog accompanies him to keep him awake.

Organizations need automation and robots to compete against countries with significantly lower labor rates and manufacturing regulations. If you can produce it for less, you can sell it for less which gives you a very significant competitive advantage. You can readily see that the time and effort required for the manufacturing engineer is much greater than the time and effort expended by the individuals who identify an opportunity and define how the organization will take advantage of that opportunity.

KEY DOCUMENTATION PRODUCT ENGINEERING PREPARATION AND DOCUMENTATION ACTIVITY

For this document, project engineering is the department that takes the research and development (R&D) concept and prepares the engineering documentation in a format that the organization can use as an official engineering document. Organizations typically assign project engineers after the project becomes part of the organization's portfolio of approved projects and the project engineers continue to have engineering project responsibilities until the organization ends the project. They develop and control all the engineering documents used in production. They have the responsibility for signing off on all production documents that impacts the product line (for example, routings, approved suppliers, repair procedures, test procedures, and operating instructions).

During this activity, the project engineer pulls together the notes in his or her notebook and the drawings on scraps of paper on his or her desk to prepare formal drawings, specifications, and directions. Up to this point in time, the organization has paid little attention to having an accurate document change control system.

You should take great care in the preparation of these documents to ensure that the documents are in line with the education level of the individuals who will use them. One of the biggest mistakes made during this activity is engineers preparing documents to impress their associates rather than having them directed at the individual who will use them.

Before release of any engineering document, it should go through a formal design review typically involving manufacturing, manufacturing engineering, quality assurance, procurement, and often someone from the field maintenance group. Every function should have their own checklist that they use to review an engineering document. Typically the quality assurance checklist would consider things like:

- Manufacturability
- Inspection capabilities
- Reliability of the output
- Repair ability
- Testability

- Readability of the documentation
- Completeness of the documentation
- Allowable variation requirements and backup data

You should have a central document control and version center responsible for keeping the documents in sync with the current product vision level. Often an organization cannot implement an engineering change activity until they change the associated manufacturing and field services procedures to reflect the engineering change. Change control is a major part of document control.

_____

MANUFACTURING ENGINEERING, TEST ENGINEERING, INDUSTRIAL ENGINEERING DOCUMENTATION

Although the headings in this documentation focus on engineering, government, service, public and private organizations and perform these activities and these organizations require engineering to have a high degree of confidence that the output will perform as required in the product specifications. I like to think of these particular documents as "how to" documents that define the processes that result in meeting the product specifications. Often these departments are tempted to change their procedures so that they become more customer-centric ignoring the engineering requirements. This is a major mistake. If the engineering documentation does not reflect the external customer requirements, the organization should change it and then modify the "how to" documents. I observed on several occasions where a change in the "how to" documents to better reflect a customer requirement resulted in immediate customer satisfaction but had a major impact upon the output's reliability.

Typical "how to" documentation prepared during this phase of the ISC include:

- Activity flow routings
- Set up instructions
- Test procedures
- Facility layout
- Approval of supplier list
- Packaging instructions

- Repair procedures
- Training instructions
- Job descriptions
- Assembly drawings
- Equipment requirements
- Reporting requirements
- Stocking requirements

Equally important to good documentation related to the required outputs is the documentation that explains how the organization obtains the desired outputs.

Quality Assurance Documentation

Although the exact job descriptions for quality engineers vary drastically from organization to organization, in this case, I'm going to consider their job is to assure that at a minimum the product delivered to a customer will meet or exceed engineering requirements and satisfy the customer's expectations. Often organizations validate these confidence levels and performance requirements using independent quality assurance during the process, and quality audits and inspections during the end process. This responsibility lasts all the way through the product lifecycle until the organization scraps the product or the product becomes obsolete. To accomplish this task, organizations need to take into consideration all the product engineering documentation, "how to" documentation, field performance reporting, and the marketing specifications for the specific output. A major input to this activity is the customer satisfaction reports, manufacturing performance reports, customer complaints, supplier input performance, failure analysis reports, employee opinion surveys, exit interviews, return rate reporting, and off-line testing (usually related to meeting the reliability specification). In most organizations, quality assurance and product assurance are the only areas that are held accountable for the product meeting its engineering reliability requirements. Where manufacturing engineering is primarily held responsible for is the efficiency of the production process; quality assurance is primarily responsible for the effectiveness of the product engineering and manufacturing activities.

The following are typical documents that quality assurance should generate. In some organizations, the quality assurance activities are primarily to facilitate performance improvement actions and problem analysis. The classical Quality Engineering responsibilities are then reassigned to another function who needs to prepare these documents.

- Sampling plans
- Inspection procedures
- Off-line testing procedures
- Equipment capability studies results
- Efficiency reports related to production
- Scrap and rework reports
- Supplier rating reports
- Failure analysis reports
- Corrective action status reports
- Product certification reports
- Process certification reports
- Quality regulations compliance reports
- Internal audit reports
- Experimental design results
- Customer after sales service performance
- Customer reliability performance reports
- Calibration schedules
- Audit plans
- Defect reports
- Scrap and rework reports
- Supplier qualification reports

Again, all the examples given are primarily product-oriented. Service, public, and governmental activities need to have the same type of documentation and follow-up as a manufacturing process. For example, at the bank the quality function has a set of documents that provide the management team with a high degree of confidence that they are meeting customer requirements. In this case, techniques like reporting individual worker customer satisfaction levels turns out to be a major part of the quality program.

Financial Reports

In the Chief Financial Officer's function, it is important to have a tight control over innovation. Too many excellent innovators have ended up in prison because of innovation activities. Putting that aside, the financial department plays a crucial role in the innovation cycle. Much of the procedures and controls in the financial area are legally and morally defined providing little room for new innovative ideas. This limitation does not mean that the functional department should not be innovative; it only means that outside factors control many of their products eliminating the possibility of making innovative changes in the processes. Without adequate financing and reporting, even the very best innovative idea is doomed or, at a very minimum, will not meet its full potential.

The following are some typical financial documentations:

- Accounts payable backlog
- Accounts receivable backlog
- Accounts payable cycle time distribution
- Accounts receivable cycle time distribution
- Budgets for each natural work team
- Budget compliance report for each natural work team
- Cash on hand investment return
- Financial performance projections

Production Control and Procurement

As you get closer and closer to going into production, production control and procurement greatly increase their involvement in establishing their document control and reporting system. The combination of production control and procurement are deeply involved in all of the activities related to supply chain management. This relation requires close scheduling controls from placing an order with a supplier to the delivery of the completed output. I will discuss supply chain management in greater detail in the next part of this book.

Typical documents that would be the responsibility of production control and procurement to create are:

- Approved supplier list
- Supplier rating systems
- Stocking levels
- Delivery levels by complement
- Purchase order status reports

- Output quantities per time
- Order processing reports
- Production status reports
- Supplier rating reports

You can prepare similar list of this type for each of the major functions. For example, human resources prepare job descriptions and availability reports. The call center prepares reports for duration of calls, subject matter, and calls to correct the problem. Information technology (IT) provides the hub for everything. For example, IT provides the means to operate the customer relations management (CRM) reports that the sales group uses. They prepare the Enterprise Resource Planning (ERP) reports used by production control, the customer satisfaction analysis reports used by quality assurance and product engineering, and the budget status reports used by finance to track compliance to budget. In most big organizations, these basic IT services are already part of the products that IT provides. All that is required is the input of accurate data.

You should require these documents to meet the change level and phase in level control as well as the engineering documents. Document review and sign off on these documents should at a minimum include product engineering, manufacture engineering, quality engineering, and manufacturing.

To provide guidelines to the service industry, government activities, and public sector, you should assign some functions within the organization with the responsibility for preparing the "how to" documents and the functions that are impacted by the documents should approve them. In these industries, organizations often assign IT the responsibility to bring together a total integrated documentation and reporting system. IT is a good place to put this responsibility as they are the best place to define standard software and equipment. In addition, IT generates most of the reports.

INFORMATION TECHNOLOGY DOCUMENTATION

IT is responsible for ensuring that adequate reporting systems are available to all areas within the organization. The initial focus is usually on accounts payable and receivable. One of their extremely important responsibilities is to maintain the knowledge management system. One of the fallacies is that with computerization of so many activities there will be less need for reports. The truth of what's happened is that with more information available and with very easy and quick distribution systems, the organization generates more reports. People are so dependent upon vast quantities of data that almost everyone has a cell phone and/or a wristwatch that provides the same functions. Many individuals find it much more convenient and less stressful to have conversations over the internet than in person. I have observed people sitting in the same room texting back and forth to each other rather than communicating directly. It's always easier to criticize an individual when you don't have to look them in the eye.

Simple Language

There are 12 tasks required to streamline and optimize a process and simple language is last so that you can apply it to the previous 11 tasks (see Figure 7.7). Simple language is a very important concept because it opens the door to effective communications between the engineering, management, and the production workers.

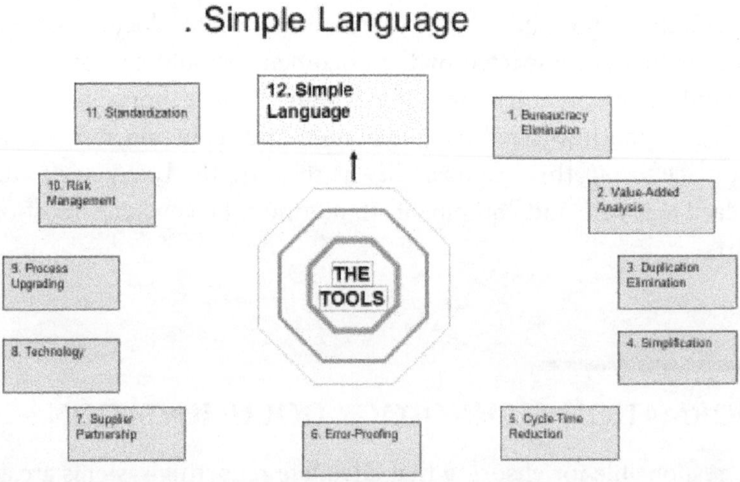

. Simple Language

FIGURE 7.7
Task 12. Simple language.

Readability Requirements

Readability requirements apply to all documentation used within the organization. This requirement includes documentation coming from functions like product engineering, industrial engineering, test engineering, quality engineering, information services, human resources, and so on. You should take great care in the preparation of these documents to ensure that they are in line with the education level of the individuals that will use them.

> Keep it simple to save time.
>
> **H. James Harrington**

Ask yourself the question: "Is all this documentation necessary? Managers spend 40–60 percent of their time reading and writing job-related materials. They never use 90 percent of the documents retained. Clerks spend 60 percent of their time on checking, filing, and retrieving information.

Reasons to Document Processes

There are at least four good reasons to document the existing process:

1. Understanding. The INT will be streamlining the current process and working with it as it fits into the organization's culture today. Without a good understanding of the current process, it is impossible for the INT to identify improvement opportunities.
2. To operate the new process. The organization needs to document the new process well so the employees who will be working in the new process will have no doubt about what they need to do.
3. Understanding customer values. It is important that the INT understand what the customer requirements are and what the major objectives are within the process. By understanding the current process, the INT can identify added value points from the customer's perspective.
4. To define current problems. The organization must understand the problems they are having with the current process to get the support to implement the new process. The organization must design the new process so that it eliminates these problems. Very often the organization does not recognize many of the problems until they put together and study the entire process.

Too many people write to impress, rather than to communicate. They write long documents that no one reads. They believe that management rates a report based upon its weight, not upon its content. They don't consider that a long report takes longer to read and costs more to communicate the information. It may take more time to consolidate what you want to communicate, but in the long run it will save the organization money. Too many people use the longest words in the dictionary rather than short, more common words that everybody understands. I have seen procedures written in English for which I had consult a dictionary to interpret them before I could understand them. Too many procedures and reports are full of acronyms and abbreviations that many of the readers do not know or understand. Studies have proven that a college graduate can read a procedure or report written at the 10th grade level in 30 percent less time with 34 percent better retention than a report written at a the college graduate level. Businesses should not write letters or procedures at a higher level than 10th grade.

The Six Writing Rules of the Road

People who don't have a high school degree often use procedures written by engineers. As a rule of thumb, you should write procedures at two grade levels lower than the education level of the least educated people reading them.

If the language you are using is not the reader's native language, you should write it at least three grade levels lower than their educational level. Some simple ground rules are:

1. Be *familiar* with your audience
2. *Understand* how familiar your audience is with the terms and abbreviation
3. *Procedures* that are more than four pages long should contain a flowchart
4. *Determine* the reading and comprehension level of your audience (write the document so that all readers can easily comprehend the message)
5. *Use* acronyms with care (don't force your reader to learn new acronyms unless they are used frequently throughout the report)
6. *Never* use an acronym or abbreviation unless you define it in the document

Good Examples

Many good documents are very short but present a very powerful message. Let me give you some examples of short and long documents:

- The Lord's Prayer: 57 words (very short)
- The Ten Commandments: 71 words (no acronyms)
- The Gettysburg Address: 266 words (easy to understand)
- The United States Declaration of Independence: 300 words (to the point)
- The U.S. Government Contractor, Management System Evaluation Program: 38,000 words (would you believe it?)
- It would take 56 years to read the General Motors Corporation repair manuals produced in 1980

Readability Index

Evaluate your writing using a readability index. You can calculate it as follows:

- A = average number of words per sentence
- B = percent of words with three or more syllables
- R = readability index = 0.4 (A + B)
- 10 or less = good
- 10.1 to 16 = caution
- 16.1 to 22 = dangerous
- Above 22 = ridiculous

Figure 7.8 provides an easy way for you to analyze your readability index. Many computers have a program built into them that will calculate your readability index. I recommend that you evaluate the readability of all the documents you prepare.

Forms are another type of document that organizations do not give the proper thought to before releasing them. Organizations allow programmers to design computer input screens and forms designed to work well with their software package. However, little thought is given to the person who inputs the data to make it easy to implement all the data.

Designing forms is an art. Organizations must direct forms at serving the person who is recording the data and at reducing input errors.

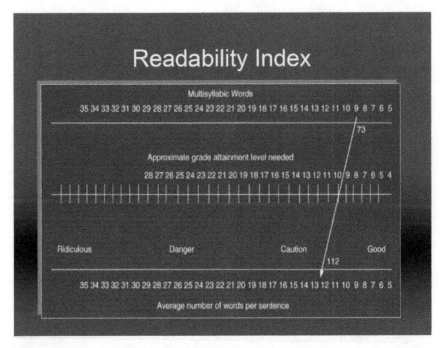

FIGURE 7.8
Readability index.

Organizations should not design forms directed at how it is best to enter the data into the computer. They should design forms for the user and then use the software to arrange the data so that the software package can use it.

Does a good form make a difference? When the British government agencies focused their attention on form design, errors plummeted and productivity soared:

- The British Department of Defense revised its travel expense form. The new forms reduced errors by 50 percent, the time required to fill it out by 10 percent, and processing time by 15 percent.
- By re-designing the application form for legal aid, the British Department of Social Services saved more than 2 million hours per year in processing time.

The National Aeronautics and Space Administration (NASA) Engineering and Safety Council developed 30 procedures that were well above average procedures from a benchmarking standpoint. The council wanted to shorten and make them more useable. As a result, they were able to cut the procedures by 60 percent without affecting technical content. Now the NASA procedures are not only short, they are also more useable.

NASA Ames Information Technology Support Center (ITSC) located in Mountain View, CA, documented their 4 key procedures in 19 pages. Similar procedures run over 100 pages.

The Eight Most Frequently Documented Complaints

The eight most frequent complaints about documentation:

1. Not enough pictures. Most people prefer pictures to words. One picture is worth a thousand words, takes less space, and is quicker to analyze.
2. Too big. Most documents are written to impress rather than to educate and train. Blaise Pascal stated, "I have made this letter longer than usual because I lack the time to make it shorter."
3. Unusable and one-size-fits-all. Too often our procedures and descriptions are not designed with the customer and user in mind, making them hard to use. Standardized forms seem more important than making them easy to read.
4. Poorly Designed Documentation. Principles such as grouping and consistency are often not followed. Good writing principles are often ignored.
5. Mixed Information Types. Policies, procedures, processes, training, and standards are often mixed together, making it difficult to understand. Each of these document types needs to be used in a different scenario.
6. Written Sequentially. Process documentation is meant to be used nonlinearly. It is not a novel and needs to be written in a manner where each piece stands alone. This allows the reader to find the information they need quickly.
7. Difficult to Find Information. Documents that are hard to read are not used and often ignored.
8. Dust catching documents. Too many documents become dust catchers rather than useful documents. Publishing online helps keep documents up-to-date.

The Six Guidelines for Good Documentation

I guess I should start this paragraph out by saying, "Don't do the eight things listed in the previous paragraph." After saying that, here are some other things that will help you in your documentation:

1. Tailor documentation and processes to the organization and each business unit.
2. Write so the new person to the process will understand it; not just so the expert will understand it.
3. Use chunking and sectionalizing to organize the document. Label the chunks so readers can quickly find what they are interested in.
4. Use information mapping to quickly find specific parts of the document that interest the individual.
5. Minimize abbreviations and acronyms.
6. Do a process map where you answer the five W's and one H.

Enough Is Too Much

Excessive handling is a worthless task. In 4 hours this morning I had six phone calls asking me to donate to a charity or trying to sell some home repair to me. Each phone call interrupted my thought pattern and made it difficult for me to get back on track. The internet has sped up the distribution of information but it has also resulted in a lot of needless information. Too often you use distribution lists rather than selecting the individuals who need to read the information. This is very costly for people who don't need or even want the information. It takes me 2 to 3 hours each day to go through my email. I estimate that 15–20 minutes of that time is worthwhile. I had my name on a do-not call list and that helped a small amount. My computer screens junk mail but this often gives me problems because sometimes it throws something I really need into the trash.

DOCUMENTATION SUMMARY

Certainly documentation is a necessary part of doing business. I thought that with the age of computers, the amount of paper used would decrease. It has not! What can you do to reduce the number of trees cut down to provide paper? Some sinful thoughts include:

1. Measure people based upon how few words they can use to communicate the needed information.
2. Document only what has to be recorded for use later.
3. Be sure that everyone on your courtesy copy list wants to get the information.
4. Measure yourself by what you are costing the organization with your documentation. Considering it takes 5–7 minutes to read every page, which means a 10-page report sent to 20 people costs the organization $500 (6 minutes × 10 pages × 20 people × $25 per hour equals $500). This calculation doesn't include the time it takes to prepare the email and send it out. Ask yourself, "What was the organization's return on investment?"

Streamlining allows you to right size, not down size.

H. James Harrington

Nothing is more dangerous than an idea when it's the only one you have.

Emile Chertier

8

Process Grouping 8: Production

OVERVIEW

You would think that production would be capable of continuously putting out excellent output. After all, they have all the procedures, documents, people, training, and equipment capable of producing good output all the time. Production has eliminated all the risks so nothing should stand in the way of smooth even flow of output from these production and service processes. However, you can be sure that the minute you look the other way, something will happen that brings that smooth flow down to a standstill. Usually first-time yields are too low. The waitress is unhappy because Johnny at table 3 creates an awful mess and she had to clean it up. On top of that they only left a 5 percent tip. The man at table 5 yells out loud enough for everyone to hear, "Where is the glass of water I ordered 5 minutes ago?" The waitress unthinkingly replies, "Why don't you order a cocktail that will put you in a better mood." The man at the window of the unemployment office sees someone trying to sneak in to the front of the line and yells, "Go to the end of the line. Can't you see other people are waiting?"

Managing the supply chain continues to be a major problem as long as organizations are delivering the output. No matter what happens at a supplier or in the process or in the process production control, the organization is responsible for seeing that customer orders are still on schedule. If your organization does not have a production control department, someone has to perform the production control activities. If Tom is out with the flu, how do you fulfill the customer needs if you only have two waiters instead of three? If your computer isn't working, how do you make flight reservations? If the final tester is down, what do you ship to the customers this week? If you start enough parts to the process but the scrap rate is so high you can't meet production schedules, who's going to do something about it?

These are all good questions and interesting problems to solve. These are the type of reasons that a very effective corrective action program needs to be extremely active during the production activities. Programs like Six Sigma, TQM, and Process Redesign are key ongoing initiatives that are required to support the production process. The innovative process is different from the initiatives like Six Sigma in that it accepts errors as part of the learning process.

Engineering change control of product benefits delivered to customers turns out to be a challenging problem. In many products you must know the exact engineering change levels at which the product is to add features such as personnel replacement parts. Just think about the complexity of this problem in airplanes with literally hundreds of thousands of parts involved.

Problems like stocking are critical in the production environment. If you have too much materials in stock, you're wasting money and if there is the change in one, it could mean scrapping out all the items in stock. If you have too little stock, you miss ship dates. Where should you maintain stock in the field? What should you stock in countries like Japan, China, Russia, and Germany and how much of it?

Customers are interested in when you will deliver the item to them, not when your organization will start to transport activities. I'm not happy if I want my steak because I'm hungry and the waiter tells me it's been ready for pickup for about 5 minutes and he or she will get it to me in 10 minutes. The customer's primary concern is not when you are going to ship something, but when you're going to deliver it to them. This concern means that you need to put a very reliable shipping system in place even though you're using a contractor for the supplier to transport the item. I had a Toyota and when the thermostat broke down, it took days before they could get a replacement item. I just bought a KIA with the hopes that the parts situation would be much better than Toyota's. I might be sorry that I made this change if the reliability of the KIA is much worse than the Toyota.

As you go into production, additional support is required. You must calibrate and maintain equipment. Governmental and international standards like ISO 9000 (quality management systems), ISO 14000 (environmental standards), and safety requirements results in several internal and external audits conducted on a regular basis.

All the responsibilities of product engineering, manufacturing engineering, manufacturing, quality assurance, industrial engineering and production control that I discussed in the previous chapter also apply to the production phase.

Overview Summary

It is too bad that most corrective action and continuous improvement take place during the production cycle. From a financial standpoint and a business reputation standpoint, the continuous improvement and error elimination activity should take place during the concept validation, business case analysis, and documentation process groupings. By the time you go into production, you should have a product design that will require no future modification in a process design that you have error proofed. You should relate a very small percentage of the product costs to the corrective action taken.

The preparation phase is less challenging and rewarding. An established organization involves many different disciplines. In many cases, it is just one more thing for which they are responsible. Usually activities related to today's customers take precedence over the Innovation System Cycle (ISC). All too often you consider these activities as boring paperwork problems on process and that will be good enough. It is true that may be good enough but good enough will not keep customers in today's competitive environment.

It's important to remember that this effort is an investment in the future and as a result, there often is less return on investment during a production cycle. It is the activities directed at helping to ensure that there are jobs in the future within the organization. For this reason, it's extremely important that you focus on the more innovative, creative, inventive activities during Phase II so that fewer errors will occur during the production cycle. It is mandatory that you are better today than you were yesterday and better tomorrow than you are today.

The big question is, "Is it innovation or continuous improvement?" Usually it doesn't make a difference; it's just something that you need to improve if you want to stay in business.

No person or company should be content to stay where they are, no matter how successful they now seem to be.

Stephen R. Covey
The Seven Habits of Highly Effective People

INTRODUCTION TO PRODUCTION

> Every assignment I have ever had had its good and bad points. All you can do is pick one that has more good than bad.

> **H. James Harrington**

Production is the life blood to the innovative cycle. Without an effective means of producing the desired service or product, you have wasted all the effort and money already invested in the project. Organization after organization has found out that the difference between success and failure is the innovative level of their production process. Not only does the production process have to be rapid, and efficient, but the output must look better, do more, work better, and last longer than the competition's output. Development engineering may be the heart of the innovative organization, but it is production that is the blood of the organization, taking life-giving nourishment to every part of the body.

Organizations seldom note the large amount of errors that occur during the first seven Process Groupings and these errors remain hidden from everyone's eyes. Organizations have no reporting system to keep track of errors, do not measure and report errors, or have no set standards for errors. If the production process has many errors as product engineering, or manufacturing engineering, or research and development, the organization can never deliver product to customers.

PIXIE DUST

Today is March 17 and as you all know, this is the day set aside every year to honor the man who drove the snakes out of Ireland—the wonderful old St. Patrick. Those of you who came from Ireland (and I feel sorry for those who didn't) know that on St. Patrick's Day the standard meal is corned beef and cabbage. To live up to this tradition, I went and bought a large corned beef, a head of cabbage, a bag full of small red potatoes, and enough carrots to make a family of rabbits happy for a week. I carefully boiled the corn beef until it was tender ending up with a large pot full of the nectar of the gods. After carefully removing the corned beef from the boiling broth, I wrapped it in aluminium foil and tucked it into my oven to give it a crispy outside covering. I then scrubbed and rubbed and scrubbed the potatoes and carrots until they were cleaner than a baby's cheek. I carefully dropped the carrots, onions, and potatoes into the boiling pot of broth. About 30 minutes later after the head of cabbage had been washed thoroughly, I added the individual leaves of cabbage to the mixture. About 15 minutes later I was ready to sit down for my delicious meal of corned beef and cabbage.

Ho!! It was all right, but it was nowhere as good as the corned beef and cabbage that my wife used to make when she was alive. Somehow, she had the pixie dust that transformed the ordinary into the extraordinary. That's exactly what an innovative production system does to a creative design destined for delivery to an external customer. Somehow, an effective and efficient production operation has the pixie dust required to make outstanding products and/or service. [**Note:** Next year I'm going to a restaurant for my corned beef and cabbage.]

> When you start the production activities, it's a lot like getting married. You have sworn on the output specification that the organization can perform as documented.
>
> **H. James Harrington**

At the "Process Grouping 8: Production" point, you have completed the proof of concept successfully and laid out the production area and the equipment has met the process capability requirements. The facilities are ready for pilot-type short runs and you have delivered beta-type product to selected customer partners. Up to this point, highly trained specialists have performed the actual production activities to identify strengths and weaknesses in the documentation. You are now ready to turn a pilot facility into a functioning continuous process.

STARTING THE PRODUCTION SYSTEM

Facilities Analysis

You cannot just throw a switch and turn the pilot line over to a production facility without jeopardizing the organization's reputation and the products' profitability. The transformation from pilot to production should be a gradual transformation. But in today's rapidly changing environment there is a great deal of pressure to bring up the production facilities as rapidly as possible. To expedite the transformation without adding excessive risk, pilot line operators should work with the production operators and basically certify them for the individual activity. Adequate training of the production employees related to the activity and the final desired outcome should always precede this process. Based upon the complexity of the production activities, you can define the transformation time statistically.

At the beginning of the facility transformation, it is desirable to have all the production equipment available and in use during the transformation. Very often this is not possible due to hard tooling delays. You should make maximum effort to at least have all the parts in storage, parts transferred, and unit assembly packaging used. In addition, it is very desirable to have all the conveyor systems operating. As you start the transformation, you should set the conveyor belt at a minimum acceptable speed and increase the speed as the assembly operator gains experience.

The production system sometimes starts by preparing the engineering and process outputs used to perform the proof of concept analysis to the production product. More often the organization starts the pilot facility after the project has successfully completed the Business Case Analysis activity. Often at first it looks more like an engineering experiment than a production facility. The organization slowly transforms these facilities into the production facility as they add equipment and release procedures. The organization uses the initial outputs internally within the organization or delivers them to selected customers as beta-production units for which the customer provides feedback on the output's performance and suggestions on ways to improve it.

Highly skilled laboratory technicians who have a tendency for creativity about the way they do things and less willing to follow specific documentation often produce the initial production. As a result, it is important to choose experienced, disciplined, and skilled employees. These are the employees who have the pixie dust to bring things together clearly defining opportunities for continuous improvement. It is important that you assign early in the process the initial cadre of experienced production employees to work with the engineering laboratory technicians. These production employees will provide the basic knowledge and technical understanding required for the demands of mass production. Initially they will serve as observers and helpers, but you will phase that rule out soon as the laboratory technicians turn the complete operations over to the production environment. Although you invested some costs in training production workers, these costs are most always offset by the initial knowledge and experience they gain.

You should design the project plan to have the complete mass production facilities up and functioning in time to evaluate the performance level of output produced in the production facilities. You are selling the pilot facilities are not highly automated for many activities within the production process will be performed by programmable devices and will depend upon the accuracy in the hard tooling customized to the individual product.

The S-curve

The S-curve is a mathematical model also known as the logistic curve. It describes the growth of one variable in terms of another variable over time. In business, the S-curve is used to describe, and sometimes predict, the performance of a company or a product over a period of time.

Figure 8.1 is the projected output status versus time. It is very important that the production line is operating before the take-off point on the S-curve.

Figure 8.2 is the predicted adoption rate versus time. This also can be used to show what percentage of the total facility capabilities are projected

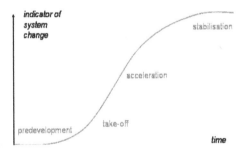

FIGURE 8.1
The projected output status versus time.

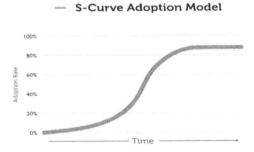

FIGURE 8.2
The predicted adoption rate versus time.

compared to operating if 100 percent equals the maximum output of the facility's delivery. I believe that the transfer from engineering to manufacturing should occur before requirements reach 5 percent of the production capability because the pilot facilities output is usually much less than the production requirements.

Production Key Activities

The critical part of the production activity occurs during the steep growth part of the S-curve. By the time the S-curve flattens off, you should resolve all the major problems and most of the minor problems. By the time the output reaches the flat part at the top of the curve, you need to redirect emphasis to new or improved outputs that can make use of the present facility. This is necessary because in today's environment the stable part of the S-curve lasts for a very short time and then starts decaying extremely rapidly. Failure to act quickly to design on demand can result in a major loss of already established customers and the very low acquisition of new customers.

Although many more functions are involved in production activities, I'm going to limit our discussion to the following:

1. Supply chain management. This is a plan of having the right things at the right place at the right time without too many that they get in your way.
2. Production support engineering (manufacturing engineering/test engineering/industrial engineering). These are the groups that provide direction and training to the people who produce the output.
3. Human Resources. If there is a good problem correction and problem preventive system, the organization can basically eliminate most problems, but the problems related to the human factors stay with us throughout the project lifecycle.

Supply Change Management Systems

The critical part of setting up an operation is the scheduling of supplies. An approach called "supply chain management" is an effective way of addressing the tools' supply chain management system.

Although there are many data systems that must be up and operating in support of the production facilities, probably the most important one is the supply chain management program.

You're only as good as your worst supplier.

H. James Harrington

Here is one organization's story. I had a perfect product with all the equipment needed. The organization had just completed a stringent capability test and also performed the stress testing so I knew the product would stand up under almost any condition. I trained the operators so thoroughly that they were overqualified; I swear they could do the jobs with their eyes closed. Suddenly everything fell apart. Immediately customers began to complain and the organization could not fix their equipment. Fixtures broke and shut the line down for days. And the paint clogged our spray guns resulting in an uneven coat of paint. Customers were complaining because they got cut when they were using the product. I was working 20 hours a day and falling behind.

The question was, "What did I do wrong?" The answer is, "I put so much effort and attention into the production facilities that I ignored the organization that provided the inputs to the process. I forgot the golden rule, 'The suppliers provide the base that the organization's function and reputation is based upon.'"

Love the supplier like you love yourself; treat the supplier better than you treat yourself.

H. James Harrington

The incredible complexity of today's products, the drive to be first in the market, just-in-time manufacturing, an increasingly quality-conscious, and the global market-place are causing all manufacturers to re-evaluate the way they do business. Supplier management now applies to many more areas other than components and materials. Organizations are out-sourcing much of the administrative and support activities like human resources, finance, quality assurance, and information technology (IT). This approach has made most organizations even more dependent upon their suppliers than ever before. Excellent suppliers are no longer a nicety; they are a necessity.

One clear trend has emerged: the top management of the leading-edge manufacturers have added supply management to their strategic initiatives. They have channeled major resources into their procurement organization with the mission to manage and develop a supply base which delivers a competitive advantage in availability, quality, delivery, and total cost improvements.

These leading-edge organizations' strategy is to get the materials and information moving faster, better, and cheaper. These top managers are truly committed to achieving excellence. They realize that they cannot achieve it overnight, nor can they buy it. They must develop excellence from *within*.

At the heart of the supply management process (SMP) is an attitude of teamwork and proactive prevention by an experienced cross-functional commodity team. The major areas of responsibilities, qualifications, and activities required have been clearly defined. The team performs their responsibilities by linking the organizations' business objectives of quality, cycle-time, and total cost initiatives within the supply base daily activities. The linking mechanism is a partnering relationship attitude and a "creative purchase agreement" which defines the targets for improvement, the plan to achieve the targets, the supply and customer team, and the performance measure and review process.

CURRENT STATE ASSESSMENT

The organization needs to do an unbiased review of the present SMP. This assessment will provide a picture of the way the SMP is working today. It is usually better if people who are not part of the present process perform the assessment, so that the assessment provides an objective picture. It should assess all sources that supply the organization with any item. To accomplish this task, the organization's budget is a good point for identifying all functions that purchase any item. You should prepare a list of the functions that pay for services, materials, taxes, parts, assemblies, and so on. Then prepare a list of the items that will become part of the SMP. You should exclude very few purchased items. Typical examples that you may not include are taxes, electric bills, national gas bills, and so on. After you define the items and the functions that you will include in the SMP, the assessment team needs to understand how the organization performs the different supply processes. For example, do the development lab, the product engineering function, and production control use the same process for procuring parts? If not, how and why do they differ?

The Sixteen Questions to Evaluate Supplier Processes

You should evaluate the different processes for items like:

1. How are suppliers selected?
2. How are suppliers measured?
3. Are good suppliers rewarded?
4. How are suppliers involved in the design process?
5. How much of the purchase budget goes to each major supplier?
6. How well is the system documented?
7. Is the SMP in keeping with ISO 9000?
8. How good is the performance feedback process to the supplier?
9. How good is the supplier history file?
10. Are poor performing suppliers dropped?
11. Who gets supplier interface training?
12. What percentage of the items goes through receiving inspection?
13. How good is supplied equipment maintained?
14. When and how were the suppliers certified, and how often are they recertified?
15. Does the organization report cost to stock?
16. How many suppliers are there per item?

This assessment should provide the management team with a view of today's process, its problems, and recommendations on how they should improve it.

SUPPLY MANAGEMENT MODEL

The Ten Steps of the Generic Supply Management Model

An SMP can be developed using the following 10 steps.

Step 1: *Establish a supplier management team.*
Step 2: *Develop an action plan.* A team should start with one supplier or a selected group of suppliers in a pilot effort.
Step 3: *Develop specifications and standards.* Organizations can achieve continuous improvement only if the customer sets and communicates explicit standards and measures for quality delivery, service, and cost.

Step 4: *Prioritize product attributes.* A product can have many quality attributes. Organizations should identify important product quality characteristics on the engineering print. Non-conforming critical characteristics can jeopardize health, safety, or welfare. Non-conforming major characteristics affect product function. A minor product non-conformance, a blemish, deals with product appearance.

Step 5: *Determine process control and capability.* After the organization devises a commonly understood measurement system and prioritizes product service characteristics, the organization asks the supplier to submit a process flow diagram and specify the most suitable locations for tracking quality and testing products. The supplier establishes effective statistical process controls to the designated product quality characteristics.

Step 6: *Measuring performance.* The measurement system indicates how quickly the organization pursues improvements. It is a key measure of the commodity team's effectiveness.

Step 7: *Improve continuously.* Continuous improvement means that the organization has set performance or specification targets and, over time, reduced gradually the variation around these targets.

Step 8: *Take ownership.* After the customer has initiated the improvement effort, the organization encourages the supplier to take ownership of the improvement effort and be responsible for it. Only a few suppliers will have the commitment and stamina for the long haul.

Step 9: *Audit performance.*

Step 10: *Continuous improvement.* Start at Step 1 and enhance the SMP by using more sophisticated tools in each step.

Develop personal relationships—just because the supplier is ISO 9000 certified does not mean he or she will provide you with acceptable outputs.

H. James Harrington

SUPPLIER MANAGEMENT

It just came to me that our extremely large federal debt is the result of buying from the lowest bidder.

H. James Harrington

If your management is your most valuable asset and your employees are second, then truly your suppliers run a very close third. One clear trend that has emerged in today's environment is increased focus on supply chain management, in which the supplier plays a central role. Top management of the leading edge organizations has added supplier management to their strategic initiatives. They have channeled into their procurement organization a mission to develop and manage a supplier base, so that it provides a competitive advantage in availability, quality, delivery, and cost. Since the 1980s, organizations have enhanced greatly the interface with the supplier and labeled it as "supply management." Companies that have organized for supply management include Motorola, Hewlett-Packard, Xerox, IBM, Selection, General Motors, Ford, Raytheon, and Rockwell. Most of these companies have developed an SMP and an integrated procurement system that uniquely fits their culture and business needs. Most of these companies with advanced SMPs consider them a strategic advantage and will only disclose the basic details. They closely guard their advanced tools and systems.

The Eighteen Building Blocks in Supplier Management

Some of the common building blocks found in the excellent organization's supply management programs are:

1. A totally new concept in management that involves purchasing, engineering, supplier quality assurance, and the supplier working together as one team early on, co-located to foster mutually set goals.
2. A long-term, win-win partnering for mutual growth and profits.
3. A process of concrete, on-site, and frequent help to each other focused on new product introductions, quality, cycle-time, cost reductions, and co-training and learning sessions.
4. The supplier is an internal partner including their chain of suppliers (i.e., early supplier involvement).
5. All benchmarked companies state that supply management is a strategic business decision.
6. Trends are to centralized price negotiations and decentralized buying.
7. Some manage production items and other commodities, while others also manage transportation.
8. Single sourcing is acceptable, but most have two suppliers for capacity and risk reasons.
9. Early supplier involvement is practiced carefully.
10. Many invest capital into their supplier base.

11. Suppliers are given firm, fixed orders covering a month's requirements: never canceled; with a 12-month rolling forecast.
12. All have a credible supplier measurement system.
13. All have "stretched" goals for improving quality, reducing cycle time, and an annual cost reduction target.
14. Most have an advanced integrated procurement system.
15. All have raised the profession levels of their purchasing staff-engineers, many with advanced business degrees.
16. Most were strongly encouraged by their key customers or competitors. Few started supply management because it was "the thing to do."
17. Most are developing partnership relationships.
18. Both parties go 60 percent of the way.

ISO 9000 AND ISO 14000

Most supply relationships start with a requirement for the supply to be certified to ISO 9000 equivalent, but this is only a beginning point. ISO 9000: 2018 is good enough for suppliers that produce commercial commodities like nuts and bolts, but not good enough if you are going to form a true partnership with the supplier. This relationship requires that the individuals in both organizations get to know each other and establish common objectives. It also requires that the customer gets to know the supplier's process well enough to understand their limitations.

A good supplier should commit to having a continuous improvement process that will more than offset inflation, rising material costs, and rising labor costs. I have negotiated contracts with many suppliers that included a committed cost reduction of 10 percent to 15 percent per year.

Supplier measurements and rating systems have also changed drastically. In the 1970s, I measured and reported back to our suppliers the percentage of lots that the organization rejected. In the 1990s, quality is only one of three supplier performance criteria. The other two are delivery and costs. A truly comprehensive rating system must include all three.

Many methods exist for calculating an overall supplier performance index, which assigns different weights to each of the three performance elements through algorithms of various complexities.

As the customer-supplier relationship becomes increasingly more important, the communication systems are continuously evolving to include much more than just these three basic elements. Organizations are preparing narrative and graphic reports regularly that include things like responsiveness, in-line fall out, and field performance. They also include comments from all the departments that have anything to do with the supplier. Departments like quality assurance, product engineering, accounting, purchasing, shipping, manufacturing, accounts payable, and so on provide monthly input that goes directly to the supplier. Today software products, like "Performance 360" sold by Market Answers, sets up an Internet superscript automatic systems that acquires data from enterprise resource planning (ERP) or workflow where each month the key stakeholders for each supplier answers a predetermined set of questions related to the product. The software then prepares a comprehensive report that is transmitted directly to the supplier. The supplier uses the same system to respond to the problem and to define their corrective action. A summary of all the supplier activities is then presented to all the relevant management within the organization in a form designed for their specific need.

> Today acceptable supplier management systems are measured in percentage of suppliers that have provided perfect compliance for the last twelve months.
>
> **H. James Harrington**

Production support engineering (manufacturing engineering/test engineering/industrial engineering)–manufacturing engineering is one of the most active engineering groups that directly support the production process. The home-away-from-home is in the manufacturing area.

The manufacturing engineer is a key player in Phase II as he or she converts the many product engineering documents into routings, training programs, workmanship standards, and determines if the organization will not produce it in-house. The manufacturing engineer breaks down complex assemblies and equipment into small building blocks that assembly operators can produce.

The manufacturing engineering group in conjunction with the industrial engineering group define workflow throughout the organization and the equipment that the organization will use to produce a specific device. Documentation related to a process includes routings, procedures, operating instructions, training materials and the flow diagram of the process. Designing tools and fixtures that are unique to an individual product is also one of the primary responsibilities of the manufacturing engineer. In many organizations, the manufacturing engineer will also define the work standards for the areas. Another major responsibility is identifying problems that occur in the manufacturing process and correcting them. They develop repair procedures for products that otherwise the organization would scrap. Automation mechanization and robotics are becoming the tools of the trade for manufacturing engineers.

Quality Assurance Responsibilities

The quality assurance documentation responsibilities include:

- Help to select suppliers
- Review and approve process control documents
- Certify the line
- The collective action cycle
- Establish a quality reporting system
- Obtain performance information for products after delivery to the customer
- Establish a quality management system in keeping with or better than ISO 9000

For those of you who believe continuous improvement should be part of innovation than the production activity is the most innovative time in the product life cycle.

H. James Harrington

The prediction activity is always a very risky one. Anything that can happen will happen. Holes drilled too big, the print used is out of date, the operator not trained to do it right, the fixture won't keep the part from vibrating during machining operation, the print and the parts don't agree, it's assembled correctly but won't work, and so on. The list of problems goes on and on. With a great deal luck, you will find most of the problems during the process, but always a few bad parts make it through. When hard tooling replaces soft tooling, nothing seems to work. Eventually through the miracle of hard work and conscientious individuals' good output, goods are ready to be shipped but the organization has no orders.

Human Resources

Throughout the project, people are a continuing problem and a continuing asset. They are both a blessing and an irritation. They are a lot like water.

When you don't need it, you don't miss it, but if you don't have it, you will die. Human resources is not something you bring in, sit at a desk, give them their job description, and forget about them. When treated right, they are truly the most valuable asset in most organizations. You need to treat them like a very expensive Mercedes-Benz, keeping it greased, changing its oil, washing the dirt off it, and reacting quickly to repair it when you hear a strange knock in the motor. Sure, you feed the Mercedes' gas tanks to keep it running just as you provide a salary to keep your employees performing but like the Mercedes, that's not enough. Your employees need a lot more than a salary to build loyalty and trust into the organization. Continuous care and maintenance is absolutely essential. I consider showing concern related to the employee and his or her family as a good starting point. Make it a point to know the names of the individual's spouse and children. Make it your job to help them grow in mind and spirit. Provide adequate training so that they feel you are concerned about their future. Keep them from getting bored by providing cross training in different areas. Remember their hire date anniversary and their birthday. I give employees a day off on their birthday. Treat the person who reports to you with the same or better respect than you have for the person who you work for. At least once a week spend a little time talking with each person who works for you. Make it a point to talk to them in their work environment, not in your office.

Develop a documented set of values related to work in your interface with people and put it up in your work area. The following is a set of values I tried to live up to over the past 50 years. I will admit that at times I strayed away from them without meaning to. When I stray, I try very hard to get back in line.

The Man I (HJH) Want To Be
  My Values and Beliefs

A man who would be concerned with how he could help others instead of himself, who would give others loyalty instead of demanding it of them, who would think of himself as the assistant instead of the boss, who would think it was his job to help others do their job better.

A man whose pride was peculiar because his pride was in his people. A man who could walk around the organization and say, "Yes, it was well done but not by me. I just happen to be lucky enough

(Continued)

to have the best team in the whole organization." That is where his pride lies. Anything worthwhile that comes out of the department, his team did. If something goes wrong, he feels that maybe he was not on the ball. Maybe he had not directed or guided or taught or led his team properly. He will take the blame for anything that goes wrong.

A man who never made a promise he didn't intend to keep, merely to slough others off. I would pick a man who might say, "Gee, I'm so busy, Jim, I just don't know if I'll ever get done. But let's not wait until tomorrow when it is more convenient for me. Let's sit down right now and go at it. Now is the time."

A man who knew that I was not a genius. If I come to him with an idea, I don't want him to give me that objective stuff. I don't want him to say, "You have a suggestion. Here is the form. Fill it out. Stick it in the box and 3 months later if it is any good we will give you an award for it."

> I want him to get excited about my brain child. I want him to treat my brain child carefully, because it is the most wonderful idea in the world at the moment. I gave birth to this child of mine. I want him to treat it tenderly, especially tenderly if it is a feeble-minded brain child. The man who is going to get an award doesn't have to worry. It is I. If I don't get one, I will feel low. I want my boss to pick me up and encourage me.

A man who would handle every grievance right now, not like the fellow who has a 40-room mansion, but no garbage pails, and who says, "We just kick it around until it gets lost."

> A man who in many ways reminded me of my father whom I loved dearly. But who had the knack if I stepped out of line, of lowering the boom so fast I didn't know what struck me until too late. But who, if he thought I had been pushed around, would fight for me every step of the way up the line even to the president of the company and the chairman of the board if necessary to see that I got a fair shake and a square break.
>
> I did not originate these values and I may never be this man but I am trying to live up to these values every day of my life.

H. James Harrington

Note: This content was originated by Dr. J. L. Rosenstein and modified by H. James Harrington.

Information Technology Support

You cannot overemphasize the importance of up-to-date functioning information systems with people trained to use them. More and more the competitive advantage goes to the organization that uses the latest technology the best to collect relevant data and provide it to the people who can act on it. Certainly, one of the primary responsibilities for the IT group is to develop a continuous flow of up-to-date information into the knowledge base and a rearrangement of it into the most practical usable form. Making effective use of today's computer explosion is a three-part program:

1. Collecting the data
2. Reducing the data down to an easy to use format
3. Making use of the analyze data to make business decisions

IT should be responsible for the first two parts of the project and have a major responsibility in providing customized training on how to use the outputs. All too often IT turns out to be a department of programmers and system operators who never really understand how the organization uses the output from the computer processes. IT should be responsible for:

1. Training the people
2. Training the field support staff
3. Standard equipment and software throughout the organization
4. Developing systems that will screen the input discarding data that is not relevant to the organization
5. Working with suppliers to receive customized software packages
6. Helping to identify new applications for automation and robotics
7. Incorporating software packages that recognize positive and negative trends
8. Reducing the cost of processing data which includes reading the output of the system
9. Putting systems in place that report items that require action based upon present information and future trend analysis
10. And, of course, getting the reports out on time

Is this a complete list of the IT responsibility? Of course not! It is just some of those that are on my hot list. There needs to be more emphasis placed on what the IT group at your organization can do to make the organization more competitive with less of a focus on buying someone else's creativity. Organizations need a great deal of the innovation that IT because IT should be a primary driver of an organization's future. When you buy a software package that is on sale to anyone, you don't get a competitive advantage, you just get a chance to spend a lot of money.

Daily Work Management Meetings

The daily work management is made up of four levels of meetings designed to follow up on all standard work and discuss problems:

- Level I meetings take place every shift, in which a team leader discusses the last shift's performance with his or her group. The group also discusses work that they need to accomplish during the up-and-coming shift as well as any problems that they are facing. These meetings should be stand-up meetings and the tools to facilitate these meetings should be part of the performance improvement plan.
- Level II meetings are the daily meeting between the INT manager and the manager of the groups that are affected by the change. At these meetings the participants discuss the top three problems of different departments. The participants define improvement activities to prevent these problems from occurring in other areas and to correct the problem where it is occurring.
- Level III meetings are a daily meeting between the innovation team (INT) manager, project manager, and the managers of the groups affected by the change. These meetings do not have an agreed-to correction strategy. Participants discuss major problems and make decisions if the problem is of significant magnitude to affect the end project performance and if they should escalate it to the project executive sponsor.
- Level IV meetings are held at key milestones throughout the innovative cycle to conduct a complete project status review with a primary focus on anything that would prevent the project from being successful. They also record any exposure to cost or schedule overruns based upon the estimates of the individuals working on the project. These are executive level meetings and at a minimum the executive sponsor should attend.

For most projects a project database is set up to track the project status and to define interrelationships dependencies. The organization updates these databases at least once a week to reflect the progress made during the week.

ACTIVITIES IN "PROCESS GROUPING 8. PRODUCTION"

The production activity is always a very risky one. Anything that can happen will happen. Holes drilled too big, the paint used is out of date, the operator not trained to do it right, Mary was filling in for Jane who is out ill and as a result did the job wrong, the fixture doesn't hold the part from vibrating during machining operation, the print did not adhere to the parts because they were dirty, it's assembled correctly but won't work. The list of problems can go on and on. With a great deal of luck, you will discover most of these issues during the start-up process, but there are always a few bad ones that go through. When hard tooling replaces soft tooling, nothing seems to work. Eventually through the miracle of hard work and the work of conscientious individuals, good output is ready to be shipped to sales but alas you have no orders.

PROCESS MANAGEMENT

> Your processes manage the organization, not your managers.
>
> **H. James Harrington**

The process management concept certainly isn't new to management professionals; it's the basis of most improvement methodologies.

Definition: A process is a series of interconnected activities that takes input, adds value to it, and produces output. It's how the organizations do their day-to-day routines. Your organization's processes define how it operates.

The Two Approaches to Process Management

There are two basic approaches to managing processes:

- The Micro-Level Approach directed at managing processes within a natural work team (NWT) or an individual department
- The Macro-Level Approach directed at managing processes that flow across departments and/or functions within the organization

Most of the work that quality professionals do is related to continuously improving our processes. Some of the tools they use include design of experiments, process capability studies, root cause analysis, document control, quality circles, suggestions, Six Sigma, Shewhart's cycles, ISO 9000, just-in-time manufacturing, and supplier qualification, among many others.

Management in excellent organizations requires each NWT (department) to continuously improve (refine) the processes they use.

The Six Factors to Manage Processes

To manage a process, you must define and agree upon the following:

- An output requirement statement between process owners and customers
- An input requirement statement between process owners and suppliers
- A process capable of transforming the suppliers' input into output that meets the customers' performance and quality requirements
- Feedback measurement systems between process and customers, and between process and suppliers
- The process must be understood
- A measurement system must be put in place for the process

You should address these six key factors when designing a process. However, the problem facing most organizations is that they never designed many of their support processes in the first place. They were created in response to a need without really understanding what a process is.

> Most individuals, teams, and groups within an organization will take the path of least resistance. Inevitably, over time, they will function at the lowest level of acceptability.
>
> **William J. Schwarz**
> *CEO Alliance and the Center for Inspired Performance*

> If you (management) create an expectation of continuous product or service improvement, but fail to deliver on that expectation, you will see a build-up of fear and negative forecasting.
>
> **Stephen R. Covey**
> *The Seven Habits of Highly Effective People*

Refining the Process

Refining the process is an ongoing activity. If the refinement process is working as it should, the efficiency and effectiveness of the total process should be improving at a rate of 10–15 percent a year. In most cases the project team focuses on the broad major problems that reflect across departments and reap this harvest within 3–4 months. At that time, the organization can disband the project team and turn over the process refinement activities to the NWT involved in the process. Area activity analysis (AAA) methodology is the most effective approach to process refinement.

PROCESS OWNER

Executives still manage most organizations using a smokestack type organizational structure. This structure means that the organization's processes flow across many different boundaries from one department to another. overall, a great deal of effort goes into managing the work efforts that goes on within a department because the measurement system emphasizes individual department performance. Unfortunately, this approach lends itself to developing a number of roadblocks, obstacles, duplications, and sub-optimization. To offset this, you should assign a process owner who is responsible for optimizing the total process performance. This approach is a very effective way to break down the walls that build-up between individual organizations and focuses the total team on what needs to be done rather than only what they are doing.

There are many other organizations without whose activities an innovative organization would not be possible. I chose not to include them not because they were not important, but because I could not do justice to their contribution in the few pages that I could devote to this chapter. I felt it was better to just recognize them for their contributions. Some of the other organizations are:

- Safety
- Security

- Maintenance
- Personnel
- Finance
- Legal
- Sales
- Call center
- Facility maintenance

SUMMARY

The preparation and production phase is less challenging and rewarding. An established organization involves many different disciplines. In many cases, it is just one more thing for which they are responsible. Usually activities related to today's customers takes precedence over the ISC. All too often organizations consider these activities as boring paperwork problems, so they just define process and think that will be good enough. It is true that this may be good enough, but good enough will not keep customers in today's competitive environment.

It's important to remember that this effort is an investment in the future and as a result, there is no return on investment during the activities. It's an activity to help ensure jobs in the future within the organization. For this reason, it's extremely important that you focus on the more innovative, creative, inventive activities during Phase II and make fewer errors. It is mandatory that you are better today than you were yesterday and better tomorrow than you are today. Is that innovation or continuous improvement? Really, it doesn't make a difference; it's just something that you need to improve if you want to stay in business.

Here is a personal example. I spent 2 years building five buildings that housed an organization that made thread from raw cotton. The organization dyed the thread to the desirable colors and then made cloth out of it. Some of the threads were used to weave sweaters. The cloth was then cut and sewed together making bluejeans, shirts, underwear, and dress pants. After installing working team equipment and training 5000 workers, I suddenly realized the organization did not have a design organization. To make up for this error, the organization went out and bought design companies. This proved to me that when you're talking innovation, you need to look at the total cycle as you will fail if any part of the cycle conforms poorly. The old saying holds true, "A chain is as weak as it weakest link." This in the first law in innovation.

> No person or company should be content to stay where they are, no matter how successful they now seem to be.

> **Stephen R. Covey**

> Every time you say something nice about a person an Angel lights another candle along the path to heaven. Every time you say something bad about a person, three candles are blown out.

> **H. James Harrington**

9

Phase III. Delivery. Process Grouping 9:
Marketing, Sales, and Delivery

OVERVIEW OF "PHASE III. DELIVERY"

You don't have an innovative product until the point that the value-added exceeds the cost of the project. The biggest gamble we take is all the money that was spent prior to an equivalent amount received in accounts receivable.

H.J. Harrington

Everything you have done so far has been in preparation to deliver products and/or services to customers that meet or exceed their expectations. To date, all your effort has been invested in the future. Now suddenly the future is here and you need to see the profits roll in. All too often people think of profit as the dirty six-letter word, but without it you couldn't have this wonderful country you live in. If developed organizations did not make a profit, our salaries would be lowered significantly and probably eventually eliminated. Soup kitchens would open until the government ran out of money. You soon would find that you didn't have a warm place to sleep at night. To make a profit is the primary reason a for-profit making organization functions. The profit-making organizations are the heartbeat of America. If you didn't have the faster-than-a-speeding-train profit-making organizations, then you would have the not-for-profit making organization that depends upon taxes, and then there would be no one to pay the taxes. The result would be the not-for-profit making organizations like our government would not exist.

Organizations that generate a profit make the world go around. It's hard for me to call a change innovative that does not result in value-added (profit) to the organization. Even the not-for-profit organizations need to make a profit, but they call it "net favorable balance" instead of profit. They use their net favorable balance to pay outrageous salaries to their management team and pay off their debts. Without profit-making organizations providing the funds to support them, they too would be out of business.

I divided "Phase III. Delivery" into four process groupings:

- Process Groupings 9. Marketing, Sales, and Delivery
  These three functions should be and must be the closest to the customer or consumer. They are the most familiar with the customer's and potential customer's short and long-term needs. They are highly motivated by money as it relates directly to their commission which often is a major part of their income.
- Process Groupings 10. After-Sales Service
  This is the group you call in to help you when you have a problem and to entertain you with music while you stay in line waiting to be served. Often the phone lines are busy, and you are put on hold for an estimated 15 minutes with a message saying that the lines are busy and there will be a 15-minute wait. Sarcastic, yes!! But that is more and more the common response. It's almost impossible to talk to a live person. I was taken back recently when I called in a complaint and the phone was answered by a real person whose first comment was "Do you want to talk to a live person or to the computer?" On another occasion, I was taken back when the call center specialist told me that she had listened to nothing but complementary comments related to a new product they were shipping. When I pointed out that I was surprised that she was not getting any complaints, she responded by saying, "If a person sounds negative, I just erase it without bothering to listen to it. Who wants to get yelled at?"

  When I refer to after-sales service, it includes the repair centers and call centers. Often it includes the salesperson who interfaces with the customer that he or she just made a sale to. I have had salesman make comments like, "Fill out a complaint form. I just sell the product. Handling complaints is not part of my job description." I was staying at a very expensive and swanky Ritz Carlton hotel and I noted that there were electrical sparks coming out of the light in the shower. It was bad enough that I decided it was unsafe to take a shower. When I informed the front desk about the problem they gave me a complaint form to fill out. If I wanted a complaint form, I would have asked for one, I just wanted to be sure that the next person who uses the room is safe.

- Process Groupings 11. Performance Analysis

  This is a very important part of the innovative process. I personally do not believe that products which do not meet their performance expectations financially and/or functionally should be considered anything but failures and should be ashamed of them, rather than hiding the truth by calling them innovative. The correct name for these products and outputs should be "**demotivators**."

- Process Groupings 12. Transformation

  All too often the organization implements a change and the targeted employees use it. Performance improves significantly, but you know that often when you direct attention at a specific part of the business, there is a temporary performance improvement. Unfortunately, when you remove the spotlight from that part of the business, it tends to slip backwards to the original performance level. In some cases, this is a worse condition than before. For example, if your boss is standing watching you, you are more productive than when he is away at a meeting. I have seen customer relations management (CRM) systems that were very beneficial when first installed, but 6 months later the sales people were back to using their old system that they were familiar with. However, now the organization requires them to input information into the new online system resulting in a decrease in productivity because no one is finding the data useful. I heard salesman say, "I know what my customer is buying I don't need a computer to tell me."

Another excellent example is the Lean concept where everything has its place and is always put back in its place. For IBM, I called this the clean desk approach where at the end of the day, employees were supposed to clear their desktop of any paperwork. IBM required everyone to comply with this new process. The way I complied with it was I had one drawer into which I pushed all the papers that were on my desk at the end of the day. The next day when I came in, my first big job was to go through the papers in that desk drawer to arrange them so that I could use them during the day. The clean desk process operated for about 30 days and slowly eroding until 6 months later when everything was back to where it was prior to the clean desktop policy.

Transformation is the formal evaluation of how an individual change impacts the long-term operations of the organization. The organization measures the real value of the change by its long-term impact, rather than by the individual's immediate reaction to the change.

Transformation relates not just to the introduction of the new concept or process, but also to its continuance over time. All too often that innovative change only lasts if someone is watching over it. After the focus is taken off from the change, the culture of the organization goes back to where it was. When this happens, the organization has wasted a lot of money and other scarce resources. If it is a temporary change in methods for the process, you should not consider it innovative.

The Seven Innovation Project Evaluators

If you have a truly innovative change, you should to be able to answer the following questions with a resounding "Yes!":

1. Do your employees accept and embrace the changes in their processes, behaviors, and beliefs?
2. Was the change in keeping with expectations?
3. Did the change bring added value to the individual employee?
4. Do your customers and/or potential customers prefer the new product and/or the way the organization operates and/or how you provide the services?
5. Was the value-added of the change great enough to offset any price differences?
6. Is the new process added value to the customer or potential customer and the investor compared to the way things were before the change?
7. Knowing what you know now, would you invest in this change?

Performance analysis is the activity of classifying the parts of the process and/or product functions and placing them into one of the following the following three classifications:

1. Value-added
2. No value-added
3. Less value-added

You then analyzed the equivalent parts of the new and old processes or products classifying them in one of the previously mentioned classifications (for example, interview process cycle time is less than the old process and the new process is adding value).

INTRODUCTION TO PROCESS GROUPING 9: MARKETING, SALES, AND DELIVERY

Let's start with some common definition for marketing and selling. There are many different definitions of marketing. One study indicated that there were 74 different marketing definitions. I prefer the very simple definition as defined by the English Oxford dictionary:

> Definition of marketing—the action or business of promoting and selling products or services, including market research and advertising. Marketing is finding out what you don't have, and sales is the task of selling what you do have. Marketing is the activity of finding out what the customer wants to buy.

> Definition of Selling—It is first and foremost a transaction between the seller and the prospective buyer or buyers (the *target market*) where money (or something considered to have monetary value) is exchanged for goods or services. Selling is the art of *closing the deal*.

> Definition of sales—is the activity of taking a lead and selling the item to the potential customer.

Note: The term *sales and marketing* are used so commonly that you assume they are the same—they are not.

As these definitions infer, marketing is the mother and selling is the child. I personally would have defined it the other way around. Marketing would be responsible for research and advertising and selling would be responsible for closing the deal with the customer. But someone somewhere defined marketing as the total and selling as part of the marketing activities. Because this is an accepted definition, I will use it in our discussion.

The Seven Major Responsibilities of the Combined Marketing and Sales Operations

In today's environment more and more companies are combining marketing and sales to eliminate any confusion. This combined total department is responsible for:

1. Conducting market research
2. Developing advertising strategy and campaigns
3. Promoting the reputation of the organization's products and/or services

4. Identifying potential customers
5. Selling the organization's products and/or services
6. Measuring after sales customer satisfaction
7. Defining target markets

The Three Different Types of Sales and Marketing Employees

The job of marketing/selling is very complex and challenging. I believe that there may need to be two different types of people and maybe even three different types:

1. Research. The research type of individual excels in preparing surveys, analyzing trends, and managing focus groups. These are the individuals who studied the technology related to their organization's output and can predict very accurately future requirements. They are the technology and application specialists. This is the group that prepares the marketing specification for new products and services. These are the individuals that identify and quantify improvement opportunities for the organization. They are the primary drivers of research and development (R&D) activities. Their primary measurements of success are when they define a business opportunity that results in increased sales and profit. The two primary interfaces are the external customer and R&D. These types of individuals really are technocrats. In the ISC, their primary activity is directed at "Phase I. Creation. Process Grouping 1. Opportunity Identification."

2. Good innovators/creators. This type is characterized by individuals who are extremely good innovators and/or creators. They work with artists, performers, and producers in developing and creating advertising campaigns. These are the people who think way outside of the box. These are the organization's advertising specialists. In most organizations this is part of the innovation movement as this group acquires or originates more creative and innovative ideas and concepts than even R&D.

3. Extroverts. The third category of marketing and sales personnel are individuals who would be considered strong extroverts. They quickly develop one-on-one relationships with potential, new, and established customers. These are the individuals who focus on closing a sale. These are the direct sales employees who

are the organization's most frequent interface with its customers and potential customers. It is extremely important that these individuals build up a personal relationship with the potential customers. This is necessary so that the customer will have a high degree of trust in the salesperson's statements. These are individuals who measure the success by the amount of money they earn, because they are compensated primarily by commission. It's easy to understand why the amount of the commission is a personal indication of how good a job the individual is doing. I personally am always surprised at the amount of take-home pay the sales-type people receive in comparison to the technologists within the organization's facilities.

From my point of view, it's difficult to find one individual who can do all three types of assignments well. To summarize, the three types of people required to do sales and marketing in an innovative manner:

- Technology and Application Specialist
- Advertising Specialist
- Direct Sales Employees

Technology and Application Specialist

This is the individual who is highly qualified and who is responsible for predicting future customer and consumer needs. They typically write the marketing specification for new products. They are one of the key people who are responsible for keeping the knowledge management system up-to-date. Typical activities include:

- Conducting focus groups and surveys with current customers and consumers
- Conducting focus groups and surveys with potential customers and consumers
- Conducting the customer satisfaction survey and associated corrective action
- Gathering information related to competition's R&D activities
- Preparing the marketing specification for new products
- Defining advertising and sales channels
- Managing the help desk

Advertising Specialist

Typical activities for the advertising specialist include:

- Preparing the booth layout equipment
- Defining the marketing strategy
- Frequently connecting with customers and potential customers in his or her region
- Negotiate advertising campaign contract
- Preparing and obtaining advertising artwork and layout
- Attending trade shows and exhibits
- Defining unique advertising campaigns for regions and/or cultures
- Relating changes in sales volume based upon advertising approach in campaign
- Studying competitive advertising approaches
- Packaging the product or service. The way the organization packages the product or service is a major influence on the sales process. Often the million-dollar advertising campaign can be brought to its knees because the product is not presented in an attractive container. Size, shape, and color of the container can make or break otherwise outstanding innovation. I observed cases where changing the packaging more than doubled sales

Direct Sales Employees

The direct-sales employee is the primary interface between the organization and its customers and potential customers. The sales group must have:

- The ability to manage and coach effectively
- Have extremely good and effective communications skills
- Effective cooperation development skills
- Have the ability to know when to shut up and allow the customer to make a buy commitment
- Have the ability to listen and understand the potential customers concerns and problems then mold the presentation so that it addresses these concerns and problems. The success or failure of the innovative conceptual idea rests in the salesperson's hands. A good salesperson can sell a mediocre product, but even outstanding products can fail without good salespeople

Typical direct-sales employee activities are:

- *Cold calls.* This is contacting customers and potential customers by telephone or by person-to-person contact to explain the organization's product and to determine how it could be used by the customer or potential customer. The organization often enters this contact information into the knowledge management system or records it in the individual records system.
- *Scheduled appointments with customers or potential customers.* The purpose is to promote interest in the organization's products and/or obtain a buy commitment.
- *Presentations at conferences.* These are initial presentations that stimulate interest in products or services that the organization offers. They are usually general in nature because organizations frown upon using this media to make a sales presentation.
- *Prepare proposal.* This is usually a basic document that defines the work the organization will perform, the time schedule for the activity, and the cost of the product or service.
- *Conduct demonstration.* This is usually a group activity where customers and/or potential customers observe the salesperson setting up and using the product or activity. Proving time for the organization to demonstrate the buying criteria.
- *Provide sales forecast.* Forecast potential sales closers over the next 3 to 6 months. This allows the production facility to schedule the workload and have product available to meet customer requirements.
- *CRM maintenance.* The sales organization often is responsible for keeping the CRM system up to date and operating. Almost every sales contact should become part of the CMR system.
- *After sales customer satisfaction.* The direct sales representative is responsible for ensuring that the organization delivers the product on time and that the product performs as required by the contract.
- *Corrective action.* They are responsible for identifying problems and improvement opportunities related to the marketing and sales systems and problems that occur because of these systems and/or products not performing correctly. They are responsible for obtaining corrective action on these improvement opportunities and providing feedback to the customer about corrective actions related to the problems the customer encountered.

- *Pipeline maintenance.* They are responsible for having, reporting, and ensuring accurate knowledgeable information related to the pipeline visibility, velocity, and produce ratios.
- *Shelf space.* Sales is always fighting for more shelf space or for different locations in the store. If the store allots room for one of your items along with a large group of similar items, sales go down significantly. What you want to do is to have a group of your products in a row allowing it to attract a potential customer during their sales cycle. Besides space location, position on the shelf can be even a more important factor. High up or low down on the shelving is bad. The ideal place for your product is at shoulder level or one shelf lower. Customer flow patterns within the store are also very important consideration to increase sales.

MARKETING PROBLEMS

Note: The following section is based upon the book entitled *Resource Management Excellence* published by Paton Press.

It is extremely important to know when to remove or change your output. The organization directs all the money and effort invested in R&D at developing the marketable assets. The art of understanding where to invest your R&D spending and to know when to replace the present offerings is all part of resource management.

Marketing's primary role is to work with future, potential, and present customers to identify their future needs and to nurture and romance the customer to the point that they are excited about buying the products and services of the organization. I believe that marketing has let most organizations down by performing poorly in the following areas:

- Poor forecasting
- Lack of accountability
- Inadequate follow-through

Poor Forecasting

Marketing's responsibility is to identify future products and target cost structures, relevant market windows, and volume. The high failure rate of new product introduction is a testimonial to the poor job that they are doing. Inaccurate market forecasting has cost a lot of equipment to be underutilized, or the other extreme, put the organization in a position where they cannot meet customer demands. Companies like Campbell Soup won many awards for their innovative products, most of which did not sell when presented to the public. In the 1980s poor market forecasting led IBM to pour most of its R&D resources into mainframe development instead of PC development, resulting in them losing the lucrative PC market.

Not only are the marketing quantity projections bad, but also their analysis of when and how long the product window will be open is also faulty. Marketing needs to better understand and project the technological developments related to the industry, the competition's strategy, and the customers' changing expectations, because their projections drive product obsolescence and R&D funding.

Lack of Accountability

The management team in most organizations accepts poor performance by marketing as being a way of life, making them think that marketing is an art, not a science. It is a guessing game, like throwing darts at a dartboard. Organizations accept marketing projections that are plus or minus 20, 30, or 40 percent without discussion. There is a need to hold marketing accountable for their projections. A management system needs to be put in place that compares actual to marketing forecast in areas like:

- Marketing product requirements to relief engineering specifications
- Sales volume for 6, 12, and 18 months
- Completeness of input into the engineering specifications
- Accuracy of the support costs comparison to actual

Follow-Through

Marketing organizations tend to develop their market forecasts and throw them over the wall to engineering, never being held accountable for their adequacy and accuracy. As a result, frequently the final product is not aligned with the marketing specifications. Marketing should have the responsibility for following-through and ensuring that product and service specifications agree with their input, or at a minimum, meet the requirements set forth within their input.

Other Functions

I do agree that other functions have a lot to do with providing high-quality products and services, functions like R&D, manufacturing, sales, customer call centers, and so on. However, I am limiting this chapter to marketing because marketing has the biggest opportunity to improve, more than any other function in most organizations; however, they have done the least to improve.

CUSTOMERS AS A RESOURCE

> The Amazons and the Priceline.coms of the world have developed an enormous franchise in a very short amount of time because they started with the customer and offered what the customer needed.
>
> **Nigel Morris**
> *President & COO, Capital One Financial Corporation*

You cannot overlook the organization's customers as an important part of the organization's resources. Too often organizations get so involved in finding new customers and growing their market share that they take their present customers for granted. It is estimated that the cost of finding a new customer is 10 times the cost of keeping the current customers satisfied. For example, if a region has 1,000 customers and they want to grow by 10 percent, the average cost to obtain a new customer is $400 and the past retention rate has been 80 percent with no special focus on the present customers. This would mean, if there is no change in the customer relationship strategy, the sales force would need to acquire 300 new customers (i.e., 200 customers) to make up for the loss of current customers and 100 to make up for the 10 percent growth in sales. That would be a total of 300 new customers at $400 each for a total cost of $120,000. If they invested $40 in each current customer, it would cost them $40,000 to keep the current customers and another $40,000 to gain the additional 100 new customers for a total of $80,000, which is a $40,000 (50%) reduction in cost.

> The best hedge against uncertainty is to be close to the customer.
>
> **Rosabeth Moss Kanter**
> *Harvard Business School*

Customer care requires a consistent and methodical, but creative approach that will turn customer outreach into collaborative innovation. This means that you need to go beyond having satisfied customers to make them loyal allies.

Customer-Care Processes

Excellent customer-care processes result in excellent customer-satisfaction results. There are four key groups that often have been overlooked in an organization's improvement programs:

- Sales
- Marketing
- Customer call centers
- Customer service centers

The average business loses 15 percent to 35 percent of its customers each year due to poor sales or customer service.

David B. Puglia
Vice President, Aspect Communications/Microsoft

Most improvement processes focus upon the products, development engineering, suppliers, and manufacturing. I agree that the products are important, but equally and maybe even more important, are the service processes that directly interface with the organization's customers. Organizations lose more customers over poor service than over poor products. These four customer-interface groups play the single most important role in obtaining and keeping customers.

The Four Major Characteristics of Excellent Delivery Organizations

There are four major characteristics that are prevalent in all excellent organizations:

1. They have a well-defined service strategy, which highlights the real priorities of their customers.
2. Their front-line employees like people and are interested in them. They make a good assessment of the customer's current situation, their frame of mind, and their needs.

3. They have developed customer-friendly systems. Their systems are designed for the customers, rather than the organization.
4. They keep their commitments to their customers. They have follow-up systems to ensure that any commitment they make to the customer they meet on schedule.

There are only two activities in any organization that count:

- Making things
- Selling them

All employees who are not directly involved in these two areas must be mindful that their jobs are supportive of these two activities. If your customers do not feel they are being served as well as they could be, they will move on to another supplier. A typical organization will lose 10–30 percent of their customer base each year, while an excellent organization will lose less than 5 percent.

The Five Drivers of Excellent Service

Customers look to these organizations exhibiting the four characteristics of excellent delivery to provide them with excellent service, as though they were the only customer that the organization has. You all hate to stand in line waiting to check-in at the airport, but when you get to the counter, you want the attendant to be friendly and to take all the time necessary to process your reservation and explain what you need to do to make our flight. These conflicting customer attitudes present a dilemma to the organization and a very important challenge. Customers expect five things related to the four characteristics of excellent delivery each time they contact an organization:

- Accuracy
- Timeliness
- Responsiveness
  - Caring
  - Polite
  - Knowledgeable
- Reliable service (dependable)
- Clean, neat, attractive tangibles things
  - Physical facilities
  - Personal appearance

The Customers' Perception

The customers' perception of organizational excellence is defined by the summarization of all the customer's perceived positive and negative evaluation of all the contacts they have with an organization. Unfortunately, negative experiences have a 20 times heavier weighting than positive experiences. Understanding the customer's perception is critical to providing high levels of customer satisfaction. It is not enough to provide excellent service—the customer must perceive it as excellent. They need to be **wowed** by the experience. They need to feel that this is an organization that knows them, respects them, and values them as a preferred customer.

> Ultimately, your goal is to enhance the lifetime value of your most profitable customers and leverage what this brings to your company.
>
> **Joe W. Forehand**
> *CEO, Accenture*

Every executive team plays a very important role in customer perception. What they do, what they say, and where they say it are all-important. Microsoft's executive team stays close to their customers by making sales calls—that includes the chief executive officer (CEO) and chief operating officer (COO). Robert J. Herbold, retired CEO of Microsoft, stated, "It (executive sales call) signals that the customer is very important, and that, consequently, the customer says, 'Wow, that's an organization that is clearly viewing me as a valued customer.'"

Jeff Bezos, founder of Amazon.com, sends e-mail to customers asking them to respond to him personally with their thoughts. Richard Branson, President of Virgin Atlantic Airlines, comes to Gatwick to apologize for late flights. The chairman of EMC Corporation, Dick Egan, spends more than 50 percent of his time with the organization's customers. These are just typical examples of how the executive team needs to lead the customer care process.

> Information about the outside is obsolete quickly, especially in today's environment when technologies crisscross, and markets and distribution channels change four times a week. The only way you can get outside information is to go out with your customers.
>
> **H. James Harrington**

THE FIFTEEN FACTORS FOR SURPRISINGLY GREAT PEOPLE

The excellent organization provides surprisingly great service to its external customers on a consistent basis. To provide surprisingly good service, you need to have surprisingly good people. What characteristics make up an organization that develops "surprisingly great people" resources?:

1. Properly selecting employees
2. Providing superb training
3. Securing competitive equipment
4. Developing great communication with management and even better communication with customers
5. Selecting management who is concerned about the employees and their needs
6. Hiring employees who are concerned about their customers' needs and expectations
7. Developing honest and straight-talking managers
8. Promoting the understanding that customers may not always be right, but they are never wrong
9. Developing managers who understand that employees are not the problem, but can be part of the solution
10. Preparing clear, understandable definitions of customer expectations and feedback systems that measure the degree of compliance
11. Hiring managers who solve problems, not place blame
12. Hiring managers who build people, not use them
13. Setting targets that challenge the individual
14. Promoting the belief that we are never good enough
15. Establishing a reward system that recognizes surprisingly good service

To follow these 15 factors requires all organizations to invest heavily in training all employees with even more emphasis on the individuals who make up organizations that exhibit the four characteristics of excellent delivery (for example, Marriott spends more than $20 million a year on training its employees who interface with their customers.) At a minimum, all employees should receive 40 hours of training per year.

In a study conducted by the White House Office of Consumer Affairs, they found out that customers who complain about products and services are more likely to do business with companies that upset them than the individuals who do not complain. If a complaint is resolved, between 54 and 70 percent of the people would do business with the company again. This number grows to 95 percent if the customer feels that the company resolved the complaint expeditiously.

The Impact of Losing a Customer

It is very important that you really consider the impact that you have on a customer and the future of the organization, whenever you take exception to a customer's complaint. The cost of losing a current customer usually has a much greater impact on the organization than providing the customer with a new product. For example:

- The lifetime cost of losing a customer in the auto industry runs $180,000.
- The yearly cost of losing a customer in the supermarket industry is $4,800.
- The yearly cost of losing a customer in the appliance industry is $210.
- The yearly cost of losing a customer in the banking industry is $110 per year in profit.

Don't ask, 'Is everything okay?' Instead ask, 'What's the one thing I could do better next time?'

The Sales Team Builds an Organization

A good salesman makes your product look good, and a good product makes a salesman look good. You need to make them both look good for customers to buy your products.

H. James Harrington

It is easy to see that supermarkets should seldom question a customer complaint relative to a product that the customer claims is faulty. An organization must not just handle complaints; it needs to go out of its way to welcome complaints and to solve them. Studies prove that less than 5 percent of people who are unhappy with products and services complain to the organization. The other percent—the silent majority—just walk away from these products in favor of the competition. It should be the organization's objective to double the number of complaints it receives, not because the products and services perform worse than before, but because the company has improved the communication system significantly, thus breaking down the customers' reluctance to share their thoughts with the organization. A restaurant owner should not ask a customer, "Was there anything wrong with the meal?" or "How was the meal?" What he or she should say is, "Can you suggest any way that we can improve our service or food?" A question like this does not put the customer in a position in which he or she is complaining, but puts the customer in a position of being helpful by offering advice and suggestions.

> We look every month at the customers we lose. To me those mean that we failed in the relationship.
>
> **Alexandra Lebenthal**
> *President, Lebenthal & Company*

The sales team needs to be motivated and competitive. They need to be individuals who are driven to win and truly enjoy working with people. There's an old saying: "Give me a person who is in debt and I will show you a great salesperson." This may be true, but it can be overdone. In excellent organizations, the sales personnel are highly motivated and driven to meet quotas, but they are also rewarded for ensuring that the products and services that they sell truly represent value to their customers. It is for this very reason that many of the excellent organizations have decreased the emphasis on sales commissions and refocused their reward system based on customer satisfaction and team selling skills.

In the movie, "Miracle on 34th Street," the Macy's Santa Claus sends customers to Gimbles when Macy's did not have what they needed or when Gimbles had it at a better price. You may reason that this only happens in the movies, but the concept is a legitimate approach to building customer loyalty.

> Your organization needs to have a long-term view but with short term results.
>
> **H. James Harrington**

The Difference Between the Old and New Type of Sales Team

I find that there are very different attitudes in the sales force that make up the organizations that I classify as "excellent organizations." The following is a list of the old type of sales force prevalent in most organizations and the new type of sales force in excellent organizations (see Table 9.1).

> You'd be surprised how much outside information about customers and noncustomers companies simply do not have, and in many cases, cannot get. And yet, you don't make your decisions on what goes on inside your company; you shouldn't, at least.

> **Peter Drucker**

Being Customer Centric

I focused the discussion to this point primarily on sales. Marketing, customer call centers, and customer service groups, also have an equal potential to detract or contribute to high levels of customer satisfaction. All four

TABLE 9.1

Old Type of Sales Force versus New Type of Sales Force

Old Type of Sales Force	New Type of Sales Force
Does what needs to be done	Knows the whole business
Knows the product	Knows the customer's business
Every sale is unique	Every sale is based upon the standard process, modified to the customer
Works hard to look good	Makes the organization look good Takes pride in the organization
Resists any type of measurements	Uses measurements to benchmark activities
Monetarily motivated	Performance motivated
Sells the products	Sells solutions
Gets new customers	Keeps the proven customers
Changes job often	Long-term commitment
Sells the product even if it is not the best answer for the customer	Helps the customer find the best answer even if it is another organization's product
Finds ways to beat the system	Changes systems that are bottlenecks to progress
Heavy-handed selling	Haggle-free buying
Measured by number of new sales	Measured by customer retention

groups—sales, marketing, customer call centers, and customer service groups—require equal focus on performance improvement and customer satisfaction for the organization to excel.

The Nine Commonly Used Sales and Marketing Tools

For the sake of brevity, I will not discuss in detail the improvement activities of the other two groups. But some of the more effective tools, which make up those interface groups' toolbox that focus on maintaining our customer resources, are:

1. CRM software
2. Customer surveys
3. Business to customer (B2C) software
4. Balanced scorecard
5. Indirect poor-quality cost measurement system
6. Knowledge management
7. Complaint handling (corrective action tracking) systems
8. Peer reviews
9. Customers being part of the design process

Buying the CR solution – that's the 1%. Making it work is the 99%.

Dr. Jon Anton
Director of Benchmark Research, Purdue
University Center for Customer-Driven Quality

Ford's past chairman, Donald E. Petersen, put it this way, "If we are not customer-driven, our car won't be either." The past Chairman of Premier Industrial Corporation, Morton L. Mandel, stated, "To us, customer service is the main event."

Customer Lead or Customer Followed

The way customers are getting serviced is completely changing.

Greg Gianferte
CEO, Right Now Technologies

Excellent organizations cannot afford to wait until the customer has a need and then fill that need. Excellent organizations must be able to project what is possible and then create the market. They need to be well ahead of their customers, offering new and exciting products that their customers had never even dreamed about. No one asked for the Sony Walkman, VCRs, electric lights, mini-vans, or the worldwide web. Customers ask for their present needs. They seldom have the technical know-how to realize what is possible. It is the excellent organization that must have the vision of the future and brings that vision to reality. This is what **wows** the customers.

> The customer cannot articulate unmet and emerging needs. If you ask them, 'How do you improve this?' you generally end up with incremental improvement. So, it's very important to start with game-changing ideas internally and then go validate or prioritize them with the customer.
>
> **Jay Desai**
> *Institute of Global Competitiveness*

The Four Points of Dow Corning's Sales Improvement Strategy

Because of Dow Corning's change to a customer-oriented focus, revenue growth has been in the double digits. In this transformation they reinforced four points:

1. A change in business strategy must be reflected in every aspect and every level of the company
2. Success is no longer about technology leadership or cutting-edge products alone
3. Success requires achieving a competitive advantage even if it disrupts the status quo
4. Companies must redefine success and regularly reinvent the business—in good times and bad

Note: Taken from Customer Relationship Management, June 2004, Charles Butter, Author.

Winning and Losing Customers

> You don't grow unless you have a high level of customer satisfaction.
>
> **Joe Hogan**
> *Vice President, Hewlett-Packard's Outsourcing Group*

TABLE 9.2

How to Win or Lose Customer

Win Customers	Lose Customers
1. Capabilities	1. Trust
2. Trust	2. Quality
3. Price	3. Capabilities
4. Quality	4. Price

You attract international customers to your organization for four reasons (see column on the left) but you lose customers for the four reasons (see column on the right). Both lists impact order with one being the highest impact (See Table 9.2).

> Good quality is a stupid idea. The only thing that counts is your quality getting better at a more rapid rate than your principal competitors. It's real simple. If you are not getting more, better, faster, than your competitor is getting more, better, faster, than we're getting less better or more worse.

Tom Peters

You drive product and service capability by using the latest technology and/or using present technology in more creative ways. People base trust upon experience and reputation. It reflects the faith that the customer has in your ability to meet your cost, schedule, and performance commitments. Price today ties in directly with value. Customers are looking at getting the best performance at the least cost. Quality reflects more than just the initial view of the products and services purchased. It reflects the quality of the total organization, the reliability of its products, and the capability of its sales and service personnel. You lose customers for the same four reasons that you attract them, but in a different order.

> The public does not know what is possible, but we do.

Akio Morita
Sony

> Of all your resources, your present customers are one of your most valuable resources.

H. James Harrington

All Customers Are Not Equal

Theoretically, all customers are equal and good always wins over evil. But you know that is not true. In the movie, "Where the Boys Are," two girls come into a restaurant and ask for two cups of hot water. When the waiter arrives, they add catsup to the water, get some free crackers, and enjoy the soup and crackers while watching the boys pass by. When they ask for a second cup of water, the restaurant owner says, "Yes, but do me a favor. Tomorrow go to my competitor across the street."

The Four Things That Make a Good Customer

Yes, all businesses have customers who cost them more to service than what the customers pays for. You would like these customers to go to your competitors. On the other hand, there are customers that stay with you allowing you to make a reasonable profit each time they buy from you. As consultants, you see this all the time. Customers and potential customers want free information. They want very detailed proposals, then take the information provided and do it themselves. Here is a typical example. A customer asked us to turn in a proposal to do a benchmarking study. They came back stating they like it but would like more detail about how we would conduct the study. We provided a detailed process flow. They then came back stating, "Before the executive team would approve the proposal, they needed to have a typical agenda for a meeting with a benchmarking partner. We supplied this and then they wanted to know the names of the organization that we would be visiting to get the information. We provided this information and then we were told it was put on hold for the time being. Later we found out that they conducted the benchmarking study without our participation. This does not sound ethical, but this is the way many organizations operate. It is important that you select your customers carefully. There is 10 percent of the market you probably don't want, and your competition is trying to unload. Robert Cole from University of California at Berkeley has offered the following relationship theory:

- Try to attract customers you can keep
- Try to keep the customers you attract
- Try to attract high-value customers
- Try to turn your customers into sales people

The Six Levels of the Customer Relationship Ladder

Murray Raphel, author of *Up the Loyalty Ladder,* developed the following customer relationship grid (the objective of any organization is to move from a suspect to an advocate customer):

1. Suspect customer
2. Prospect customer
3. Customer
4. Repeat customer
5. Loyal customer
6. Advocate customer

You can manage and design the customer's experience—or the customer will do it for you.

Wendy Close
Research Director, Gartner Group
CRM Magazine, Dec. 2004, p. 22

Good advertising equals good sales, the two go hand-in-hand

H. James Harrington

THE SIXTY-FIVE WAYS TO ADVERTISE

People want to buy something—anything. All you must do is tell them how it will help them, make them more beautiful, make it easier to do, or save them money. A friend of mine took a cruise to Mexico, not because he wanted to take a cruise, but because he saved so much money by taking it right then.

For years, Japanese automobile advertising within the United States was far better and more frequent than U.S. automobile advertising in the United States. If you tell me enough times that I will like something, after a while I will buy it to see if I will like it. All too often you accept what you see on television or read on the internet as being fact when, in truth, it is often exaggeration. So much of the information you are receiving is opinions, not facts.

Sheldon Nesdale (Email: sheldon@marketingfirst.co.nz) lists 65 different ways to advertise your products or services (see Table 9.3).

TABLE 9.3

List of Ways to Advertise Your Products and/or Services

CINEMA ADVERTISING
1. Pre-movie advertisements
2. In-movie product placement

TELEVISION ADVERTISING
3. 15/30 second television advertisements
4. Infomercials
5. Television programmed sponsorship
6. Television interviews

NEWSPAPER ADVERTISING
7. Regional community newspaper, freely distributed
8. Regional daily newspaper
9. National daily newspaper

RADIO ADVERTISING
10. 15/30 second radio advertisements
11. Radio interviews

OUTDOOR ADVERTISING
12. Billboards
13. Video billboard
14. Bus shelters
15. Bus backs
16. Truck sides
17. Car signage
18. Outdoor signage on your building
19. Miniature billboards: core-flute signage stabbed into grass verges
20. Posters around town
21. Free standing displays in shopping malls
22. Hot air balloons/blimps
23. Paint a sports field with your logo
24. Burn your logo onto the side of a mountain (check with the local council for permission first)

MAIL
25. Direct mail/addressed mail
26. Un-addressed P.O. box mail drop—flyers/postcards
27. Un-addressed residential mail drop—flyers/postcards

ONE-ON-ONE
28. In-person cold calling (unannounced)
29. Telemarketing
30. Participate in networking groups (e.g., Chamber of Commerce, BNI)

(Continued)

TABLE 9.3 (*Continued*)

List of Ways to Advertise Your Products and/or Services.

ONLINE ADVERTISING

31. Text ads (e.g., Google AdWords)
32. Display advertising (banner, skyscraper, video, applications/software (e.g., msn messenger))
33. Organic search engine optimization
34. Email marketing/newsletters
35. SPAM
36. Online directories (e.g., Yellow Pages online and country-wide business directories)
37. White papers/e-books
38. Blogging
39. Social networking sites (e.g., Facebook, Twitter, LinkedIn, Pinterest)
40. Contribute to special interest forums (e.g., Google Groups)

MAGAZINE ADVERTISING

41. Gossip style magazines (e.g., Woman's Day)
42. Industry specific magazines (e.g., Needles and Pins Weekly)

PRINTED DIRECTORIES

43. Yellow Pages
44. Local directory

WEBSITE

45. Your website
46. Campaign specific mini-websites

SPONSORSHIP

47. Sponsor a sports team's t-shirts
48. Sponsor a community event or non-profit organization

BRANDED OBJECTS

49. Branded pens, coffee cups, t-shirts, bags, clocks etc.

PUBLIC DEMONSTRATIONS

50. Set up in shopping malls (or in the supermarket)

GUERRILLA ADVERTISING/ALTERNATIVE ADVERTISING / STEALTH MARKETING

51. PR stunts
52. Word of mouth
53. Viral (video, email, postcards, CD's)
54. Legal graphite
55. Chalk on the sidewalk
56. Logos in the snow/sand
57. Flyers under car windscreen wipers
58. Video projection onto side of building
59. Night-time shop window video or laser light show
60. Sponsored humans (to tattoo your brand on their forehead, or, a not quite as exciting, wear a branded t-shirt)

(*Continued*)

TABLE 9.3 (*Continued*)

List of Ways to Advertise Your Products and/or Services.

SMS TEXT MESSAGING
    61. SMS text messaging

PUBLIC RELATIONS
    62. Distribute press releases (for print & online publication)
    63. Contact journalists/reporters directly with something newsworthy

TRADE SHOWS & EXPOS
    64. Exhibiting at trade shows and expos

SEMINARS
    65. Seminars

The internet programs I personally use the most are Amazon, YouTube, Facebook, and LinkedIn. I realize Table 9.3 gives an extremely long list providing the innovator with many possible combinations. It is my experience that the advertising strategies change depending on the time of year and economic situations within the country. It also will vary based upon the maturity level and competitive position of the product or service.

FAILED SALES PRESENTATION

The following is a real example of a failure in the sales system that I was assigned to improve. The organization had outstanding products that had excellent reviews, but the burn rate for the organization was almost twice the sales rate per month. The salespeople were typically given 2 hours to make a sales presentation of the new and progressive software package. I had two of our very best people making the sales pitch. They were part of the initial group that defined the software package and were very proud of the work they did (and rightly so).

My observation of a number of their sales presentation follows:

The two men started out with an excellent audience including the president of the organization, the controller, the IT functional manager, the head of the project management department, and number of software engineers and project management. The presenters really understood the product. They described all the safety features, the software applications, and how each icon in the software package was designed to accomplish a specific task, the different ways you can look at the outputs, and so on.

I noticed about 30 minutes into the presentation that the president of the organization would sneak out the back of the room closely followed by the controller. Then the manager of the Project Management Office magically disappeared even though there was a great deal of discussion going on between the presenters, the project managers, and IT employees. The presenters were so proud of their package that they kept going deeper and deeper into it to show how it manipulated the data to get meaningful reports out. At the end of the 2 hours the conversation was still hot and meaningful. Some of the potential client's people stayed on fascinated in exchanging information with the two excellent systems engineers. This should have been a sure sale, but the presenters never asked for the sale. The whole purpose of sales is to get someone to sign a contract, not to entertain the audience.

The Three Critical Lessons Learned

The next time I appointed two less competent people to make the presentations with the instructions to tell the audience that we would be glad to set up a meeting or phone call so that we could get the people responsible for the specific functions to answer their detailed technical questions. We developed a standard sales presentation where we started with, "We're going to present to you a black box. We will focus on what inputs are required to this black box and then what type of outputs you can get and how you can use them to make your life easier, reduce costs, and allow you to shorten schedules." The presentation was designed to take 1 hour. At the end of the hour we instructed the presenters to say, "This is a package made for your application, don't you agree?" Then 15 minutes before the end of the 2-hour scheduled presentation, the presenter asked, "It's obvious that there is a very good match between your applications and our software package. When would you like us to start installing it?" With this new tactic, we ended up closing three out of five of the next presentations we made. From that starting point, things took off. These were the lessons learned:

1. The customer cannot buy a product if the presenter does not give them a chance to commit.
2. A quiet time interval puts the pressure on the buyer to speak up. They cannot buy your product when the salesperson is talking.
3. Focus on what the sales will do for the customer, not upon what the product will do.

Why Is Sales and Marketing the Most Innovative Function in the Organization?

Based upon the following list, I believe that the sales group and the marketing group lead the innovation movement within most organizations:

1. They are the primary organization responsible for identifying innovative opportunities.
2. Unique creative thought patterns drive the promotion and advertising activities.
3. They develop, refine, produce, and deliver the promotion advertising opportunities to the potential customers. This is the broadest definition of innovation in medium and large companies.
4. Each potential customer to whom the sales person makes a presentation has their own unique personality. This requires the salesperson to be very creative and innovative when he or she presents her or his products and/or service to the potential customer.

Sales and marketing play a key role in the innovative cycle and the organization must integrate them into the organization's planning cycle. The following are four planning activity where the sales and operation planning fits into the planning cycle:

- Strategic Planning
- Business Planning
- Sales and Operations Planning
- Detailed Planning, Scheduling and Execution

The sales and operation's planning plays a key role in the decision-making process as it relates to balancing demand and supply to integrate into financial and operating plan. There are four fundamental crossroads in sales and operations planning. It is essential that these four crossroads maintain the correct balance (see Figure 9.1).

The key ingredient in any sales activities is the accuracy of the forecasting which drives the entire production process. Figure 9.2 provides a view of the forecasting activities as they relate to the sales and marketing organization.

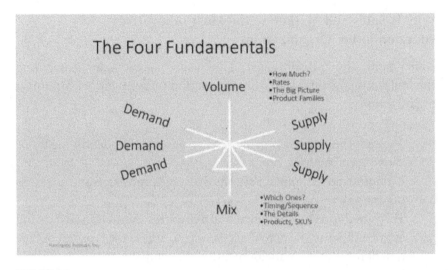

FIGURE 9.1
The sales and operations planning fundamentals crossroads.

The Forecasting Process Inputs and Outputs

Inputs
* Current Customers
* New Customers
* Competition
* Economic Outlook
* New Products
* Planning Strategy
* promotions
* Bid Activities
* Management Direction
* Intera-company Demands
* History Data
* Miscellaneous

Outputs Forecasts That Are:
* Reasoned
* Reasonable
* Reviewed Frequently
* Represent the real demands

FIGURE 9.2
Overview of the forecasting process.

The Five-Step Sales and Operational Plan

Figure 9.3 provides a view of the five-step sales and operational monthly planning cycle. In reviewing this, it may look like it is redundant in some places, but it is absolutely essential that these estimates be as accurate as possible.

It is essential to have a good measurement system that allows you to react to unexpected and unplanned-for variation. Figure 9.4 is a comparison of projected demands for actual sales orders for two different products.

The Monthly S&OP Process

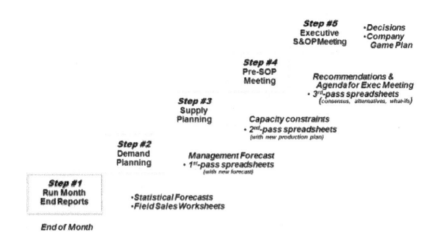

FIGURE 9.3
Monthly sales and operations planning cycle.

Accuracy????

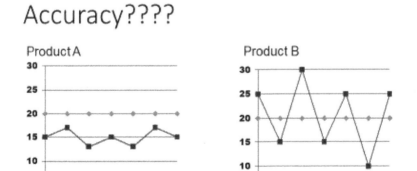

- Which is more accurate?
- Which can be fixed more easily?
- Which is more "dangerous?"

FIGURE 9.4
Comparison of projections to actual orders.

PACKAGING AND DELIVERY

Here you sit with a warehouse full of deliverable product orders scattered all over the warehouse. The question you need to address is, "How are you going to accomplish the physical movement of the product in the least expensive way in a package that would be very attractive to consumers around the world? Frequently an organization is shipping directly to a retailer who provides the interface to the consumer. It doesn't make any difference if your customer is a large company, small company, or an organization that delivers your product to the consumer, the design of the packaging makes a huge difference in the sales volume. If two products from different organizations sit on the shelf side-by-side, the one that is most attractively packaged will generally sell twice as many units. Innovative attractive containers and packaging design is one of the most important competitive advantages an organization can have. In today's comprehensive knowledge system it is difficult for any organization to produce output that is significantly better than the competition. As a result, sales are often driven by the way the organization packages and promotes the product.

Another packaging concern is how the organization packages the product to move from the organization's warehouse to the consumer's home. That means that packaging must be designed so that it can take the rough handling it will receive in the luggage departments of airline, boxcars, and trucks. You should drop test and vibrate all shipping packaging design to ensure that the packaging provides adequate protection for the product that you will transport in it. Shipping costs are often a major consideration that can be the difference between a product's profitability and a product's failure.

SUMMARY OF MARKETING, SALES, AND DELIVERY

As I indicated before, the marketing, sales, and delivery activities very often are the most innovative functions in an organization. They are the few functions that generate an idea and process it all the way through to measuring its impact on the customer. The activities within sales and marketing that require a high degree of creativity and innovation are:

1. Advertisement design
2. Container design
3. Packaging design
4. Opportunity recognition
5. Sales strategy

10

Process Grouping 10:
After-Sales Services

INTRODUCTION TO AFTER-SALES SERVICE

So you worked hard and sold one of your products. You had a good idea, you got funding to develop it, you produced the product, you talked to many potential customers, and now you have a customer who is satisfied with your product and it is performing well. This certainly is a customer who will come back and buy from you again, right? Not necessarily so. You still have one more hurdle to go over before you have a loyal customer. That hurdle is after-sales service. Many companies leave you with the impression that after they've got your money, they could care less about you. I have seen car salesmen who seem to be very interested in making you happy and you felt they were on your side before you bought the car. Two months later when the door handle fell off the back door, they had little or no time to talk to you when you bring the car in for service. I personally try to avoid the companies that have automatic computer-run customer care facility. These facilities that use a series of – dial 1 if, – dial 2 if, – dial 3 if, and so on. It's like no one wants to react to your problem and just sends you to somebody else because they do not have time for you. These are the organizations that after dialing in 2 to 9 numbers come back saying, "You are a very valued customer, but the repair center is very busy. There will be a 40 minute wait before a repair technician will be available to talk with you." As bad as that is, it's much better than the computer that talks back to you after you have been on hold for 15 minutes saying, "If you still having problems, call back and we will try to help you later."

So many times in the automated systems there is no way to talk to a human. The computer has no sympathy for the problems you're facing nor does the computer have the responsibility for providing you with the correct answer. I often choose to buy a product from a particular organization just because I could talk to a real person, not a computer, if I have a problem. I don't know about you, but I get mad when I am waiting on the phone and every 3 to 5 minutes the computer comes on the line stating, "Please stay on the line. Your call is important to us." We talk about how poor quality costs money all the time and being put on hold is a good example. I will bet few organizations would keep you waiting for long periods of time, like they do today, if they had to pay for the customer's time. But wait—they do pay for the customers' time because that customer does not come back and buy from them again. They turned loyal customers into mad customers who would rather go without then buy from them again.

Last week I had an experience of how a call center should operate. I called into their helpdesk and after two rings a young lady with a very pleasant voice answered the phone saying, "Would you like to talk to the computer or can I help you?" Now there's a company that is customer centric.

> Personally I hate these computerized call centers. If my suppliers don't care enough about me to talk to me, then I don't care enough about them to buy from them again.
>
> **H. James Harrington**

Six of the After-Sales Service Activities

The following are included in the after-sales service activities:

- The call center activities
- Repair activities
- Customer inquiries
- Helpdesk
- Delivery schedule
- Complaint centers (I recently called into a top-of-the-line hotel informing them about a safety hazard in my room. The answer was, "Stop by the front desk and get a complaint form.")

The Call Center Activities

Definition: Call center. A call center is a centralized office for receiving and transmitting a large volume of requests by telephone. Company call centers should track the incoming product support and information inquiries from customers. They can also handle outgoing calls for telemarketing, data collection, and follow-up. Often a call center collectively handles letters, faxes, and email. It is sometimes called "contact center."

A call center can range all the way from one person on a switchboard to a large open room layout with many individual computer workstations. Each workstation is manned by an individual who has a telephone, computer, and headset. They perform three types of activities:

1. *Making Outgoing Calls.* This approach is typically used for telemarketing, debt collection, and/or various types of surveys. Typically the operator has a predefined presentation that is designed to create interest and/or cooperation from the individual receiving the call.
2. *Reacting to Inbound Calls.* These are often related to a problem an individual is having with the product or service that was provided by the organization. In these cases, the individual working in the call center must be technically competent to provide meaningful answers for 75 to 85 percent of all the questions. When they are unable to provide an acceptable answer, they need to know who to transfer the call to so that the customer's question can be answered. Support desks are often used by companies in the computing, telecommunications, and consumer electronics industries. Answers to the commonly asked questions are programmed into the computer so they are directly available to the call center operator when contacted by a customer.
3. *Customer Service Call Centers (sometimes called customer contact centers).* They answer specific queries relating to customer issues. This type of service may even be used to respond to customer complaints and undertake retention strategies for unsatisfied customers.
4. *Contact Call Centers Perform Sales and Marketing Activities.* They are used to make cold calls, to do the initial qualification of the potential customer prior to turning a customer over to a sales representative. Often a major part of their activities is computer-generated requiring no human intervention. There are often used to conduct surveys.

Typical Call Center Service Performance Metrics

Like all operations within an organization, after-sales service is primarily driven by how the organization measures its performance. Typical center service performance metrics are:

- Customer satisfaction
- Cost per call
- Average handling time (also average hold time)
- Revenue per call

- First call resolution
- Total problem resolution
- Active and waiting calls
- Quality reports
- Service level agreement

The Eight Call Center Design Considerations

1. Call center jobs usually are low-paying jobs in a less than desirable environment. Efficiency of the individual worker is closely monitored providing regular feedback on comparisons between individual workers.
2. Frequently call center activity is performed in an individual's home. This results in increased communication problems and standardization activities.
3. Frequent customer complaints are transferred because the individual does not have the necessary skills and/or authority to resolve the problem
4. One of the most frequent complaints is the long wait time on incoming calls.
5. Often the outgoing calls are to individuals who are rushed, doing something else, or just plain rude making it a bad environment for the call operator.
6. Due to the large amount of calls at specific times of the day for short periods of time, several part-time workers are used. They do not have the benefits of being trained as well as the full-time employees. They will often work as little as 2 hours a day 4 days a week.
7. There is little or no time available to build up working relationships between the individual operators.
8. Because many of the outgoing calls are computer-generated without costing the organization any human resource cost, they use mass regional telephone lists without considering the cost and time of the person on the other side of the phone line. It may be value-added to the organization but it sure is negative value-added to the potential customer.

The Three Types of Repair Activity

There are three different types of repair activities that established organizations conduct:

1. *Separate Repair Facility.* The organization sets up repair centers where the organization's technicians make repairs to the product that

they sold to the consumer. The auto industry is an excellent example of the repair facilities and service facilities. For repair problems that occurred during the warranty period, the organization is responsible for the total cost of the repair. Usually the customer is responsible for delivering the defective item to the repair facility. The organization charges the customer for repairs made outside of the warranty time-frame. No consideration is given to the consumer's cost of delivering the defective item to the repair center or the cost of the loss of use of the item while the company is repairing the item.

The cost to the customer that is realized because an item is not available for use during the repair cycle and the value of the customer time and expense to deliver and pickup the repaired item is paid for by the customer even when the defect was covered under its warranty. At a minimum, it costs the customer an hour to drop off the defective item and another hour to take it up. Assuming it is 5 miles to the repair station, the travel cost is $8.50. Assuming the person works at Burger King with minimum wage of $15 an hour, his or her lost wages cost is $30. That's a cost of $38.50 to the customer even if the product is under warranty and the company pays for the repair. If the customer is a programmer who is receiving $32 an hour, that would be a total cost of $72.50 to the customer. (The cost of an error increases proportionately to the hourly rate of the customer.)

2. *Home Service Repair.* These types of repairs are used by organizations that sell primarily commercial products. These organizations have contracted with a number of maintenance organizations to repair their product using the selling organization's name. These individuals respond to a phone call to a local distributor expressing a problem related to a product that was either still on warranty or outside of the warranty conditions. From the customer's standpoint these individuals represent the organization that sold the product so the repair technician needs to be carefully trained. The reputation of the selling organization is highly dependent upon the service that was provided by the home service repair individual. Everything is important in making a good or bad impression on the customer. They are concerned about the cleanliness of the repair persons clothing, his or her friendly nature, and their ability to fix the problem. Sears is an excellent example of this type of home service repair.

3. *Remote Service Repair.* For this type of repair the customer must return the product to the producer of the product. The producer of the product will analyze the condition of the returned product and determine if it can be economically repaired. If producer does not recommend getting the product repaired, they will frequently replace it with a new one. If it is not under warranty, the producer will recommend that it be replaced with a new unit. Often the producer will offer a reduced price to the consumer so they will agree to by a new unit to offset some of the cost of replacing the defective item. Dell Computer is an excellent example of this type of repair service. Another good example is the restaurant that takes off the cost of the dinner because the steak was overcooked.

Call Center Personnel

Call center personnel are unique individuals. Consumers often receive their telephone calls with a very negative greeting. It seems like they always contact me in the middle of eating my dinner or talking on the other line with a customer. Customers often treat these call center personnel very rudely. Customers swear at them, complain because they are wasting their time, or what they are selling is not that the customer needs or even wants. But still the call center operator needs to place the next call treating the potential customer as a close and dear friend with a smile in her or his voice.

When the customer is calling in to complain or to get something fixed, they are frequently put in hold for long periods of time. Often music and commercials are continuously playing with the hopes that they can keep the customer waiting. The longest wait time that my organization has been subjected to is 3 hours and 18 minutes. The maximum wait time for incoming calls should be no more than 4 rings and on average all calls should be answered within 2 rings.

Many major call centers are run as separate businesses with between 10 to 200 phone stations in a single room. Operators report to work usually not knowing what product or products they would be pushing today. Usually detailed scripts were prepared for each and every product. The sales center operator assignment was simply to read the script as though she was talking to a close friend. These large call centers get paid based upon the number of phone calls they made. These operators are offered a great deal of latitude as it relates to starting and stopping time. Often a call center operator works as little as 3 hours per day 3 days a week. You can see how these factors put a great deal of stress and challenges on many of these call-center activities. Usually a call center agent is hired to manage these challenges.

Call Center Agent

Call center agent responsibilities include the following:

- Obtain client information by answering telephone calls
- Interviewing clients
- Verify information
- Determine eligibility by comparing client information to requirements
- Establish policies to enter client information and confirm pricing.
- Understand the changing customer needs and requirements
- Stay close to customers' future needs through customer interviews, customer service, and direct phone calls.
- Identify future call center customers by analyzing the external customer contact needs.
- Prepare and approve contracts including pricing
- Develop friendly relationships with potential and current customers through personal contact and professional contact.
- Schedule work assignments.
- Maintain communication equipment by reporting problems.
- Ensure quality results by adhering to standards and guidelines; recommending improved procedures (sample review of recorded telephone calls)
- Update job knowledge by studying new product descriptions
- Participate in educational opportunities.

What Kind of Skills Does a Call Center Agent Need?

A call center agent should possess the following skills:

- Verbal communication
- Telephone
- Human relations
- Problem-solving
- Motivational

- Listening
- Data entry
- People
- Customer service
- Attention to detail
- Multi-tasking

Call Center Representative

The front line person for call centers is the call center representative. This is the individual who makes direct contact with the potential customer. They need to build up a customer's trust in the organization to the point they are willing to commit financially to the organization without physically seeing, touching, or operating the product or services. Although the call center representative can be either a male or female, for cold calls a female seems to have the advantage. For repair activities usually the male has a tendency to build up the required trust faster than a female.

The call center representative duties typically include the following:

- Determine requirements by working with customers
- Handle inquiries by clarifying desired information; researching, locating, and providing information
- Resolve problems by clarifying issues; researching and exploring answers and alternative solutions; implementing solutions; escalating unresolved problems
- Fulfill requests by clarifying desired information; completing transactions; forwarding requests
- Sells additional services by recognizing opportunities to up-sell accounts; explaining new features
- Maintains call center database by entering information
- Keeps equipment operational by following established procedures; reporting malfunctions
- Updates job knowledge by participating in educational opportunities
- Enhances organization reputation by accepting ownership for accomplishing new and different requests; exploring opportunities to add value to job accomplishments

Call Center Representative Skills

Not everyone makes an acceptable call center representative. It's a much more difficult assignment than it would seem at first glance. The call center representative has the most challenging job. Every time the phone rings the person on the other end of the line has a different personality, different priority, different problem, and different tolerance levels related to interruptions. The following are some of the inherent skills and qualifications that a manager should look for when he or she is selecting a call center representative:

- Verbal communication
- Interpersonal understanding
- Phone skills
- Customer focus
- People skills
- Customer service
- Data entry skills
- Listening skills
- Building relationships

Repair Representative

Call center personnel infrequently are in physical contact with the potential customer. The repair representative typically is working with a customer who has already purchased a product or service. The impression that the customer has related to the repair representative's capability goes a long-way in determining if the customer will buy from the organization again.

Customers do not expect the call center personnel to have detailed technical knowledge related to the product they are trying to get the customer to buy. This is not the case with the repair representative. Their appearance is a very important part of the interface. Oily spots on their coveralls or uniform immediately makes the customer feel that the individual does sloppy work. Inability to respond quickly to a technical question immediately decreases the confidence that the customer has in the repair personnel. The repair representative must have all the skills that the call center personnel have, plus they need to look neat, clean, and behave in a very professional manner. The repair representative's first impression sets the stage for the customer's conclusions related to their capability. You never have a chance to make a new first impression.

AFTER-SALES SERVICE SUMMARY

The after-sales service is a very important factor that must be considered when a customer has a need to purchase a replacement item or the next generation item. Some of the studies indicate that a person who is dissatisfied with the service and/or product but who has a pleasant experience in resolving the problem is more likely to buy again from the supplier than a customer who has not had a problem.

The key to real effective after-sales service is empowerment. The individual first interfacing with the unhappy customer should have the authority to resolve the problem without escalating it up the management chain. Allowing the service representative to have the ability to offer the customer alternatives goes a long ways in transforming customer attitude from offensive to cooperative. Organizations should empower the call center representative to give the unhappy customer things like offering a free replacement item, giving them 30 percent off on their next trip, send someone free of charge to make the repair at the customer's location, and so on. These types of actions build confidence in the organization's desire and ability to satisfy their customers. Some studies indicate that a dissatisfied customer's satisfaction level goes down by the number of individuals the customer must talk with to get the problem solved. This attitude is because the customer correctly draws the conclusion that they wasted their time talking to somebody who could not solve the problem.

When an unhappy customer or potential customer calls in and is kept waiting on the telephone line for more than 5 rings, this does not leave the impression that the organization has a great deal of work to do, but rather that the organization is understaffed and probably will not have time to do the quality job that the customer is expecting and needs.

> After-sales service rates number 3 in driving customer satisfaction after product engineering and the sales and marketing.
>
> **H. James Harrington**

11

Process Grouping 11: Performance Analysis

INTRODUCTION TO PERFORMANCE ANALYSIS

Innovation Rule #1: For a project to be successful from an innovative standpoint, it has to add sufficiently more value to the receiver (customer) than they paid for the output and the output has to be produced at a cost that is significantly lower than the purchase price.

H. James Harrington

In reality, the value-added content of the item should exceed the initial purchase price and the lifecycle costs of the output combined. However, in general, decisions are made based upon the initial purchase price without considering lifecycle costs. The key word in all innovation projects is value-added. The following are some definitions related to key value words and/or activities.

Definition: Value—The worth of something in terms of the amount of other things for which it can be exchanged for in terms of some medium of exchange.

Note: The amount of *value* of an *innovation (outcome)* is relative to, and determined by the perception of, the *stakeholders* involved. Value can be realized, redistributed or destroyed for different stakeholders (e.g., in a value chain or across industry sectors). The *stakeholders* involved can be producers, consumers, suppliers, customers, partners, competitors, innovators, users, networks, clusters, and society.

Definition: Value-Added: The difference between what the producing company paid for its inputs and the price it charges for the finished goods. In practice, the term is used more commonly to describe how a service or component can add to a product's usefulness, and thus potentially to the final price charged to customers.

Definition: Value-added analysis: The procedure for analyzing every activity within a process, classifying it as value-added, organizational value-added, or non-value added, and then taking positive action to eliminate or at least minimize the non-value-added activities or tasks. A value-added analysis can either be positive or negative when all the stakeholders are considered. (For example, productivity is increased but there is a 10 percent rise in employee layoffs because of the increased productivity. For the investor this project is probably a positive value-added. For the employees it probably is a negative value-added.) Quantifying the nonfinancial value-added impacts is very difficult.

Definition: Value analysis: Identifying the required function for a product, estimating value for the required functions, and suggesting an approach to provide the required functions and the lower overall cost without performance loss to optimize cost performance. The analysis of a system, process, or activity to determine which parts of it are classified as real-value-added (RVA), business-value-added (BVA), or no-value-added (NVA).

The Four Helpful Hints

The following list provides four helpful hints:

1. During "Process Grouping 11: Performance Analysis" and "Process Grouping 12: Transformation" is where a project proves itself as being innovative or a failure. This is the point in the cycle where the organization measures the project's value-added contribution to the organization and customers. The organization considers projects that have a combined positive contribution as viewed by the stakeholders as innovative in nature. The organization considers those that have a negative impact on value as a failure unless there is a special condition where the organization will use the results as a springboard for newer better results.

   Theoretically you don't know if a project is innovative or a failure until you have enough information available to accurately measure the impact the project has on the organization's stakeholders. Typically, an organization's stakeholders are:
   - The investors
   - The customers or consumers

- The employees
- The employee's family
- The organization's executives
- The local and national government
- The suppliers

Many projects have positive impact upon some of the stakeholders and negative impact upon other stakeholders. I see too many performance analysis summaries where the only thing that is discussed was the positive impact areas, ignoring the negative impacts. I know some of companies that installed very effective Six Sigma programs and during the same time their customer satisfaction index dropped significantly.

Another example is a process that was streamlined reducing the amount of human resources required by 25 percent. This reduction resulted in a significant decrease in the production costs, but it had very negative impact upon the employees who were laid off because of the process redesign efforts. In addition, the number of defects that the customers experienced increased by 15 percent.

2. Although not everyone agrees, I believe that to be classified as an innovation a project has to add value based upon its total stakeholder impact. At the very minimum it must add value to the organization and to the external customer.

3. Transformation relates to how well the changes were adopted and how long they continued to be used. Many of you have heard the story about the *Hawthorne Works* in Cicero, Illinois. The original research at the *Hawthorne Works* in Cicero, Illinois, was originally interpreted by *Elton Mayo* and others to mean that paying attention to overall worker needs would improve productivity. It is believed that the novelty of being research subjects and the increased attention from such could lead to temporary increases in workers' productivity. The study and results are referred to as "The Hawthorne Effect" (also referred to as the observer effect). The Hawthorne Works had commissioned a study to see if their workers would become more productive in higher levels of light. The workers' productivity improved when the company made the changes, and slumped when the study ended. They then lowered the light level and repeated the experiment again and productivity increased for a while. It was suggested that the productivity gain occurred as a result of the *motivational* effect on the workers of the interest being shown in them.

4. In another case the CRM software package was installed with the promise that it would provide the organizations with a significant competitive advantage by greatly improving sales. Thousands of dollars later the equipment was installed, the software was up and running, and the salesmen were using the new and improved processes but sales did not increase. The reason that sales did not increase was that the competition also installed the same software eliminating any competitive advantage for the organization although they spent many thousand dollars in upgrading the sales process. Of course, if the organization hadn't installed the new software, that organization would have realized that their competition had a very significant competitive advantage over them.

What you should learn from these stories is that productivity will increase when management's attention is focused on the specific area. It does not mean that the new process is better or worse than the old process. When evaluating the impact of a project on stakeholders, you need to run a control sample along with the project sample. That's the very reason why new drugs are tested by providing one group of people with sugar pills and the other group of people with the actual drug. In both cases, no one knows if he or she is taking the new drug or not.

I have seen several CRM systems that had been installed for hundreds of thousands of dollars and were initially used extensively when management was closely examining the data. It wasn't long before the salesperson slipped back to his or her own methods, but still had to input the information into the computer system but did not use the output reports. The CRM system only served to increase his or her nonproductive work time. Management rated the CRM system implementation as a very successful project because it provided the salesman with so much more information but the information is worthless if the transition to using it is not lasting. By the way, sales did not go up for this organization because their competition also implemented a CRM system. As a result, both organizations had an excellent database and spent more money on advertising. The bottom line was there were very minor changes in the organization's percentage of the market at a much higher cost. The question is, "What would have been the results if one organization had installed a CRM system and the other one did not?" Sometimes, you have to spend money just to maintain where you are.

THE TEN REASONS WHY IT IS HARD TO MEASURE INNOVATION IMPROVEMENT

There are number of reasons why you may be receiving false, or at a very minimum misleading, indications of improvement when trying to measure innovative improvement. Some of them are:

1. Special attention to an activity naturally results in improvement in the basic entities' activity that could greatly distort the results you get after you innovative change.
2. When attention is focused on an improved innovation, a bubble of creativity occurs while the obvious or delayed observations are highlighted and reported. This bubble last for a short time and then dies out. This bubble occurs for as much as of 12 to 18 months before it stabilizes at a nominal level for innovative ideas.
3. Decisions related to continuing or discontinuing innovative initiatives usually have to be made in a very short period of time with no sustained database to work from.
4. Often the database is not available to measure and compare before and after effects.
5. All the projects that have a positive value and impact on one or more stakeholders can have a negative impact upon one or more other stakeholders. It is difficult to make a comparison between these two conditions. In most cases, these types of analysis have never been done in most organizations.
6. Most organizations accept new projects based upon improvement results, rather than value-added results. (For example, the project could be completed to reduce development cycle time without ever calculating value-added. This example could either be a negative value for the organization or add significant positive value-added.)
7. Many innovative projects are based upon changes in technology that is available to add value. However, not implementing them can have a very negative impact upon the organization. This is particularly true for software packages that are sold based upon

improving the customer interface implemented by the organization and its competition. This could result in a great deal of additional resources expended for no improvement in comparison to the competition.

8. In most organizations the data collection system is not designed to measure improvements that result from the specific changes.
9. An important part of the value-added as a real result of an innovative change might have a non-financial impact based upon most organization's accounting system. There is a high error rate in projecting value-added content in the subjective areas.
10. Innovation improvements are hard to measure in your organization.

Value-added only occurs when the organization eliminates something or improves its performance. Saving 30 minutes a day for 20 employees may sound like you saved 600 minutes. In most cases, it may sound like improvement, but there are no bottom-line results if the organization does not remove these 10 people from the process. What typically happens is the employee takes longer coffee breaks or is given an assignment that did need to be done before. If it didn't need to be done before the change, it certainly doesn't need to be done after the change. When the value-added results in reducing processing time, the department should be required to identify the surplus employees resulting from the change initiative

The Eight Typical Innovation Performance Measurements

Keeping all these problems in mind, you still must provide a legitimate evaluation of the value-added content for the innovative changes. Some of the more frequently used measurements are:

1. Increased sales
2. Reduced production costs
3. Increased market share
4. Return on investment
5. Reduced cycle time
6. Increased customer satisfaction
7. Reduced accounts receivable cycle time
8. Improved reliability

STAKEHOLDER VALUE-ADDED

After you define the change measurement methods, you need to then define how these measurements impact each of the stakeholders. To accomplish this, you need to define what the stakeholder's priorities are and from that you can estimate the impact the change has on the stakeholder.

The Thirty Stakeholder Priorities

Each stakeholder classification has a unique set of priorities and desires. I find there is some variation in the name and priority some individual organizations give stakeholder classification. The following is my interpretation of the highest-priority impact by stakeholder classification:

Management
- Return on assets
- Value added per employee
- Stock prices
- Market share
- Reduced operating expenses

Investors
- Return on investment
- Stock prices
- Return on assets
- Market share
- Successful new product

Customer
- Reduce costs
- New or expanded capabilities
- Improve performance
- Ease of use
- Improve Responsiveness

Suppliers
- Increased return on investment
- Improves communication/fewer interfaces

- Simplify requirements/fewer changes
- Longer cycle times
- Longer contracts

Employee
- Increased job security
- Increased compensation
- Improved growth potential
- Improved morale
- Improved job satisfaction

Community/mankind
- Increased employment of people
- Increased tax base
- Reduced pollution
- Support of community activities
- Safety of employees

As you can see, for every measurement related to innovative change there are 30 priorities that you need to consider to determine if it is truly a value-added change. When you do this, you need to look at each measurement and evaluate its impacts on each of the 30 priorities classifying them as:

1. The change has no impact on the priority being evaluated.
2. The change has a negative impact on the priority being evaluated.
3. The change has a positive impact on the priority being evaluated.

You then can go back and estimate the impact each of the measurements had on the positive and negative impacts. Some people try to do this from a financial standpoint, but evaluations focused just on financial returns favor management and the investor distorting the impact upon other stakeholders. As a result, I moved to a five-point scale. For its positive impact, the priority is rated:

1. Very little positive impact
2. Minor positive impact

3. Significant positive impact
4. High positive impact
5. Major positive impact

The following five levels of rating used for the changes that have a negative impact upon the priority.

1. Very little negative impact
2. Minor negative impact
3. Significant negative impact
4. High negative impact
5. Major negative impact

Types of Major Performance Indicators by Functions

If you include continuous improvement as part of innovation, it opens up many other performance measurement indicators. The following is a list of major performance indicators for just one of the stakeholders—your customers:

Customer Perspective

1. Number of customers (No.)
2. Market share (%)
3. Annual sales/customers ($)
4. Customer lost (No. or %)
5. Average time spent on customer relations (No.)
6. Customers/employee (No. or %)
7. Sales closed/sales contacts (%)
8. Satisfied-customer index (%)
9. Customer-loyalty index (%)
10. Cost/customer ($)
11. Number of visits to customers (No.)
12. Number of complaints (No.)
13. Marketing expenses ($)
14. Brand-image index (%)
15. Average duration of customer relationship (No.)
16. Average customer size ($)
17. Customer rating (%)

18. Customer visits to the company (No.)
19. Average time from customer contact to sales response (No.)
20. Service expense/customer/year

This list of customer performance measurements is an excerpt from the paper, "Translating Strategic Intent into Action and Budgets," by Mark Gitlin of the Corporate Training Warehouse.

When doing a value analysis, the innovative process could impact any one of the previously mentioned measurements. To keep the process manageable, limit your number of value-added measurements to less than 10, remembering that you need to collect information on each performance measurement as it was operating before you installed the change.

INVENTORY MANAGEMENT

Inventory management is the skill of minimizing the cost and risk of incoming, in process, and final goods inventory. Inventory is a costly part of every organization's operation. It represents the costs of the materials and labor that go into producing the inventory, plus the cost of the floor space occupied by the inventory. Inventory costs also include the costs of the money used to produce the item. These very high costs have driven organizations to develop a number of inventory reduction approaches. Among them are one-minute-process change over, SMED, Kanban, TPM, Lean, cellular manufacturing, Poka-Yoke, Kaizan Blast, Just-Time-Production Flow, single unit build, and build to order. Much of the effort to date has been directed at reducing in-process inventory. Toyota Motor Company led the auto industry in Just-in-Time. Just-in-Time is good, but I believe that controlling finished goods inventory is even more important. When Toyota was having their suppliers deliver components to their assembly line every day to keep in process inventory down, they had thousands of cars sitting in the receiving docks in the United States that they could not sell. I believe that if you are going to have inventory, it is best to have it at the component level, rather than in finished goods, because your investment is much less.

Although low levels of inventory are desirable, low inventory levels also represent a very significant exposure. Out-of-inventory costs run in the billions of dollars per year for U.S. companies. Larry Kellam, Director of Supply-Network Innovation at Proctor and Gamble, notes that reducing out-of-stock products by 10 to 20 percent could boost its annual sales by anywhere from $400 million to $1.2 billion.

Another disadvantage of low inventories is that any disruption in the supply chain can shut down an organization due to parts' shortages. One trucking strike in Germany cost the country 3 percent of its yearly gross national product. With the increased trends in single-source suppliers, a fire or a natural disaster like a flood or a strike can quickly shut down its customers.

The challenge for inventory management is to keep the correct balance between customer demands, inventory costs, and risks related to the supply chain. This is a delicate balance that requires a well-designed risk and cost analysis.

PERFORMANCE ANALYSIS SUMMARY

There are almost as many ways to measure performance differential (hopefully improvement) as there are projects to implement. Each project team has its own set of values and subtracted impacts for that project. One of the ones that is most popular and understood by the executive team is a cost benefit analysis. The combination that I have found to be extremely effective is changes in costs for employee, return on assets, and increased sales. The major difficulty most organizations have is how to measure the positive and negative impacts a change has on the various stakeholders. Is difficult to answer questions like, "What is the difference in impact of laying off three employees versus saving $150,000 over the life of the product?" When you are considering this, take into consideration the cost of replacing the experienced employee with a new employee at some later date. I have found that the value of an individual employee varies greatly from organization to organization based upon the organization's value.

Four Very Important Points

Let me repeat four very important point.

1. Run a control sample in parallel with the measurement sample to get legitimate results.
2. Never make an organizational change unless you can define the value-added that the restructuring will bring about. There's just too

much restructuring in U.S. companies that accomplish nothing, by putting off the inevitable and never addressing the real situation. IBM was an excellent example of this in the 1980s.

3. A project is only as good as the results it achieves.
4. Every failure can be considered a learning experience, but you can't be in school all your life.

It may be only human to make a mistake, but to make the same mistake twice is ridiculous. But to be paid for making mistakes is stupid.

H. James Harrington

12

Process Grouping 12: Transformation

![section divider]

INTRODUCTION TO TRANSFORMATION

> Developing an 'I can do it' culture is required to become an innovative organization.
>
> **H. James Harrington**

Very simply put, you can think of transformation management as the conversion of resistance to the project to commitment to the project. We need to change the attitude of everyone from "it can't be done" to "we will get it done." That's what is meant by changing resistance into commitment.

The Twenty-One Change Drivers

To make this transformation, we need to use the 21 change drivers:

1. Define the pain related to the current state
2. Define an achievable remedy
3. Prepare a future-state vision statement
4. Define what's-in-it-for-me scenario (for the target, the organization and the team)
5. Understand the reasons for resistance
6. Respect those who put up resistance
7. Be truthful with the targets
8. Listen intently to the targets
9. Develop win-win scenarios
10. Align the change to the organizational culture
11. Don't move so fast that we overstress the system
12. Set up reward systems that encourage people to change
13. Maintain open communications

14. Stop talking and start listening
15. Look at the situation from the eyes of the person who is putting up the resistance
16. Recognize that resistance is normal
17. Understand the emotional cycles related to change and specific bail-out points related to how the individual perceives the individual change
18. Help targets over the bail-out points
19. Provide everyone with required change training
20. Build models where the targets can observe the change and gain hands-on experience with the change before it is implemented
21. Involve as many of the targets as possible in the change decisions.

Too many people who are implementing a project take resistance to the project personally. In truth, resistance is good and normal for resistance to change is just human. You are trained to question everything that can impact you from the beginning. Your mother warns you not to touch the stove because you may get burned, or to put on your coat in the winter because it is cold outside. You are taught to question everything, every change before you accept it, to be sure that it is good for you.

Mentally every change that comes down the road meets resistance. Individuals stop to ask the question: "What's in it for me?" Each person performs a cost-benefit analysis of the change to determine if he or she chooses to accept or reject the change. The degree of resistance to the change varies from individual to individual based upon their experience, age, and culture. In general, the more bad experiences an individual has experienced related to changes that impact him or her or the older the person is, the more resistant the individual has to change. Many managers feel that if the organization institutes any change, the employees need to embrace the change and make it part of their personal habits. In reality this is not the case. The level of transformation will be based upon the individual change and how it impacts the individual.

BUILDING COMMITMENT

Building commitment within all of the projects' stakeholders is essential, but few project managers seem to understand how important it is and know how to do it. They also don't know how easily it can be eroded. The commitment process is made up of three phrases:

- Phase 1—Preparation
- Phase 2—Acceptance
- Phase 3—Commitment

The Eight Change Stages

Each of these three phases represent a critical juncture in the commitment process. Each phase has several degrees of support (stages) for the change project (see Figure 12.1).

As an individual or organization moves from one stage to the next, the commitment to the change increases. Also, the degree of effort and time required to invest in the change management process increases based upon the degree of commitment required to support the change project. Figure 12.2 depicts the pluses and minuses for each stage in the commitment model.

When implementing major organizational change, there is a continuum of change management strategies that the organization can use depending on the change and the degree of acceptance that change must have by the individuals affected by the change. At one end of the commitment level is "internalized commitment" and at the other end is "institutionalized commitment" which is forced compliance (See Figure 12.3).

Phase I: Preparation
- **Stage 1: Contact**
- **Stage 2: Awareness**

Phase II: Acceptance
- **Stage 3: Understanding**
- **Stage 4: Positive Perception**

Phase III: Commitment
- **Stage 5: Installation**
- **Stage 6: Adoption**
- **Stage 7: Institutionalization**
- **Stage 8: Internalization**

FIGURE 12.1
Commitment model.

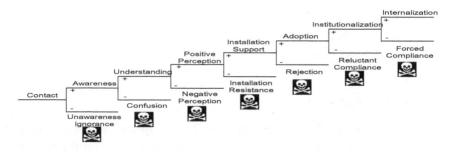

FIGURE 12.2
Stages in the commitment model: Pluses and minuses.

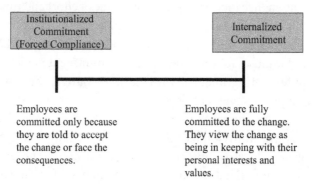

FIGURE 12.3
Institutionalized/internalized commitment.

Institutionalized Commitment

Not all changes require the people who are affected by the change to believe in the change. They may only be required to comply with the change. These changes that are forced upon the targets may be accepted by the targets because they wish to comply with the organization's activities. The organization motivates the targets to comply by rewarding those that comply and punishing the individuals who do not comply. Targets often mimic acceptable behaviors and learn to do and say what they consider acceptable to the organization. Of course, this approach does not have a positive impact on the targets attitude towards the change. In today's fast changing environment most organizations are realizing that their employees need to understand and support the change. With institutionalized commitment the return on investment (ROI) is often greatly reduced.

Internalized Commitment

Internalized commitment occurs when the targets believe that the change reflects their personal beliefs, needs, and wants, as well as those of the organization. This level of commitment results in the people impacted by the change (targets) to take ownership for the success of the change because it satisfied their own needs and they believe it is good for the organization. At the personal level the change is more embraced and supported than the organization could ever mandate.

RESILIENCY

> Change is not something that just happens. The CEO and his or her key people have to make the case for change in innovation and they have to create an environment that fosters it.
>
> **Charles Kalmbach, Managing Partner, Accenture**

> One key to survival in today's rapidly changing environment is to develop a resilient organization. Resiliency is not invented; it is liberated.
>
> Definition: Resiliency is the ability to absorb high levels of disruptive change while displaying minimum dysfunctional behavior.
>
> **Daryl Conner**

To increase an organization's ability to absorb change, the resiliency of the project team and those who are impacted by the change (change targets) is an important factor. The more resilient the organization is, the greater its speed of change. A resilient organization has five characteristics:

The Five Characteristics of Resilient People

1. *Positive*: Resilient people display a sense of security and self-assurance that is based upon their view of life as complex but filled with opportunity. Positive individuals or groups:
   - Look for the good, not the bad
   - Look forward to a better future
   - Have a high level of self-esteem
   - Feel they can influence what is going to happen
   - Have a can-do attitude
   - Are energetic

2. *Focus*: Resilient people have a clear vision of what they want to achieve. Focused individuals or groups:
   - Know what they want
   - Prioritize their efforts based upon impact
   - Align personal and organizational goals
3. *Flexible*: Resilient people demonstrate a special ability in thinking and in working with others when responding to change. Flexible individuals or groups:
   - Bend with the wind
   - Can adjust to change
   - Can see things from different perspectives
   - Are open-minded
   - Are open to other people's ideas
   - Like to be a member of a team
4. *Organized*: Resilient people can develop and find order in ambiguity. Organized individuals or groups:
   - Like structure
   - Group information effectively
   - Plan their activities
   - Are not impulsive
5. *Proactive*: Resilient people encourage change, rather than defend against it. Proactive individuals or groups:
   - Have lots of new ideas
   - Take risks
   - Like to see things moving along
   - Question the status quo

Resilient Employees

I liken the resilient person to a capacitor and the resistant person to a resistor. In an electronic circuit the resistor just sets there burning up energy, but the capacitor stores up energy so that it can use it when needed.

Definition: Assimilation points is a measure of the stress level within an individual or organization that is the result of a change activity. Each individual has a personal maximum number of assimilation points that they can withstand without behaving dysfunctionally.

"Assimilating change" involves not only the effort necessary to deal with what is causing the change (i.e., new technology, reorganization, new process), but also the short-term and long-term implications of the change (e.g., power base shifts, new skills must be learned, new relationships formed, new expectations established).

Definition: Future shock is the point in time when people can no longer assimilate change without displaying dysfunctional behavior.

The resilient person can increase his or her future shock level up to 1,500 assimilation points and at the same time reduce the peak assimilation of the individual changes by as much as 50 percent while reducing the change impact duration by as much as 25 percent. This provides the organization with a very competitive advantage.

Resiliency is not a tool or a methodology; it is an attitude, a culture, the way we behave, and our beliefs. No organization can transform itself into a resilient organization overnight. It takes time to bring about the transformation. When an individual's original level of resiliency is raised through training, coaching, and rewards, it is referred to as "raising baseline resiliency to an enhanced level." As the individuals who make up the organization base resilience level move up to the enhanced level, the organization's cultures and behaviors will change to reflect this new level of resiliency.

Organizations can measure the resiliency enhancement level by monitoring the organization's changes in behavior as defined by the five resilient characteristics. It is my experience that when change impacts a group of resilient people, a great deal of synergy occurs. Resilient employees live with the same change challenges that everyone else had, but they usually possess traits listed in the following section.

The Six Traits of Resilient People

- They are physically and emotionally healthier
- They rebound from the change faster and with less stress
- They achieve more of the objectives
- They are more productive
- They have a higher level of implementation capacity
- They develop a resilient culture

Winners look at change as building blocks. Those that fight change, find themselves as the foundation that someone else builds upon.

H. James Harrington

THE EIGHT CHANGE RISK FACTORS

There are eight risk factors that must manage during any major change initiative. They are:

- Defining the cost of the status quo
- Developing a clear vision
- Obtaining sponsored commitment
- Developing change agents and change advocacy skills
- Understanding targeted responses
- Aligning the change with the culture of the organization
- Anticipating internal and external organizational events
- Developing sound implementation architecture

The Gartner Group estimates that inexperience, overextension, or under-committed executive sponsorship will account for 50 percent of the enterprise change-initiative failures. Fewer than 35 percent of the change-management initiatives will include customized strategies for managing change resistors or leveraging early change adaptors unnecessarily constraining the organization's overall capacity. They also state that 75 percent of change leaders will employ one or more levers to help drive change without possessing even a rudimentary understanding of the implications, directly causing destructive organizational behaviors.

> Unfortunately, many organizations go for buy-in on new processes or systems after they introduced it, and the results can be catastrophic.
>
> **Robert Kritgel, Consultant**

WHAT PROJECTS NEED CHANGE MANAGEMENT?

Organizational change management (OCM) is not a stand-alone project. It usually supports some other projects. You should not apply it to all projects as some progress well without the additional change efforts. Projects that should have OCM applied to them are ones with any of the following characteristics:

- All major project changes
- Projects with a high cost as a result of implementation failure

- Projects with a high risk that human factors could result in implementation failure
- Projects with an unusually short project cycle

For all the projects that meet any one of these four conditions, you should apply a comprehensive change management plan to them.

> Change management can be the difference between long-lasting meaningful improvement and short-term superficial improvement.
>
> **H. James Harrington**

TRANSFORMATION SUMMARY

To consider a project successful, it must meet the desired level of transition before the organization assigns innovation team (INT) members and must maintain that level of transition until the organization implements a new change activity that adds greater value to the stakeholders.

BOOK SUMMARY

The word *innovation* is on everybody's tongue today, but unfortunately some use it to describe every day activities when they should set it aside for unique and creative ideas that produce value to the organization and its customers. Although the definition of innovation is becoming a very holistic terms covering any positive change, the emphasis in most of the training initiatives is focused upon the advanced creative approaches that make a significant difference in the organization's performance. To bring additional complexity to the situation, most of the formal training limits innovation to concept design. I believe that coming up with an outstanding solution that is not implemented can't and should not be classified as innovative or even creative. It may be an outstanding invention, but it is not an innovative invention unless it can be produced and deliver value to at least the customer or the organization without having a negative impact upon the other stakeholders.

Many very good organizations wait for other organizations to do the research and development work and expense. Then they come out with an equivalent or slightly better product directed at capturing a major part of the same market. This allows them to produce the item at a lower price because they didn't have to absorb the development costs.

Many other companies are innovative as they manage the total innovation system activities starting from concept identification all the way through transformation. Even though the organization is considered innovative very few midsize or larger organization have innovative employees. The silo organization construction that they have brought about produces outstanding performers in parts of the innovative system with only the executive team managing the total system. Of course, you do find innovators in a start-up and small companies where an individual is completely dedicated to a concept or idea.

The Ten Steppingstones to Innovation

1. **Management Innovation:** Executives must set the example by demonstrating their personal creativity and innovation in the way they operate, strategically plan, and measure the organization. They should be more innovative than the products they sell to the consumer. They need to learn how to be **Angel** advocates rather than **Devil** advocates. Rather than trying to find something wrong with the employee suggestion, they need to help the employee improve on making a good idea a great idea.

2. **Training Your Employees**: You should train everyone from the board room to the boiler room to have a basic set of creative and innovative skills (not knowledge but skills). You should provide a common fundamental set of basic creative tools and methodology across the organization with more complex training related to specific assignments like marketing, sales, research and development, management, and so on.

3. **Make innovation an important priority:** The three-legged stool that has been used in the past to support most organization; it consists of quality, cost, and schedule. Unfortunately, this is an unstable situation that can quickly lead to bankruptcy even though each of the three measurements are performing well. Today our three-legged stool has turned into a four-legged chair; the fourth leg is innovation. Without innovation, you can have Six Sigma plus quality at no cost to produce and you will end up with warehouses of surplus stock. Today you need a pull-delivery process in place of the push-delivery process. You want

the system where customers are clamoring for more output rather than debating if they should buy it from someone else.

4. **Employee involvement:** You need to have a culture where every individual feels that innovation is part of their job assignment. Management should restrain their natural tendency to talk and develop their ability to listen. Involve everybody in the planning session particularly as it relates to them or impacts them. Make it a *we* organization not a *me* organization. Develop internal career path for all employees making the organization something they are investing in rather than working for. Ask the employee, "What can we do better?" instead of, "Do you have any good ideas to improve the processes?" You go out for dinner and the waiter asks you," How did you like the meal?" and you answer saying it was good or it was okay. But if the waiter had asked, "Do you have any suggestions on how we can improve?" You would tell him or her that the soup was cold, and the steak was so tough you couldn't cut through it. Be proactive in employee involvement, not reactive.

5. **Hire innovative employees:** You can train your present employees to be more innovative, but it is the new employees that bring a breath of fresh air and unpolluted creativity to the organization. These new employees challenge the regular staff to try something new, different, and risky. It is often better to hire an engineer with a 3.5 grade point average than one with a 4.0. You want the free-thinkers, not the individuals who can regurgitate something they read or been told.

6. **Install Innovative rewards and recognition systems:** If you want to get something done, set up a system that rewards people for doing it. You need a system where you recognize and reward innovation. The system has to be broad enough to meet the needs of a broad range of people as everyone should be innovative. As a result, there is a need for a reward and recognition system that gives a pat on the wallet and at other times a pat on the back. Only 44 percent of the companies surveyed had systems designed to reward creativity and innovation.

7. **Measurement of innovation:** There's an old saying "What management wants done, they measure." If you want to improve innovation, you have to have some way of measuring progress or lack thereof. Many organizations have not actively measured innovation and/or creativity in the past. As a result, they find themselves in a difficult position in coming up with an innovation measurement system. Typical measures are percent of income generated by product that was not in existence

2 years ago, number of patents generated, comparison to competitive products, percentage of projects that generate real value added, and so on. One measurement that covers everyone in the organization is to set targets for each natural work team related to the number of suggestions per month that they made that the organization implemented. We have seen organizations that average 2 implemented suggestions per month per employee. And other companies that were averaging 2 implemented suggestions per hundred employees per year.

8. **Risk Taking:** An innovative organization is one that encourages its employees to stick out their necks and take a prudent risk. They encourage their employees to sail in uncharted waters greatly increasing the potential failure. Innovative organizations turn the other cheek with employees who failed particularly when they are trying to meet stretch goals. Failures are looked at as a learning experience, at least the first time.

9. **Thinking time:** Design work schedules and workload so that everyone is given a regularly scheduled opportunity to be creative and come up with innovative ideas. In some situations this time needs to be coordinated through organized team meetings that make effective use of techniques like brainstorming techniques to create new and unique ideas. With other groups it is better to give the individual time by themselves to identify improvement opportunities.

10. **Turn the world upside down:** It's imperative that everyone within the organization looks for new ways of doing things and different product that will attract customers. Yes!! OK, you need to stop thinking that that's good enough; it worked last time, so you should be good enough for this time. Instead, everything you look at you should be thinking, "Could it be better? What should be done to improve it?" Be careful if you're content with the job you have. If you are, you probably should've been moved to a different job some time ago. Often changing jobs turns your world upside down.

11. **Don't say it if you're not going to do it:** An innovative organization is a doing organization. It believes it is better do something wrong rather than to sit and do nothing. Creativity is good, but innovation is great. Even the best ideas that stay within your mind are worthless. It's only when ideas are converted into action that they can have a positive impact upon the organization, its customers, and its other stakeholders. The best way to demoralize an innovation initiative is to not follow through on your commitments. For example, I just looked

at the strategic plan for an organization and compared to their 1987 strategic plan. It looks like they just changed the heading on the front cover of the 1987 strategic plan and released it as the 2018 strategic plan. If you had no strategy, you are without a plan and without a plan you can't take action and with no action, you get no results. If the results are bad, you can learn from the mistakes you made; if the results are good, you have an innovative idea.

"Innovation is like a cold Arctic stream flowing gently off the iceberg. If it's done right, it is very invigorating, but too much of it and it will make the whole organization shiver and shutter."

H. James Harrington

RECOGNITION AND COMMENTS

The following books and/or PowerPoint presentations of H. James Harrington were used as references and information from them was included in many of the chapter of this book.

Presentations on Innovation

- *Innovation* –IAOIP annual conference by H. James Harrington (Boston 2016)
- *Hmmm—Creativity*, conference presentation by H. James Harrington (Jamaica 2008)
- *The Innovation Process* presentation by H. James Harrington at ASQ Section Meeting (Sacramento 2017)
- *Creating a Creative Culture* presentation by H. James Harrington (UAE 2012)
- *Status of Innovation* presentation by H. James Harrington (Mexico 2017)
- *Using TRIZ* presentation by H. James Harrington (Dubai 2016)
- *Innovate or Evaporate* presentation given by H. James Harrington (Abu Dhabi UAE 2010)
- *Organizational Excellence* given by H. James Harrington (Shanghai China 2003)
- *The Innovation Works* given by H. James Harrington (UAE 2014)

Books Authored or Co-Authored by H. James Harrington Used in This Book

H. James Harrington is a very prolific author, publishing hundreds of technical reports and magazine articles. He has authored or co-authored over 55 books. The following list of books were written or co-authored by H. James Harrington and were used as reference for this book.

- Innovative Change Management (2018)
- The Innovation Tools Handbook, Volume I—Organizational and Operational Tools, Methods, and Techniques (2016)
- The Innovation Tools Handbook, Volume II—Evolutionary and Improvement Tools (2016)
- The Innovation Tools Handbook, Volume III—Creative Tools, Methods, and Techniques (2016)
- Maximizing Value Propositions to Increase Project Success Rate (2016)
- Effective Portfolio Management Systems (2014)
- Making the Case for Change: Using Effective Business Cases to Minimize Project and Innovation Failures (2018)
- The New Project Management—at the publishers now (2018)
- Developing Innovative Shared Values—at publishers now (2018)
- Innovative Organizational Structures—and publishers now (2018)
- Innovation Infrastructure Handbook—at the publishers now (2018)
- Total Innovative Management for Excellence (TIME)—manuscript being prepared (target release date 2018)
- Innovation by the Numbers—manuscript being prepared (target release date 1st quarter 2019)
- Innovative Greenbelt handbook—classes being taught/ manuscript being prepared (target release 1st quarter 2019). Technical paper published 1st quarter 2018
- Innovation Black Belt Handbook—classes being taught/technical paper published 2018

Appendix A: Glossary

Activities: are small parts of a process usually performed by a single department or individual.

Business case: captures the reason for initializing a project or program. It is most often presented in a well-structured written document, but, in some cases, also may be in the form of a short verbal argument or presentation.

Business case analysis: is an evaluation of the potential impact of correcting a problem or taking advantage of an opportunity in the organization to determine if it is worthwhile investing resources to correct the problem or take advantage of the opportunity.

Concept validation: (proof of concept) is a realization of a certain method or idea to demonstrate its feasibility, or a demonstration in principle, with the aim of verifying that some concept or theory has practical potential. Concept validation is used to validate the performance of the activities defined in the value proposition (concept validation and proof of concept are often used interchangeably).

Create: is to make something: to bring something into existence.

Creative: is using the ability of people to make or think of new things involving the process by which new ideas, stories, products, and so on are created.

Cycle: is any input that goes into a series of processes and/or systems and part of the output circles back to trigger a new input into the cycle.

Entrepreneur: is a person who organizes and manages any enterprise, especially a business, usually with considerable initiative and risk. He or she does not have to create the idea or concept.

External customer: is an individual or organization not within the supplier's organization who receives a product, a service, or information from the supplier.

Innovation: is a new or unique idea or concept that adds value to the organization and its customers. Innovation is the act of taking new unique and creative ideas developed, funded, produced, and distributed to external customers that result in creating value to the organization and the consumer or customer.

Innovation systems cycle: (ISC) is the way a typical project for products would progress through the innovative activities from identifying opportunities to measuring the value added to the stakeholders.

Innovative idea: is an innovative idea is one that adds greater value to the customer and the organization then it cost to produce it.

Innovator: is an individual who ca create added value for the organization and its customers by being capable of taking new and unique ideas or concepts all the way through the ISC from recognizing an opportunity to evaluating the actual value-added.

Internal Customer: is a person, process, or department within the organization who receives output from another person and/or process within the same organization.

Intrapreneur: is an employee of a large corporation who is given freedom and financial support to create new products, services, systems, and so on and does not have to follow the corporation's usual routines or protocols.

Manager: is an individual who accomplishes an assigned task using other individuals to whom the work is delegated.

Marketing: is the action or business of promoting and selling products or services, including market research and advertising. Marketing is finding out what you don't have and sales is the task of selling what you do have. Marketing is the activity of finding out what the customer wants to buy.

Natural work team: is any group of individuals who report to the same individual. It could be employees who report to the first-line manager or first-line managers who report to a second line manager, and so on.

Organizations: are systematic arrangements of entities (people, departments, companies, divisions, teams, agencies, and so on.) aimed at accomplishing a purpose, which may or may not involve undertaking projects. They are often documented in an organization chart that shows the relationships of the individual organization to the total organization.

Organization: is a company, corporation, firm, enterprise, or association of any part thereof, whether it is incorporated or not, public or private, that has its own function and administration (Source: ISO 8402–1994). It can be as small as a first-line department and as large as the government in United States.

Organizational: refers to those activities, projects, programs, processes, and systems that apply to the total organization, not just one or two departments or units.

Organizational culture: is the value and behavior that contribute to the unique social and psychological environment of an organization. Organizational culture includes an organization's expectations, experiences, philosophy, and values that hold it together, and is expressed in its self-image, inner workings, interactions with the outside world, and future expectations. It is based on shared attitudes, beliefs, customs, and written and unwritten rules that have been developed over time and are considered valid. Also called corporate culture, it's shown in:

1. the ways the organization conducts its business, treats its employees, customers, and the wider community,
2. the extent to which freedom is allowed in decision making, developing new ideas, and personal expression,
3. how power and information flow through its hierarchy down the rest of the organization.
4. how committed employees are towards collective objectives (business dictionary).

Organizational structure: is a system used to define a hierarchy within an organization. It identifies each job, its function, and where it reports to within the organization. This structure is developed to establish how an organization operates and assists an organization in obtaining its goals to allow for future growth. The structure is illustrated using an organizational chart.

Process: is a series of interrelated actions and/or tasks performed to create a pre-specified product, service, or result. Each process is comprised of inputs, activity, outputs, tools, and techniques with constraints (environmental factors), guidance, and criteria (organizational process assets) taken into consideration.

Process Adaptability: is the flexibility of the process to handle future, changing customer expectations and today's individual, special customer requests. It is managing the process to meet today's special needs and future requirements. Adaptability is an area largely ignored, but it is critical for gaining a competitive edge in the marketplace. Customers always remember how you handled, or didn't handle, their special needs.

Process effectiveness: is the extent to which the outputs of the process or subprocess meet the needs and expectations of its customers. It is a lot like quality, but includes more things. Effectiveness is having the right output at the right place, at the right time, at the right price.

Process efficiency: is the extent to which resources are minimized and waste is eliminated in the pursuit of effectiveness. Productivity is a measure of efficiency.

Process grouping: is groups of processes and systems grouped together due to the way they interact with each other or in some cases are alternative processes (for example, you can do something by hand or electronically. In either case, the task involved is very different). In the case of the ISCs I defined 12 process groupings.

Proof of concept: is a realization of a certain method or idea to demonstrate its feasibility, or a demonstration of whose purpose is to verify that some concept or theory has the potential for use. A proof of concept is usually small and may or may not be complete. The proof of concept approach is often used for start-up companies or new products to show how the concept will perform out in the real world.

Program: is a group of related projects, subprograms, and program activities managed in a coordinated way to obtain benefits not available from managing them individually. They may include work outside the scope of projects. A program will always have projects contained within scope.

Program and project management: is the application of tasks, tools and techniques, and skills and knowledge to meet program requirements and to obtain benefits and control not available from managing them individually. It is harmonizing projects and program components and controlling interdependencies to achieve benefits outlined in the business case and value proposition.

Project: is a temporary endeavor undertaken to create a unique product or service. Projects should always have a time related to them

Project manager: is an organizational employee, representative, or consultant appointed to coordinate the project or program. This individual plans and organizes the resources required to complete a project or program, prior to, during, and upon closure of the project or program lifecycle.

[**Note:** Project manager is also the term used for individuals who are managing programs.]

Project portfolio: is a centralized collection of independent projects or programs that are grouped together to facilitate their prioritization, effective management, and resource optimization to meet strategic organizational objectives.

Project team manager: is an individual who is truly accountable for the success or failure of a specific project or program. They usually will have many, if not all, the people working on the project or program assigned directly to them. They will be responsible for getting people from other organizations to work on their project as needed.

S-curve: is a mathematical model also known as the logistic curve and describes the growth of one variable in terms of another variable over time. S-curves are found in fields from biology and physics to business and technology. In business, the S-curve is used to describe, and sometimes predict, the performance of a company or a product over time.

Sales: is the activity of taking a lead and selling the item to the potential customer

Selling: is first and foremost a transaction between the seller and the prospective buyer or buyers (the *target market*) where money (or something considered to have monetary value) is exchanged for goods or services. Selling is the art of *closing the deal.*

Structure: is the arrangement of and relations between the parts or elements of something complex.

Systems: are groups of related processes that may or may not be connected.

Tasks: are steps that are required to perform a specific activity.

Value proposition: is a document that defines the benefits and negative impacts that will result from the implementation of the change or the use of output as viewed by one or more of the organization's stakeholders. A value proposition can apply to an entire organization, parts of the organization, customer accounts, product, service, or internal process.

Work breakdown structure (WBS): is a deliverable-oriented breakdown of a project into smaller components. A work breakdown structure is a key project deliverable that organizes the team's work into manageable sections.

Appendix B: List of Most Used and/or Most Effective Innovative Tools and Methodologies in Alphabetical Order

	IT&M	Book III	Book II	Book I
1.	5 Why questions	S	P	S
2.	76 standard solutions	P	S	
3.	Absence thinking	P		
4.	Affinity diagram	S	P	S
5.	Agile innovation	S		P
6.	Attribute listing	S	P	
7.	Benchmarking		S	P
8.	Biomimicry	P	S	
9.	Brain-writing 6-3-5-	S	P	S
10.	Business case development		S	P
11.	Business plan	S	S	P
12.	Cause and effect diagrams		P	S
13.	Combination methods	P	S	
14.	Comparative analysis	S	S	P
15.	Competitive analysis	S	S	P
16.	Competitive shopping		S	P
17.	Concept tree (concept map)	P	S	
18.	Consumer co-creation	P		

(*Continued*)

	IT&M	Book III	Book II	Book I
19.	Contingency planning		S	P
20.	Co-star	S	S	P
21.	Costs analysis	S	S	P
22.	Creative problem solving model	S	P	
23.	Creative thinking	P	S	
24.	Design for tools		P	
	Subtotal number of points	7	7	10
25.	Directed/focused/ structure innovation	P	S	
26.	Elevator speech	P	S	S
27.	Ethnography	P		
28.	Financial reporting	S	S	P
29.	Flowcharting		P	S
30.	Focus groups	S	S	P
31.	Force field analysis	S	P	
32.	Generic creativity tools	P	S	
33.	Harmful-Useful (HU) diagrams	P		
34.	I-TRIZ	P		
35.	Identifying and engaging stakeholders	S	S	P
36.	Imaginary brainstorming	P	S	S
37.	Innovation blueprint	P		S
38.	Innovation master plan	S	S	P
39.	Kano analysis	S	P	S
40.	Knowledge management systems	S	S	P
41.	Lead user analysis	P	S	
42.	Lotus blossom	P	S	

(*Continued*)

	IT&M	Book III	Book II	Book I
43.	Market research and surveys	S		P
44.	Matrix diagram	P	S	
45.	Mind mapping	P	S	S
46.	Nominal group technique	S	P	
47.	Online innovation platforms	P	S	S
48.	Open innovation	P	S	S
49.	Organizational change management	S	S	P
50.	Outcome driven innovation	P		
	Subtotal number of points	15	4	7
51.	Plan-do-check-act	S	P	
52.	Potential investor present	S		P
53.	Pro-active creativity	P	S	S
54. P	Project management	S	S	P
55.	Proof of concepts	P	S	
56.	Quickscore creativity test—	P		
57.	Reengineering/ redesign		P	
58.	Reverse engineering	S	P	
59.	Robust design	S	P	
60.	S-Curve model		S	P
61.	Safeguarding intellectual properties			P
62.	Scamper	S	P	
63.	Scenario analysis	P	S	
64.	Simulations	S	P	S
65.	Six thinking hats	S	P	S
66.	Social networks	S	P	
67.	Solution analysis diagrams	S	P	

(Continued)

	IT&M	Book III	Book II	Book I
68.	Statistical analysis	S	P	S
69.	Storyboarding	P	S	
70.	Systems thinking	S	S	P
71.	Synetics	P		
72.	Tree diagram	S	P	S
73.	TRIZ	P	S	
74.	Value analysis	S	P	S
75.	Value propositions	S		P
76.	Visioning	S	S	P
	Subtotal—number of points	7	12	7
(P) priority rating*		CREATIVE	EVOLUTIONARY	ORGANIZATIONAL
TOTAL		29	23	24

Note: IT&M = Innovative Tools and/or Methodologies.
IT&M in Creativity Book 29
IT&M in Evolutionary Book 23
IT&M in Organizational Book 24
Book I—Organizational and/or Operational IT&M
Book II—Evolutionary and/or Improvement IT&M
Book III—Creative IT&M
P = Primary Usage, S = Secondary Usage, Blank = Not used or little used
*Each of the 76 innovation tools and/or methodologies were classified related to 3 categories (creative, evolutionary, or organizational). The P – stands for the category that the tool is primarily used in, the S – is the secondary usage category and a Blank - indicates that the tool is not used or seldom used in this category.

Index

Note: Page numbers in italic and bold refer to figures and tables respectively.